to Frank,
Fighting for a Conservative
environmental alternative!

Best -
Bill Tudderdof
10-6-11

POTOMAC FEVER

POTOMAC FEVER

a memoir of politics and public service

J. WILLIAM MIDDENDORF II

NAVAL INSTITUTE PRESS
Annapolis, Maryland

Naval Institute Press
291 Wood Road
Annapolis, MD 21402

Library of Congress Cataloging-in-Publication Data
Middendorf, John William
  Potomac fever : a memoir of politics and public service / J. William Middendorf II.
    p. cm.
  Includes bibliographical references and index.
  ISBN 978-1-59114-537-0 (hardcover : acid-free paper) 1. Middendorf, John William,
date 2. Politicians—United States—Biography. 3. Goldwater, Barry M. (Barry Mor-
ris), 1909–1998—Friends and associates. 4. Ambassadors—United States—Biography.
5. Cabinet officers—United States—Biography. 6. United States. Navy—Officials and
employees—Biography. 7. Bankers—United States—Biography. 8. Organization of
American States—Officials and employees—Biography. 9. United States—Politics and
government—1945–1989. 10. United States—Foreign relations—1945–1989. I. Title.
  CT275.M51348A3 2011
  973.91092—dc22
  [B]
                                    2010052835

Printed in the United States of America.
19 18 17 16 15 14 13 12 11   9 8 7 6 5 4 3 2 1
First printing

Book layout and composition: Alcorn Publication Design

To so many I owe so much. Especially to Isabelle,
our children—each an expert in their very diverse fields—
and their children (who will have to wrestle with some of
the issues noted at the end of this book). Frances, an artist teaching
art in Italy; Amy Givler and her husband Don are parents of three teenagers
(Martha Grace, Pete, and John) and are both in family practice medicine
in Louisiana; John, a computer mapping expert living in Australia
with his wife Jeni and their baby Rowen; and Roxy Paine,
a sculptor living in Brooklyn with his wife Sofia and infant daughter Laila.
And to our daughter Martha, who left us for Heaven much too soon.

Contents

Preface

In 1969 I was living in Greenwich, Connecticut—a lovely place to bring up a family, and a refuge for many financial industry types who were astonished when I told them that I was leaving a seven-figure-a-year Wall Street partnership for a forty-thousand-dollar job as ambassador to the Netherlands. Wall Street—indeed, much of Greenwich—was all about money. I suppose it still is. Well, I had learned how to make money. I wanted to learn how to make a difference. And, truth to tell, it was an ego thing; I was greatly flattered to have been called. Along the way I was bitten by the bug of public service, which so overwhelmed my immune system that over the next eighteen years or so I never looked back. For me it certainly was, to quote my friend (and idol) Robert Frost, a journey on "the road less traveled by."

A small irony: In our senior year at Harvard, classmate Hamilton Fish (the fourth) and I vowed that we would *never* go into government service. Ham had deep personal experience with the topic; his father and grandfather had been congressmen and his great-grandfather was Ulysses S. Grant's secretary of state. My experience, such as it was, was from watching politicians screw things up.

Well, Ham went into Congress. I soon enough saw government service as an opportunity to push free-market systems as an antidote to the Bolsheviks (my favored, and historically correct, name for a faction of the Communist revolutionaries who threatened to take over—or annihilate—our civilization and the world) and to improve in some fashion the lives of others. Overall, I ended up serving in the Nixon, Ford, and Reagan administrations as secretary of the navy, in three ambassadorial postings, and several presidential assignments that required Senate confirmation, in each of which I believe my background in politics, finance, and economics was helpful.

This is the tale of my service, and a few other pursuits before, during, and after; a recounting of programs and events, some that were vital, some merely important, but most, I hope, of interest. A memoir that might prove helpful to anyone contemplating a life in politics or government service—a handbook, perhaps, a guide, something I wish I could have found almost fifty years ago to help me anticipate challenges and avoid mistakes. As I learned, largely through trial and error, there is a vast difference between the hard-hitting world of business, where you gather information, make decisions, and success or failure is quickly measured, and the world of politics and diplomacy, where compromise and persuasion are the tools of the trade and "success" may be hard to define and measured only after years.

When she heard of this project, my wife Isabelle said, "This is not going to be another 'I' book, is it?" I understood her concern: Was I going to be like so many elder statesmen and memoirists, unwilling to take the chance that my accomplishments might be overlooked in the judgments of history? Well, I want to give history something with which to work, but in a recounting of the critical events of my life and times and the wonderful people who have been so important along the way. There are very few things for which I can claim personal credit, except a most fortunate selection of partners, associates, and friends. So, yes, an "I" book because I don't know how else to tell the story, but as any legal scholar will tell you, eyewitness accounts are notoriously inaccurate. I've buttressed my eighty-six-year-old memory with rather extensive personal files. All my life I followed my early training as an analyst to collect memoranda, letters, and clippings; to keep methodical records; and to save almost everything.

This is also an acknowledgment—call it a warning—that public service may bring penalties, especially to family. An unexpected crisis somewhere in the world may seem to take precedence over your son's soccer game and your son will not understand, nor soon forgive. I hope this modest effort will cover some of the distance and—perhaps—fill in some blanks for Isabelle and our children, who I know so often wondered just what it was I did when I was away from home.

Prologue

My lifetime journey got off to a rocky start: I flunked kindergarten at Towson (Maryland) Normal School. They told my father that I was not ready to go on to first grade and would have to repeat. Six years later my mother left us to go and live in England. I must have tried to make some connection between those two events—there was none, of course—but both were traumatic.

Being set back in school turned out to be a good thing: For the rest of my grade-school years I was always, on average, about six months older than my classmates. This gave me an advantage in sports and made it easier for me to appear to be smart.

Being abandoned by my mother was emotionally devastating. How else can I put it? I don't intend to dwell overlong on this, but to know the man, understand the child. Sarah Boone Kennedy and my father, Harry S. Middendorf, were married in the early 1920s and had four children: my brother Harry Jr., my brother William Kennedy Boone (or "Took"), my sister Sally, and me (1924), named John William for both my grandfather and my father's twin brother, called Billy.

However, Mother was not happy as a housewife in what she saw as the dull and boring world of Baltimore investment banking, my father's profession. Dad was all business; Mother wanted to be more in the world. In 1935 she journeyed to England to be presented at the court of St. James. This was the "in" thing for the in crowd, and a gaggle of Baltimore society women were on the trip. My mother's distant cousin, Wallis Warfield Simpson, married to a shipping executive and then living in London, gave them a warm insider welcome.

Mother was enchanted with England; she was captivated by the pomp and circumstance, but more to the point, she fell in love with a much older, well-connected nobleman. Mother's vacation romance proved stronger than her family ties, and she divorced my father. In the meantime, Mrs. Simpson had become involved with the prince of Wales and divorced Mr. Simpson. The prince of Wales soon became King Edward VIII and wished to make the former Mrs. Simpson his queen. Church and state were reluctant to have a ruler married to a non-noble American divorcée and would not allow her the title of queen, nor for any issue of the marriage to be in the line of succession to the throne. Therefore, he resigned. Everyone knows that story: giving up the crown for 'the woman I love.'

Mother's story did not have such a romantic ending: Her lover dropped dead. Eventually she came back to Baltimore and tried to talk my father into remarriage; however, my father—angry, hurt, and with very little respect for my mother's "decadent" family and none at all for dissolute royals—said no.

Here's another family story that had significant impact on a growing boy, but with a better outcome. Around the turn of the twentieth century my grandfather, John William Middendorf—one of the leading investment bankers of the South—acquired the Seaboard Air Line railroad, in partnership with John S. Williams. They raised necessary capital with corporate bonds; however, they were hit by a market crash in 1903, and Grandfather was wiped out. He not only lost all of his money, but was left with a personal debt of $5 million. The world of high finance was a small one, a club. I have a scrapbook filled with sympathetic letters and cables that Grandfather received from all over the world, especially from railroad executives such as William G. McAdoo, just then building tunnels under the Hudson River (and who later served as World War I secretary of the treasury): "What can I say," he wrote, "that will adequately express how deeply I feel for you and Williams in your troubles? Words seem so empty under such circumstances." In this club, reputation was everything; it was unheard of for a member to declare bankruptcy. Gentlemen incurred obligations, and gentlemen met them. Grandfather worked to pay off his debt, every penny. In 1928, the debt discharged, he died.

My father and Uncle Billy had joined Grandfather at Middendorf, Williams in the 1920s, helping to work down the debt, and carried on the business after his death. They survived the 1929 crash, but they ran into some problems in 1937 after they acquired a company with hidden debts; as had their father, they soldiered on.

About all *my* father ever wanted to talk about was economics—not about the good things that could happen, but about the bad things that did happen. In those days the economy went through many more cycles than today, boom, bust, and in between. He had seen it all, firsthand. Economics might seem like a pretty heavy dinner topic for a teenager, but I found it fascinating, and, living in the middle of the Great Depression, real-world lessons were everywhere at hand. President Hoover had raised interest rates and taxes when he should have been doing the opposite. We soon saw the unintended consequences of the protective tariff of the 1930 Smoot-Hawley Act. Rather than shield American industries from international competition, it brought higher consumer prices and provoked a tit-for-tat game of international trade barriers.

President Franklin D. Roosevelt distorted the economy to meet social goals. For example, Roosevelt's National Recovery Administration (NRA) set price controls—not to keep merchants from charging too much, but to dampen competition and "level the playing field," so to speak. In 1934, a New Jersey tailor was thrown in jail for three days because he charged only thirty-five cents to press a suit of clothes, rather than the government-mandated forty cents. Father had started out as an FDR supporter—he made us listen to the weekly radio broadcasts—but turned away from "that man" as the excesses of the New Deal became clear.

Father also was involved, but briefly, in a flirtation with politics. In the 1930s he had attracted some notice as head of the Maryland Taxpayer's Association, and Sen. Harry Byrd Sr. dropped by the house to try—unsuccessfully—to persuade him to run for governor. I listened in awe to that great Virginian, known even to me as a budget cutter and for standing almost alone against his fellow Democrats and the New Deal.

Thus, much of my childhood was absorbed in talk about Grandfather's problems, the 1929 crash, and living through the long Depression that followed. Money was tight; once-proud Baltimore businessmen were standing on the corner of Calvert and Redwood streets peddling apples, a nickel apiece, and "Brother, Can You Spare a Dime?" was not just the title of a song. To bring in a few extra dollars, some summers my two brothers and I worked at a nearby farm, pitching hay. In 1938 I worked for my father's firm—twenty-five cents a day—as a runner, picking up or delivering certificates for stocks and bonds that had been bought and sold. And I have to say, I took the term "runner" seriously. I got a lot of healthy exercise.

One special memory has stuck with me all these years: the annual Memorial Day encampment of Civil War veterans out along Joppa Road. This small and diminishing band of men, at least as old as I am today and some well into their nineties, would proudly march in the parade, cheered on by the crowd lining the street, symbolic on so many levels—reconciliation, remembrance, reflection.

The economy improved for a time, but there was a recession in 1937 exacerbated by labor issues and ever-higher taxes (the top marginal tax rates eventually hit 91 percent). By late 1938 the growing threat of war in Europe turned everything around. Industry began churning out vast quantities of war matériel and the export business was booming. Then, in September 1939, threat became reality when Germany invaded Poland—a reality brought to the screen of my local movie theater, with newsreel footage of Stuka dive bombers raining death.

The *New York Times*, as I recall, looked for a short, sharp contest. I remember this because I had been following developments with avid interest and decided to get a scrapbook and save newspaper clippings on the war. The clerk at Reed's Drugstore in Towson asked if I wanted the thirty-two-page scrapbook for twenty-five cents, or the ninety-six page version for seventy-five cents. I said that, based on the *New York Times* prediction, thirty-two pages should be just fine; the war should be over in a month.

Chapter 1

Down to the Sea, in a Ship

I was in prep school soon after the European war began and at Harvard by March 1943. Harvard in wartime was a great place to be. For one thing, the university was glad to have us; students were in short supply. Class enrollments were wide open and we could study with some of the finest professors in the world, and it was relatively easy to be accepted onto any of the sports teams—mine was rowing. Then, there was the general excitement of a nation at war: rationing, air raid drills, the nightly blackout with heavy drapes on the windows, no streetlights, car headlights taped over so that only a tiny slit remained at the bottom.

In some respects Harvard was *too* great, because it offered too much freedom. I was so relieved to be out of the strict regimen of my prep school, Middlesex (which had temporarily put me ahead of some of my Harvard freshman classmates), that, for a time, I literally stopped going to classes. Then, to make matters worse, I was invited into the Owl Club, one of those exclusive eating-and-drinking clubs. This carried on a family tradition, as both my father and uncle—the twins—had been members. I discovered that socializing was more fun than studying, and fell victim to a triple whammy: too much freedom, too much drinking, and too much ego.

I became president of the Harvard Jazz Club, which offered, perhaps, a bottle of whiskey, a place to crash for the night, and a modest sum to cover transportation to whatever jazz musicians we could induce to come up from New York for a concert. In that era before television, before LP records, before "stadium" concerts with mega attendance, your typical jazz musicians were delighted to have the chance to play before a live audience of any size. And I did enjoy some personal benefit, as I sharpened the negotiating skills that would come in handy throughout the rest of my professional life.

But at the time, I darn near got thrown out of school.

It wasn't long, though, before the reality of the war began to hit home and it was time for me to stand up and be counted. But if I were to serve in the military, I knew that it should be as a naval officer. This wasn't Harvard snobbishness; it was because I'd learned too much about the Army from the veterans closest to me. My father and uncle had served as Army officers in World War I, and my cousin Alex Smith was a colonel in the Army Reserve as I was growing up. His stories of impoverished training—recruits drilling with wooden rifles, right up to the very eve of the war—reinforced my negative impression of Army life. Therefore, when the Navy established a V-12 Officer Training Program at Harvard, I was one of the first to sign up.

Around this time, I was presented with one of those "what if?" events. I'd played some baseball (as a fast but wild pitcher), and in February 1944 the mail brought the following from John S. Schwarz of the New York Giants baseball team:

Dear John:
This is to notify you that you are invited to report to our training camp on March 12, 1944 for a spring training trial at our expense. We have notified Mr. Dave Beck of the Southern Railway to have your local railroad representative supply you with a railroad ticket to Lakewood. Please bring your uniform, shoes, and glove with you.

P.S. You are to report to Manager Mel Ott at the Hotel New Yorker, Sunday, March 12, 1944, in New York City.

Because of the war, the Giants were having as much trouble as Harvard in getting fresh talent. At any rate—also because of the war—I was already under contract to the U.S. Navy, so the New York Giants' All-Star player and manager Mel Ott had to soldier on without me.

I soon learned that V-12 was limited—it prepared men for Officer Candidate School (OCtS), but it offered no degree. On the other hand, once in the V-12, I learned that I was eligible for another program, an accelerated wartime version of the Naval Reserve Officer Training Corps (NROTC). This was a degree-granting program offered at a number of universities, and because naval science courses were included as a part of the curriculum, the NROTC was considered to be, academically, more or less equivalent to the program at the Naval Academy at Annapolis. More or less: Graduates were commissioned in the Naval Reserve, rather than the "regular" Navy. (Soon after the war, the program was modified and U.S. Navy [USN] commissions were given to some NROTC graduates.)

I signed on to the NROTC. I assumed that I would just continue with the already-established unit at Harvard, but, as it developed, there were not many openings in the unit there. A few of my classmates got that assignment, but most were transferred to units at Yale and Brown and other New England universities. As for me, I was sent to Holy Cross.

It bothered me to be sent off to another university because a Harvard degree meant more to me than one from anywhere else. I was certain that I would never be allowed back into Harvard, but my brother Harry—showing a fine legal mind so early in life (he later was on the Harvard Law Review)—offered a winning suggestion: See the dean and get a letter of "withdrawal with permission to return."

The dean knew me—rowing had been his sport—and gave me a sympathetic hearing and a letter that addressed my request to be re-admitted after the war, even *if* I had a degree from another school. In the event, when the war did end, a huge group of returning veterans came home to Harvard, and every applicant for admission who already had a degree (as from the NROTC at another school) was turned down—including me, initially, until I produced the letter. I think I may have been the only exception.

I did not choose Holy Cross, and in normal times I doubt that Holy Cross would have chosen me. My group of NROTC midshipmen may have been among the first Protestants to attend this solidly Catholic university, where, along with naval science and other core courses, we studied philosophy and theology from a Catholic viewpoint. My mother had been Catholic so I had some exposure when I was quite young—some, but not enough to withstand the challenges of epistemology, ontology, cosmology, and the infallibility of the Pope. However, the teaching Fathers, good people, all, offered sympathy and enough extra attention that I survived.

The naval science courses, on the other hand, were of great interest—navigation, naval history, engineering, gunnery, ship stability, rules and regulations—and I quickly realized that having to cram the essence of a normal four-year program into a year and a half would require efforts more focused than any I had exercised at Harvard. I gave up carousing for the duration.

By the time I finished Holy Cross the war was ending, but not my commitment to the Navy. Graduation brought an accelerated BS centered on the thermodynamics of steam (a miserable subject for a future career, but a degree nonetheless); a commission as ensign in the United States Naval Reserve (USNR); and orders to report to the headquarters of the Pacific Fleet, at Pearl Harbor, for further assignment.

I journeyed by train to California, and then on board the troop transport USS *Doyen* to Hawaii. En route, a most unpleasant shock: I was subject to almost constant seasickness. Ah, well, the die had been cast; play it as it lays (to mix a couple of metaphors). Arrival at Pearl Harbor brought a more pleasant surprise. I had exchanged a chilly New England for a lush, tropical paradise. Well, "paradise" may be a bit over-the-top; Honolulu had just come through a bloody riot staged by servicemen, ostensibly protesting the slow pace of repatriation (although I think that some of them had been fighting over access to the women of the Hotel Street brothels). But, in truth, everyone wanted to go home . . . and here I was, swimming against that tide, off on my great adventure.

Here also was my first true look at the wartime Navy, and it was awesome. The piers were crowded with ships, some moored four or five deep, some parked bow-to-stern in the shipyard dry docks, where the sounds of pneumatic chisels cutting away damaged steel mingled with the smell of burning metal as new plates were welded in place. The remains of the battleship *Arizona*, victim of the December 7 attack, had been cut down to about the main deck but were still very much in view. When the water in the harbor was calm, one could see a sheen of fuel oil floating on the surface, steadily seeping from a sunken hull in which a thousand sailors lie entombed. It was a clear reminder of where the Pacific War had begun . . . and where, for many, it was now winding down.

Except, of course, for me. Where should I be sent for duty? I was offered an assignment to PT (patrol torpedo) boats, but I was pretty sure that chronic seasickness and eighty-foot wooden boats would not be a good match. "Send me anywhere else," I asked, otherwise seeking to enlarge upon this experience, "as far out into the Pacific as possible."

In the geography of the Pacific Theater, that was determined to be somewhere on the coast of China. I was duly issued orders to the LCS (L) 53 (then anchored in the Whangpoo River, Shanghai) as replacement for another officer whose turn had come. LCS stood for "landing craft, support" and the (L) for "large," although in usual practice the cumbersome (L) was dropped. LCS 53 was a floating rocket-launcher, armed with some 150 rockets mounted in fixed position on the bow. The rockets were aimed by pointing the ship at the target. LCS 53 was twice as long as a PT boat and therefore considered a "ship," more or less. It was powered by eight GM 671 diesels, arrayed four to a shaft. Well, so much for that degree in steam engineering. Wartime complement: five officers and sixty-eight enlisted men. (With the fighting over, as I was to learn, the complement was as few men as possible as soon as possible.)

The rest of my westward journey was by air: Honolulu to Johnston Island (the wettest place I have ever been, I think "torrential downpour" is a synonym for Johnston Island), then to Okinawa (where mopping up operations were still underway against scattered Japanese holdouts), then China, handled from one leg to the next by teams of sailors with a practiced but disinterested efficiency. The final leg was by small boat from the fleet landing in Shanghai—weaving through a river crowded with tramp steamers, huge Chinese junks, and businesslike destroyers—to catch first sight of my new home. If you've ever seen the 1961 movie *The Wackiest Ship in the Army* (starring my Harvard classmate Jack Lemmon), you have a sense of this experience: Lemmon's character thinks that his new duty station is a spit-and-polish Navy ship just ahead when, slowly, that ship pulls away to reveal a grimy, decrepit hulk. For me, it was—voila!—LCS 53.

I managed to lug my sea bag up the companionway to an apparently deserted ship, but, true to my midshipman training, I did the proper thing: I stood at attention, faced aft, and saluted what I assumed would be the flag hanging at the stern. Of course, I couldn't actually see the flag (part of the ship was in the way), but I took no chance at being caught in a violation of naval courtesy. I was about to say, although there was no one to whom I could say it, "Ensign Middendorf reporting for duty, sir," when an officer popped out of a doorway, guessed at my identity and purpose, and shouted with glee, "That s—head Middendorf is here! I can go home!" So much for the formalities of the hallowed quarterdeck.

The wartime skipper went home soon after I reported on board, and his duties were taken over by the communications officer one rank higher than I, a lieutenant (junior grade, or jg). LCS 53 had been through two of the heaviest actions of 1945, Iwo Jima and Okinawa, and in my judgment both the ship and the new skipper were considerably the worse for wear. This class of ship was built basically for one event: the invasion of Japan. No one in authority expected them to last much longer, and no one on board was trying very hard to upset that prediction.

There were six Japanese flags painted on the superstructure, the tally for the destruction of kamikaze aircraft for which the crew could claim some credit. There was no way to know for certain who may or may not have brought down an attacker, because everyone for miles around was taking each one under fire. The kamikaze phenomenon was bizarre: These were young men in their late teens, early twenties, who had been taught enough to get the plane off the ground, follow a leader to the target area, and then try to fly the plane into one of our ships. During the Okinawa campaign, they sank five ships and damaged another eighty-seven. I think LCS 53 had been hit by some pieces of a kamikaze aircraft that had been shot down just in time.

How shall I describe the Shanghai of 1945? The culture shock I found in Hawaii rested largely on cosmetics: crystal blue-green waters, palm trees swaying in the warm breezes, brightly colored birds, and everywhere (except in the shipyard) the sweet smell of ripening pineapples. Shanghai was war-torn, filled with what must have been millions of starving people, most with nowhere to go and nothing to do except, perhaps, to die in the streets. Many did so, and the smells were far from sweet.

At any hour of the day or night, thousands of destitute people wandered about, looking for food, looking for work, looking for solace, but they seemed always to be moving. When I went ashore, I quickly became a target, I thought, of curiosity. I was tall, well fed, well dressed, polite; anywhere I went, crowds—real crowds—would follow. Some people just stared, some asked for money, some reached out and patted my arms or legs or buttocks in a manifestation of a different sort of curiosity: They were trying to locate my wallet. I learned quickly to stay alert, and to keep moving.

At first, catching a ride in a rickshaw seemed like a good way to avoid the crowds, and it was, but not the danger. The driver—if that term fits a man who stands between the traces and pulls you along like a horse—might maneuver the rig into a back alley where his confederates were waiting, and then suddenly tip the rickshaw up, throwing the passenger backward. If smashing the back of the passenger's head into the pavement didn't knock him out, the driver's cronies did. A number of sailors were thus robbed, and several killed, before the word got around. The city was put off limits for a short time, and the pace of the armed shore patrol was increased. I must admit, I have never felt so powerful in my life as when taking my turn at shore patrol, driving around in a Jeep with a Colt .45 automatic on my hip.

Inflation was rampant. When I arrived in December 1945, the exchange rate was something like one hundred CNC (Chinese national currency) to the dollar; in two months, as I was leaving, the rate hit four thousand; and I later heard that within another month or two it had topped out (or, more precisely, bottomed out) at hundreds of thousands to the dollar.

Americans were about the only source of fresh money: "Hey Yankee sailor! Buy souvenir?" Some of the merchandise was legitimate, especially items of embroidered women's and children's clothing, great gifts for the family back home. Some was highly questionable: Japanese "battle flags" and "samurai" swords—I think practically every Yankee sailor in Shanghai came home from the war with at least one or the other.

Mothers, pulling alongside our ship in a sampan, were selling their daughters. ("Hey Yankee sailor," they would yell up to anyone who could hear, "want a cheap f—k? Twenty-five cents!") This was a transaction that left many a purchaser with a souvenir of a different sort, overwhelming the meager skills of the LCS 53 medical department. One night when I had the duty, I found a group of sailors hanging around the engine room hatch, waiting their turns with a young girl down below. The term coitus inter-ruptus usually is applied to a method of voluntary birth control, but I, in my naiveté, gave it a new definition by ordering a sailor to cease and desist. That sailor was not pleased and tried to attack me with a knife. Such was the state of affairs in this chaotic postwar environment, or perhaps, in the com-manding officer's desire to avoid confrontation, that no official action was taken; however, a few days later, the skipper was handed a warrant from the Chinese civil authorities for the arrest of that same sailor. I believe he was charged with killing a prostitute ashore.

Every morning I watched drab gray trucks full of Chinese soldiers head out of the city and into the hills—headed out, someone told me, to fight "some guy named Mao." The government and Mao's rebels had been wrestling for power for some time, but an ongoing "peace conference" had not stopped some of the fighting. I heard that General of the Army George C. Marshall had visited officials on both sides without noticeable result. At midday we could hear a distant *Boom! Boom!*; by dusk, all of the trucks had returned to the city. I suspect that "some guy named Mao" was not so punctilious about working hours.

Soon enough our squadron commander called us all in for a briefing: We had orders. Eastward, home! The thirteen ships in our squadron would be sailing together, and there was an immediate rush of activity among all of the officers and crews, largely confined to running ashore and celebrat-ing. But I had been assigned as engineering officer, and did, after all, have a degree of sorts in engineering, and was smart enough to be terrified. Here we were, about to set out across seven thousand miles of trackless ocean with a tired power plant and tired pumps and tired motors and no spare parts. I took our chief engineman and a couple of sailors on a scout-ing party, and we located a supply of spare parts in a building a bit upriver. I requisitioned every spare injector, gasket, belt, and anything else we could find that looked as if it might be useful. We spent almost a week getting the stuff, bringing it on board, and finding places to stow it.

Our diligence paid off. Not so much for LCS 53, although we had a few problems under way, but other ships in the squadron kept breaking down and we had the parts they needed. We passed them over on a light line: You throw one end of a long line (attached to a small weight) to the other ship, tie the spare part in the middle of the line, and hold on to your end while they pull the part across. We all made it as far as Pearl, but, as I recall, a couple of ships with more serious problems dropped out at that point.

But, I'm getting a bit ahead of the story. Finally loaded and ready, we headed down the Whangpoo for the deep blue sea. Now, please understand:

I had no training in the operation of any ship, let alone this one. My NROTC experience was limited to classroom work; we didn't have the summer training cruises of today's program. LCS 53 had in fact gotten under way a few times while in the Whangpoo, primarily to turn the ship around, to flush sediment out of the intakes, and to make sure we weren't about to be stranded on an island of our own coffee grounds, but I had been learning about engine room operations, not ship driving.

Once we were about to get under way for home, the skipper posted the watch bill. If your name was on the list (and whose was not?) you were qualified officer of the deck. If that seems pretty cavalier, it is, but the rest of the crew had been on board for a long time and they knew how to run the ship, even if I didn't have a clue. So I took my turns at watch—four hours on, eight hours off—and watched the quartermaster and the boatswain's mate and the helmsman, and I took my cues from them. After a few days of steady steaming (and except for occasional bouts of seasickness) I felt like an old hand.

In addition to my duties as engineering officer and watch officer, I was assigned—in an even greater leap of faith by the commanding officer—as navigator. It was my off-watch job to figure out where we were and to tell the skipper how we were going to get to our next port of call. If I thought that I could count on the other ships in our squadron, I was quickly put straight: We were the lead ship, and they would all be relying on me. In this, I was blessed by having a chief quartermaster who knew what he was doing. Celestial navigation—in those days of yore before the invention of global positioning systems (GPS)—was the only way to determine position at sea, when out of range of radar or long range navigation (LORAN) aids; in other words, almost always. Both at dusk and just before dawn, when the sky is dark enough to see some stars but there is still enough light to see the horizon, sailors use a tool called a sextant to measure the angles between some selected stars and the horizon, and note the precise time of that measurement. That information is matched against tables published by the Navy's Hydrographic Office (covering the particular part of the world in which your ship is operating) and that's about all that is needed to "fix" approximate position. The skill comes in making the measurements in the first place; the more accurate the measurement, the more accurate the fix. A special skill is required by a seasick navigator on a rolling ship, and an even greater skill comes in trying to figure your position after a week of solid overcast.

Our first stop, eight days out of Shanghai, was Saipan, ostensibly for some rest and recreation (R&R); in reality, it was a quarantine to screen for venereal disease and smallpox. A team of medics came on board, and a few crewmen apparently failed one or the other test and were taken ashore. As for the R&R, it was real enough, although a bit limited. After the medical formalities, we shifted our berth to nearby Apra Harbor, Guam, where we were allowed to take our turn at a barbed-wire enclosure on the beach, a party spot, furnished with tables already set up with booze—an unlimited stock of government-supplied Johnny Walker Red or Black Label—and piles of Lucky Strike cigarettes. We began to celebrate at about 3:00 PM under a blazing hot sun; within an hour, we had become a crowd of glorious, roaring, drunks regaling each other with great song ("There's none so fair as can compare with an LCS at sea!"). The rationale for the barbed wire became clear, and it was not to keep the uninvited away from the party.

Off on the next leg of our journey, I produced one superb fix after another, growing more and more confident of my skill as a navigator—until I lost Wake Island. My plot said we were within a couple of dozen miles, and the mountains should be looming over the horizon at any moment. We slowed down, circled around for a while, and someone finally spotted the island—when we were almost aground. Nothing looming, I learned the hard way: no mountains. Wake Island is flat as a pancake and the highest point was the top of some palm trees. The lesson: You can learn a lot by looking at the chart.

Under way once again, with Pearl Harbor the next port of call, some of my Holy Cross non-theological book learning was to be put to a real-world test. The weather began to turn sour, and then got really rotten. You know when you've reached "rotten" when, standing on the bridge—the conning station, some thirty feet above the waterline—you are looking *up*, way up, to the top of the waves.

I was officer of the deck, effectively in charge of driving the ship for my four-hour watch, when we began some very heavy rolling. Now, I had learned that a ship can roll from one side to another in safety, even fairly heavy rolls, if the recovery is quick and the period of the roll, from one side to another, remains about the same. However—as I learned—you are in big trouble if a ship rolls over to one side and hangs there for a moment, or two or three moments, before slowly coming up.

Bear with me on this; it may seem complicated, but is the key to my next action.

The timing of the rolls is influenced by the "metacentric height," the relationship between the center of gravity—that point which is the mathematical average of the mass of a ship—and the center of buoyancy, which is the geometric center of the mass of water displaced by the hull. In basic terms, the lower the center of gravity, the better. However, the center of gravity does not remain fixed on a ship under way, it is constantly *raised* as fuel and water are consumed.

The design of LCS 53 put six feet of hull, with the heaviest machinery and fuel and water tanks, below the surface, and about sixty-one feet, with superstructure, mast, and so forth, above the waterline. The nominal stability was marginal and the ship could handle moderately heavy rolls—*if* it was in normal trim, with tanks largely full. However, we had been at sea for some time, our tanks were far from full and, as the weather deteriorated into a full-blown typhoon, the term "moderate" could not be applied to anything we began to experience. As waves hit, the ship would tip over to a frightening angle and shudder for a terrifying moment before slowly coming back, temporarily, to the vertical. Every roll brought sounds of things crashing to the deck, things that should have been secured for heavy weather, and maybe had been, but not against a rolling so great that gravity seemed to be working sideways.

The skipper had literally locked himself in his cabin; I may have been driving the ship, but as commanding officer, he was responsible for the safety of the ship and crew. No matter: He refused to come to the bridge, leaving one very seasick, very young, very inexperienced officer of the deck to do the best he could. I had been struggling to keep the bow pointed into the violent seas, trying to minimize the roll, but a shallow, flat-bottomed hull does not provide much directional stability. I then took what the Navy calls "bold corrective action" and ordered empty tanks to be flooded with seawater. I called the skipper on his cabin telephone and told him what I was doing; he ordered me not to do it. "You'll contaminate the tanks," he yelled. "We'll never get them clean!"

I did it anyway, and soon enough, the rolling was not so dramatic and the recovery more dynamic.

Did I save the ship from foundering in the storm? I don't know for a certainty, but I do know that the other ships in company with us took the same action, and that removing all traces of saltwater was not all that much of a problem once we were safely berthed at Pearl. Does this story sound vaguely familiar? Possibly: It's very close to the fictional account at the center of the movie *The Caine Mutiny*, where (in the middle of a huge storm) Van Johnson ("Lieutenant Maryk") dramatically relieved his commanding officer, a frozen-with-fear Humphrey Bogart ("Captain Queeg"), and assumed command. Captain Queeg would not change course—the better to ride out the storm—because the fleet commander had ordered the course they were on, and Captain Queeg would not disobey an order. Lieutenant Maryk was court-martialed later for mutiny but found not guilty.

Author Herman Wouk, who had been a World War II naval officer, based his drama on several real-life incidents. Mine was not one of them, but huge storms in the Pacific claimed a number of ships. In December 1944 three destroyers capsized and sank in a single storm—790 men lost with another twenty-five ships severely damaged—in part because they continued to try to steam on an ordered but increasingly dangerous heading. They held on, and held on, and held on, until they had sustained too much damage to recover. The loss of the destroyers was most certainly due to the fact that they were low on fuel and, because they were scheduled for ship-to-ship refueling the next morning, had not ballasted the empty tanks.

Adm. Chester Nimitz, commander in chief, Pacific Fleet, sent a strongly worded message to all commanding officers to remind them that, when sailing into heavy weather, the skill and judgment of professional seamen must always take precedence over often arbitrary "orders" from higher authority. "No rational captain will permit his ship to be lost fruitlessly through blind obedience to plan or order," he wrote, "since by no chance could that be the intention of his superior."[1]

Regarding my own disobedience of orders, I find both moral and legal support in the final words of the Nimitz message: "The time for taking all measures for a ship's safety is while still able to do so. Nothing is more dangerous than for a seaman to be grudging in taking precautions lest they turn out to have been unnecessary. Safety at sea for a thousand years has depended on exactly the opposite philosophy."

At Pearl Harbor, our crew was reduced: six officers down to four, fifty-eight enlisted now at forty-nine. One of the departing officers was the skipper and another more-or-less old hand took over. We sailed to San Francisco, where more of the crew were released. Our next stop: the Kaiser Shipyard on the Columbia River in Portland, Oregon, for decommissioning, where, in the biggest leap of faith ever (or was it just attrition?), I was eventually appointed acting squadron commander. Our mission was to put the ships into "mothballs," long-term storage in the Reserve Fleet to be ready in the event of some future need. Before we approached the shipyard, an omen: We passed a little riverside tavern identified by a large sign, "Jack's Lighthouse." We passed close enough for some of the crew to have conversations of sorts with some idle women, and I knew we were in trouble when I heard them inviting the sailors to come back for a visit. It was straight out of Homer, gorgeous Sirens luring seamen to death on a rocky shore. One seventeen-year-old country waif, not more than six months off a Nebraska farm, was married within three days.

I had trouble of my own, which could have ended any hope I might have had for a naval future. Over time, the pounding of waves against a steel hull turns a ship into a big magnet, making it a sweet target for magnetic-influence anti-ship mines. Every once in a while, a ship needs to sit in an electric field in the middle of a special "deperming" dock, a U-shaped affair floating in the river but tethered to the shore. Our ship had to be demagnetized before heading for our assigned berth. I may have been legally in control of LCS 53, but I came to realize how little technical control I had when I tried to make a turn through the swiftly running current. My ship-driving experience to that point, other than the big storm, had been pretty much straight and steady. My training barely touched on "parking," and certainly not parking under these conditions.

I headed upstream, started a gradual turn, and the huge current hit the bow—*wham!* I ordered all engines back full, with full rudder, and we backed off and got stabilized more or less backing up against the current. Well, the ship may have been stabilized, but I was shaking like a leaf. On my next approach, I saw that I was too close to the shore, so I ordered all back two-thirds and another big rudder order. By this time, the helmsman was more flustered than I and he swung the wheel in the wrong direction. Thus, instead of my intended graceful slide to a stop, we were headed straight for the dock—straight, actually, for a brand-new three-thousand-dollar generator sitting at the edge. We knocked it into the river while at the same time pushing the floating dock halfway up on the shore.

This mightily upset a lieutenant who was standing on the dock; whether he was upset for the destruction of government property or jeopardy to himself, I'm not sure. "A—hole!" he yelled, along with a string of vivid obscenities more appropriate to a boatswain's mate. We finally got in position and were depermed and shifted to our berth. However, I bought the lieutenant a fairly liquid dinner that night to assure him that I was a decent sort of guy, albeit inexperienced, and merited his understanding, not the court-martial charges I'm certain he had considered filing. The generator, of course, was fished out of the drink, dried out, and because it had been immersed in freshwater, not salt, was probably none the worse for wear.

Preparing a ship for mothballing was pretty routine: Inspect every piece of equipment, and clean it up; or, if not worth keeping, such as a worn-out battery or a broken pump, get rid of it. Getting rid of it the proper way meant weeks and weeks of paperwork. Even a burned-out light bulb had to be accounted for. The innovative American sailors preferred a more straightforward method of disposal: a late-night evolution they called the "Splash Detail." Of course, had I known about it, I would not have approved.

I seem to have given one class of material special treatment: A bunch of autographed movie-star photos, Betty Grable and friends in bathing suits, had been taped on the bulletin board in the communications shack. These must have seemed like pretty exciting stuff to this naive young naval officer, because when I began sorting through a lifetime's collection of files in preparation for writing this memoir, I found four of them, tucked away in a scrapbook

We devoted a month to cleaning everything that could be cleaned, draining anything that could be drained, and putting on a fresh coat of paint on anything that could be painted. We must have done a pretty good job, because some twenty years later several of our ships were pulled out of the Reserve Fleet and transferred to the Vietnamese navy (LCS 53 was not among them; it was sold for scrap in 1949). Another LCS of our vintage was in active service in Thailand until recently, the only survivor of some 130 built for the war. A few years ago I teamed up with a group of former LCS sailors, along with Secretary of the Navy John Lehman, whose father served aboard an LCS, to pull that ship out of Thailand and bring it home as a floating museum and memorial. Here's a truly international pedigree: This American ship was with the Japanese Maritime Self-Defense Force, then the Thai navy, and came back to the United States as deck cargo on a heavy-lift freighter that flew the Panamanian flag, was manned by a Chinese crew, and was owned by a company in the Netherlands.

Mothballing finished, I was sent back east and mustered out of the Navy in Boston in August 1946, three and a half years from the time I signed up for the V-12. With about a month to go before going back to Harvard, I took a job at the Graves Shipyard in Marblehead. Well, it was more a boatyard than a shipyard, and I was relegated to scraping barnacles and painting; it was mindless work, but good exercise. To get the job, I had to join a union, and this gave me my first taste of union work rules and attitudes. The other workers came to me and said, "Slow down!" I was upsetting the standards. I thought if you had a job you were supposed to do some work, so I quit. By the end of September, I was back at school.

Chapter 2

Postwar

T he "letter of withdrawal" put me back in Harvard, and the GI Bill helped pay the way. The campus was full of veterans, but it was the unwritten rule that we did not discuss our wartime experiences, great or small. We demonstrated that we were veterans by wearing our old khakis, and the more beaten up, the better. It's funny, but I didn't find out what some of my classmates had done in the war until twenty-five years later at a class reunion, from a brochure of capsule biographies.

I knew that my earlier time at Harvard and the accelerated BS from Holy Cross would allow me to finish a Harvard degree in a year; but, with only a year of freedom before I had to find a job, I reverted to some of my earlier bad habits and often found socializing more interesting than studying.

I worked a bit harder at some courses than at others, but I was not going to win any awards for scholarship. I signed up for one fine arts course because I'd heard it was easy, a gut course in which one might catch up on sleep during the slide shows. True enough, for most people, but I became hooked, riveted by paintings by Monet, Rembrandt, Van Eyck. It changed my life, turned me into a champion and occasional collector of great art, and, later in life, led to my participation as a board member of several art museums, including the Baltimore Museum of Art and the Corcoran in Washington, D.C., and as founding chairman of the Friends of the American Wing at New York's Metropolitan Museum.

By great good luck—because only a few students had signed up—I was able to enroll in a graduate-level course taught by Austrian Libertarian economist Joseph Schumpeter, which also changed my life. He put forth the "entrepreneur" as the hero of economic growth, introducing new products, new methods of production, new competitive strategies, all of which give rise to new clusters of business investment that propel economic expansion. It is the individual entrepreneur that drives the economy, not the government, which was just about the opposite of the Keynesian school of economics then so prominent at Harvard.

Schumpeter introduced the concept of "creative destruction." As entrepreneurs bring new products and services to market, they are likely to displace companies (instant photography creator Polaroid overwhelmed by digital imaging) or whole families of products (the electric refrigerator displacing the icebox). There may be—and often has been—entrenched resistance to change. I own a 1901 Crestmobile single-cylinder gas-engine automobile that came complete with an installed buggy-whip holder. This accessory was required by a law engineered by the buggy-whip industry of Massachusetts, on the grounds that should the engine fail, a horse would surely be needed to move the machine.

Schumpeter was also a champion of business cycles—highs and lows, he suggested, can be predicted with some accuracy because they recur at relatively consistent periods. There was the Kondratiev Cycle, signaling a sharp recession about every fifty-four years, and shorter cycles with equally exotic names: the Kitchin Inventory Cycle, three to five years, the Juglar Fixed Investment Cycle, seven to eleven years. I won't make the effort, here, at further definition. At the time, as a young student, I was impressed with the concept and pleased to find such a handy set of measuring sticks. I would later learn that things in the real world don't work with such comforting predictability.

I was later told by another of my economic heroes—Ludwig Von Mises, whose course I was able to audit in graduate school—that Schumpeter, while finance minister of Austria, had screwed up that nation's economy. Perhaps, but no matter: those who teach may not always be as effective at doing. Schumpeter himself told me that he had only two ambitions: to be the world's greatest horseman and the world's greatest lover. I admired him greatly, and hope that he succeeded in the time left before his passing in 1950.

On the downside, I failed an economics course on the Federal Reserve. I will agree that holding a low regard for the Federal Reserve—an attitude I made clear to my professor on the first day of class—is not a cogent reason for screwing up my record, but at the time it made perfect sense. I went into the course telling all who would listen that Woodrow Wilson was one of the world's great sinners for creating the Federal Reserve, as well as the individual income tax (it was to be "only" one or two percent but hit that 91 percent high within a generation or so—so much for government promises). With great bombast, I argued that the Fed enables a welfare state and a spendthrift Congress. The professor—to my mind at the time, a hamster-brained sociopath—rewarded my arrogance with a failing grade. In truth, I deserved to fail.

I had to repeat the course in summer school and did not receive my degree until two months after the rest of my class. However, I was allowed to attend the June graduation ceremonies. The commencement speaker was previous General of the Army and then–secretary of state George C. Marshall. His topic: a new plan to bail Europe out of postwar bankruptcy, a plan that Arnold Toynbee would call "the signal achievement of our age," and Winston Churchill described as the most unselfish act in history. It was a brilliant, sunshine-filled day and Marshall was perhaps the most boring speaker we had ever heard. Whatever the significance of his remarks, it escaped many of the graduates. Europe was three thousand miles and many generations away from most of us; the graduation parties couldn't begin until he stopped rambling on. Twenty-five years later, when serving as ambassador to the Netherlands, I was so often reminded of that day—that speech— when grateful Dutch citizens would offer a toast "to the United States and the great Marshall Plan that pulled us out of devastation."

Most of my classmates went into one industry or another; America had emerged from the war with industry intact and robust, many senior executives would soon be retiring, and there were limitless opportunities. I was one of a very few who chose the long-depressed world of finance, but it was a world that I understood. I had the benefit of those nightly discussions with my father, and some personal, albeit low-level, experience from that summer job with my father's firm. In any event, I knew early on that I wanted to be an investment banker. I do, however, admit to a short—very short—flirtation with show business. At Harvard, I had a choice role in a "Hasty Pudding" theatrical extravaganza with Jack Lemmon, George Plimpton, Dave Binger, and Fred Gwynne—showmen, all. I blew my lines.

My embarrassing senior year encounter with the Federal Reserve notwithstanding, I had several job offers in Boston and New York City and picked the Bank of the Manhattan Company, starting as a trainee. Although we were making only two thousand bucks a year, my fellow trainees and I were swept up with the fact that working for a bank was such an enormous privilege, that in the period before World War I candidates actually paid the bank for a job.

The trainee's first three months were spent in the security vaults at 40 Wall Street. Here, the wealthy old-family New Yorkers kept their stocks, bonds, and jewelry. They were satisfied with the protection offered the paper, but expected some extra services for the jewelry—especially pearls. We were told that one of the richest women in the world, Hetty Green, had swapped the Fifth Avenue plot on which Tiffany's now stands for a string of pearls. However, we were warned, natural pearls deteriorate over time unless occasionally worn against the skin. It didn't seem to matter whose skin, so we trainees took turns wearing those damned pearls for a few hours at a time.

My next assignment was handling bonds, the prime investment tool in those post-Depression days. Bonds had coupons, which, on a stipulated schedule, were redeemed for cash. However, the coupons must first be cut away from the bond—no doubt you've heard the phrase "clipping coupons," a favored activity of the idle rich—and at our bank they were then fastened together with a straight pin. I cannot begin to explain the reason for this awkward practice, but I can affirm that unless properly inserted, with the point tucked back into the stack of coupons, the pin posed a hazard to unwary clerks. My skill with this maneuver earned my first positive performance rating: "Middendorf, you're the best pin-pusher-under we've ever had." I was clearly on the cusp of a promising career.

After about a year, cycling through a couple of branches and a long stint in the credit department, I figured that basic training was over and it was time to take my knowledge and skills to a higher level. I applied to, and was accepted by, the Harvard Business School. My father's reaction was, "Who's going to pay for it?" I said, "I was sort of hoping you would, since I did Holy Cross on the Navy and Harvard on the GI Bill," and he said, "You sure got that wrong: Get back to work!"

I stayed at the bank for about four years, working on commercial loans, which were essentially loans to credit-worthy businesses that didn't really need the money but were looking for opportunities to expand, or were temporarily swapping assets. On one transaction, for example, we accepted collateral in gold—from Brazil, as I recall—for the full amount of the loan. Another transaction stands out in my memory, for two reasons. First, the nature of the loan itself: about $50 million, ten years at 2 and ⅝ percent, to the Socony Vacuum Company, *interest only* (at about twice the then-going rate), with a balloon payment for the total when the loan came due. Second, our boss, Fletcher Gill, was so pleased with this deal that he jumped up on a desk, champagne in hand, to offer congratulations to all. Very soon he announced his retirement, married his (much younger) secretary, moved to Cape Cod, and dropped dead—all, I think, within the space of a few months.

I became involved in politics with the presidential election of 1948: Republican Thomas E. Dewey against incumbent Democrat Harry S. Truman. The keynote speaker at the Republican Convention, Illinois governor Dwight H. Green, praised the Republicans as "the party of faith in the individual American," and tagged the Democrats as the party of "bosses, boodle, buncombe and blarney." In my own (admittedly partisan) judgment, not much has changed.

In my judgment, some Democrats (and some Republicans, as well) believe that the government is a working tool that should be used to shape society. I believe that society is shaped by individuals. Some politicians have expressed the belief that earning a profit means abusing workers, that employing hundreds of people is a form of exploitation. The demonizing of businessmen, of course, makes no sense: They provide the jobs in which most Americans earn a living. The demonizing of "big" business just because it's big makes even less sense. In contrast, however, planning the economic and other aspects of the lives of those same abused people is somehow a liberal holy calling. Toward the end of the war, Friedrich Hayek had written a seminal work, *The Road to Serfdom*, subtitled, "A classic warning against the dangers to freedom inherent in social planning." Hayek wrote of encroachments on liberty and human dignity. His writings echoed my father's sentiments vis-à-vis the New Deal: the wrongful abuse of government power and policies to further social goals.

In the 1948 election, I served as Republican precinct captain for the 9th Assembly District—the so-called Blue Stocking district on the Upper East Side of Manhattan—and worked sufficiently hard that I was honored to get an invitation to go to Albany and meet with the Republican state chairman. I soon discovered that every other precinct captain in the state was being honored at the same time. We waited in an auditorium for something like an hour and forty-five minutes for His Highness to show up; he popped out from the curtain, gave a two minute talk, ordered us to "get out there and move your butt," and popped back behind the curtain. Having received this wisdom from the great oracle, we slunk back home.

Perhaps the state chairman thought he didn't really need our help: Everyone knew that Dewey was going to win. The Gallup poll had Dewey at 50 percent, Truman trailing at 37 percent. The Republican pols were already making lists of candidates for jobs with the Post Office Department. That was how the politicians rewarded local party leaders: There were post offices everywhere, and every post office needed a postmaster. (A few years later, Nixon's postmaster general, Winston Blount, presided over the transition of the post office from a cabinet-level department of the federal government to a quasi-commercial entity—an action that abolished the patronage system.)

Everyone now knows that Truman won in an upset, and a great part of his reputation today rests upon that achievement. His administration was largely in shambles; and, while he recognized the Communist threat to world peace and took actions to stand up to the Soviets, he nonetheless defended mass murderer Joseph Stalin, who, he said, was a "decent fellow" but a "prisoner of the Politburo." Truman may have been a prisoner of our own far left.

I had my first lesson in Communist duplicity from an expert, Alexander Kerensky. He had been prime minister in the provisional government established after the February 1917 version of the Russian Revolution. In the 1940s he was living on the fifth floor of a house on 92nd street, owned by the parents of a Harvard friend, who were kind enough to offer me temporary lodging on the same floor. I believe Kerensky was in his early sixties, but he appeared to be much older, a truly broken man.

He talked at some length about the Revolution and its aftermath. Kerensky, a Socialist, had been seeking reform. He greatly misjudged the Communists, who were only seeking power. As one effort at conciliation, he ordered the release of the tsar's political prisoners—including Stalin. "I didn't think he was capable of doing anything," he told me. "That was a mistake." Anytime he thought he had a settlement of differences with the opposition and could get on with running the government, he was fooled. Soon enough, the Bolsheviks overthrew his provisional government and Kerensky, disguised as a sailor, fled to save his life.

"Never trust a Communist," he warned me. "They lie and break the rules."

My time as a Bank of Manhattan loan officer came to a logical end in 1951, when, following a friendly squash game with one of our vice presidents, I made so bold as to assay a personal inquiry. "When" I asked casually, "might *I* expect to make VP?" His answer, "Oh, easily in fifteen or twenty years," sent me on a search for a job with better prospects. I was hired on at Wood, Struthers Company, a member of the New York Stock Exchange (NYSE), as a research assistant; starting salary was $15,000 a year.

This was the perfect time to become involved with the stock and bond markets. For one thing, the federal tax code greatly encouraged certain types of investment—that top tax bracket of 91 percent provided a powerful incentive for investment in tax-free municipal bonds. A ten-year bond yielding 0.78 percent was equal to about 8 percent of taxable return. For another, the rules governing investments by New York–based trusts and pension funds had just changed to allow them to own stocks, greatly expanding the marketplace. Volume of sales on the NYSE began to rise dramatically: in 1949, a big day on Wall Street would have seen one million shares traded. By the 1960s, that number had grown to twenty-five million (and today, a slow day may involve more than one billion shares).

This also was a good time to start a family. Isabelle Paine and I were married in 1953, and we eventually had five wonderful children. We lived at Peter Cooper Village in Manhattan for a couple of years, and then moved up to 1170 Fifth Avenue, where we had purchased a cooperative apartment for

$40,000: seven rooms, high ceilings, a pretty nice place overlooking Central Park. The price was so cheap because co-op owners needed to bail out of debts piled up during the Depression, which occurred when other owners moved out to avoid paying their share of maintenance, leaving those who remained stuck with all the bills.

My first challenge as a Wood, Struthers research assistant was to assess the viability of some railroad bond issues by studying the turnaround time in the Chicago railyards. Busy work? No, it was an excellent measure of efficiency; boxcars did not earn money while sitting idle. I soon became an insurance and bank stock analyst, teamed with another analyst, Austen Colgate (of the "Colgate" Colgates. Toothpaste. The university.). Austen and I quickly became close friends—and remained so until his passing a few years ago.

Wood, Struthers was a wonderful place, serious, professional, but not at all stuffy. The management was willing to encourage youngsters with bright ideas. Austen loved to run the numbers in the back office; I liked to get out front with our customers. I visited insurance companies and banks—acting almost like an old-time Dunn and Bradstreet "reporter"—to assess their operations and prospects. After I had shared my observations with Austen, we made our recommendations. It was not as easy as it sounds. Compiling and analyzing the data was tedious—no computers, of course—and we enjoyed a lot of late-night work poring over the Pink Sheets newsletter covering obscure over-the-counter (OTC) stocks, and the A.M. Best "bible" for insurance stocks. But we got a lot of business. Our clients included the Union Pacific and GE Pension Funds, J. P. Morgan, National City Bank, and ITT, for which we recommended investments. Most Wall Street firms in those days were simply brokers, buying and selling. Few did any in-depth research because it cost money to run a big research department, and firms that specialized in trusts and estates were relatively rare. I turned some of what I learned into my 1954 book, *Investment Policies of Fire and Casualty Insurance Companies.*

At the same time I became treasurer of the Investment Association of New York and a member of the Monetary Advisory Committee. Several times a year, we journeyed down to D.C. to meet with the secretary of the Treasury to advise on bond issues. Also, to improve standards of analysis, our Financial Analyst Federation created the Chartered Financial Analysts Society. Membership was limited to people who were truly expert or influential in the field.

Austen and I took advantage of opportunities for Wood, Struthers' own account. We developed a special interest in insurance stocks—searching for undervalued, obscure, and thinly traded companies, usually locally owned. Because of the Depression their stock value may have slipped, but they often had equity backed by treasury bonds worth more than the value of the whole company. I began advertising in selected newspapers around the country, soliciting information about well-established old-line insurance companies that might be for sale.

One night I got a call from a trust officer who had control of the stock of the Lincoln Liberty Life Insurance Company, in Lincoln, Nebraska. He said that the trust had a dispute with the president of the company, who wanted to buy all the stock at an unreasonably low price, and, while they were willing to sell, they wanted fair value. Was I interested? Yes. "Well," he said, "if you can get out here tomorrow I'll sell it to you."

I caught the next plane out and traveled all night. Less than an hour after my arrival, we had a deal: I could buy controlling interest in the company, 75 percent, for $1.5 million. I called Jerry Gantz, one of the partners. Jerry was one of the old hands at Wood, Struthers, a solid performer who had helped hold the company together through the Depression.

"What's the problem?" he said.

"I need a million and a half dollars," I said, "wired out here right away." I explained the deal.

He said, "I've never heard of that company . . . are you sure you want to do this?

"Well," I said, "I already did."

A month or so earlier, Dale Clark of the Union Pacific Pension Fund had called and asked if he could send over a brilliant young man from Omaha, someone I should meet and who might be a candidate for a job. It was Warren Buffett, who was so relaxed and so confident that he admitted that his goal was to come into Wall Street for a year, make a million dollars, and then go back to Omaha. Warren was very impressive, with a solid family background (his father was an investment banker and two-term congressman), and I had no doubt but that he could do exactly what he wanted to do. However, it was obvious that, although Warren would have been a fabulous addition to the staff at Wood, Struthers Company, it was too small for him. But I made so bold as to pass on some advice.

I was by this time working on my MBA at New York University— Harvard was left to the past; I needed a school I could attend in the evenings while earning a living and raising a family. It was a miserable way to live, with not much time for anything else, but I was highly motivated, spurred on, in part, by the competition from NYU classmates from a less privileged background than mine who were absolutely determined to get somewhere in life. I atoned for my earlier academic failings and pulled straight As to prove it. One of our textbooks was *Security Analysis: Principle and Technique* (better known for the names of the co-authors, "Graham and Dodd," literally a handbook for buying companies under book value, and still in print). When I mentioned the book to Warren, he said that he had not only read the book already, but he had enrolled in the MA program at Columbia, where Graham was a professor.

The story is told that Warren earned the only A+ ever given by Ben Graham. Warren then took his natural skills to a job with his father's company in Omaha, and then went with Graham's firm, Graham-Newman in New York. Somewhere along the line he did, indeed, make his million (and a whole lot more) and moved back to Omaha.

While they were living in New York, Warren and Susan Buffett had Isabelle and me over for dinner a few times. Warren and I shared a passion for insurance stocks (my special interest) and for the laws of compound interest that they embodied. I brought Warren into the Lincoln Liberty Life deal; he and I each invested $25,000. We tripled our money in six months and a day (the waiting period for treatment as a capital gain), selling our shares to the owner of a mutual fund in Boston. To return the favor, Warren later asked me if I wanted to go in with him on buying the entire press run of a forthcoming United Nations stamp issue; for a $50,000 investment, we would control the market. I got cold feet.

After Isabelle and I had our first child and with another on the way, we decided it was time for a more suburban environment and picked Greenwich, Connecticut, where we already had some friends. We rented for about a year, and then bought a house on four acres, a really nice place. My neighbor was Prescott Bush Sr.—U.S. senator, father of George H. W., and grandfather of George W. Bush. It was quite a family. At that time, George H. W. (whom everyone then called Poppy) was just getting started in his Texas oil business, Zapata Off-Shore.

They were good neighbors. Some evenings, when the clan had gathered, I could sit on my back porch and hear the sounds of the Whiffenpoof Song—yes, Yale people really did sing it a lot—drifting out across the lawn from the Bush house, where the senator, Poppy, and his brothers Pres (Jr.) and Johnny made a pretty good quartet. They had wonderful voices and it was a joy for me to sit there and listen, especially after a tough day at the office and an overheated ninety-minute commute back home.

By the mid-1950s I was a partner in the firm; by the end of the decade, a dozen years out of Harvard, my $15,000 starting salary had grown twentyfold. There was irony in this: Not many of my Harvard classmates, who saw no future in Wall Street and who pursued careers in industry, had yet reached that level. Nonetheless, Austen and I left Wood, Struthers in 1961 to set up our own firm, Middendorf, Colgate and Company. We bought a seat on the NYSE for $155,000, and the price for a seat quickly dropped to $90,000. We took that to be bad timing, not a bad omen. We saw an opportunity to carve out a needed but largely overlooked niche, became specialists in insurance stocks, and prospered mightily. I brought my father and uncle into the firm—then in their early seventies—to show them how much I really appreciated their support over the years, but they easily earned their keep. We soon had offices in Boston, Baltimore, San Francisco, as well as New York.

With a bit of what the economists call "discretionary income," I was able to indulge a growing interest in art. At first I focused on several well-known contemporary American artists whom I had met thanks to Lloyd Goodrich (director of the Whitney Museum), such as Edward Hopper and Andrew Wyeth, but I was intrigued by an ad placed by a lady who offered a Frederic Church painting, "acquired directly from the artist in the 1860s." Perhaps no one else had seen the ad, or even knew that Frederic Church was a giant of the 19th century; in any event, no line of suitors stood at her door. It was "a dark and stormy night"; the painting was hanging in a solarium with a very leaky roof and the only light came in from a streetlamp nearby. The painting was torn, partly out of the frame, flopped down on a bunch of plants and drenched by rain blowing through some broken windows. Not an auspicious introduction, but upon prodding the lady produced a flashlight, and, with a quick look at the grimy, over-varnished four-by-seven-foot canvas—whether through knowledge or intuition or both—I knew this was a wonderful painting. In truth, *Rainy Season in the Tropics* is now rated as one of Church's best. Many years later, pinched for cash from living on a government salary and putting five kids through college, I sold it to John D. Rockefeller III, and it is now at the DeYoung Museum in San Francisco.

Also at this time, I developed a fascination with the poetry of Robert Frost and was determined to meet him in person. Boston book dealer George Goodspeed called a friend who lived at the foot of the hill where Frost lived part of the year—no telephone, not even electricity. The neighbor asked the poet for an appointment on my behalf, it was granted, and Isabelle and I went up to the little log cabin in Ripton, Vermont, in which he lived, spring and summer. Frost looked like a down-east rustic, a stone-wall builder with big paw hands, but he was a very sophisticated man with passionate loves, hates, and a load of insecurities. However, he made us feel welcome; sitting on the hillside, he took a book and wrote the poem "Stopping by Woods" on the flyleaf and signed it to Isabelle and me. We remained friends until his death.

Over the years, I collected a number of Frost originals, one of particular note. In 1961 president-elect John F. Kennedy invited Frost to write something for the inauguration. Frost said no, and he and Kennedy agreed that he would read his poem "The Gift Outright." However, a couple of days before the ceremony, Frost changed his mind and began a new poem, finishing some forty-two lines. At the inauguration, Frost was so blinded by the sun that he couldn't read the new poem, but he easily quoted "The Gift Outright" from memory. I have one of his handwritten copies of "Dedication" (which Frost later renamed "For John F. Kennedy His Inauguration").

It is not a very good poem; let the first verse suffice:

> Summoning artists to participate
> In the August occasion of the state
> Seems something artists ought to celebrate
> Today is for my cause a day of days.

I had taken my own interest in politics along with the 1957 move to Connecticut, where I was encouraged by a friend, Orson St. John, to become a member of the Greenwich Representative Town Meeting. There I discovered what I call the "stoplight" mentality of local politics. Most people cannot get their arms around a really large civic project, and thus leave the details to the experts, but if it's small—like where to put a new stoplight— not only will everyone understand, but they will contribute to the debate.

Greenwich wanted to install a new stoplight out on a back road, with a contractor's estimate of $24,000. That sparked a spirited debate: was $24,000 the right cost, or should it be $17,000 or $28,000? Should the yellow light be set to a thirty-second or forty-five-second cycle? The argument went on for weeks, while a proposal for a new $15 million high school sailed through after a few meetings with the architects and some consultants.

I learned another thing at the town meetings: Few residents of the town knew the party affiliation, let alone the names, of most local political leaders, although they had a ready complaint or opinion on every issue of the day, from Communism in the schools to universal military training. I brought a certain missionary zeal, encouraging one and all to "get involved," to become volunteers for the Republican or Democratic parties.

I certainly became involved in election politics. I well recall one Greenwich town election, 1960, in which young Pres Bush, Everett Fisher, Jeremiah (Jerry) Milbank, and I worked behind the scenes to defeat two candidates who were running on a liberal platform: Grif Harris, running for first selectman (mayor, to you non–New Englanders), and Lowell Weicker, running for second selectman (deputy mayor).

After his resounding defeat, Weicker came to me and my chief partner in electioneering, Jerry Milbank, and said, in essence, "Okay, you got the votes and knocked us out—so how do I get to be on your team?" We told him: Support our libertarian, conservative ideas. "We have to stop this Santa Claus mentality that has permeated so much of our lives," I said. Weicker said, "On those terms, I have always been a conservative." So we backed him in a series of successful races, ultimately leading to terms in the House and the Senate. However, over time, his voting record became more and more liberal.

This takes us ahead of our story, but not ahead of our theme.

Chapter 3

Presidential Politics: Goldwater, the Draft

On November 10, 1962, I was invited to join a clandestine group of some fifty-five politically savvy men and women who were determined to make Sen. Barry Goldwater the next president of the United States. I had just finished working on the losing congressional campaign of Connecticut advertising executive John M. Lupton. (My children even sang on a TV commercial for John: "We love John Lupton, yes sireee—we love him for the GOP!") F. Clifton White, a New York City PR man and political mastermind, sent me a kind note: "Congratulations on the tremendous run," Clif wrote. "I'm sure you feel as I do that it was a very important vote." Then he asked me to join him at a meeting at the Essex Inn motel in downtown Chicago, set for December 2. "This," he emphasized, "is *the* important one."

Clif's invitation was to seal my fate, the beginning of a transformation from Wall Street to a life of public service. I already knew about his group and their efforts. Jerry Milbank and John Lupton were both members, and Jerry and I had been paying the rent for the group's anonymous two-room New York City office. In tribute to our willingness and ability to produce needed funds on short notice, Clif called us "the Brinks Brothers." In his own 1992 memoir of the campaign, *Suite 3005: The Story of the Draft Goldwater Movement* (Ashbrook Press), Clif was kind enough, on page 116, to give me credit for many things—not just paying the rent—as "the man who stood at the dike and kept it from crumbling around our ears."

There was no name on the lobby register or on the door to the office, and correspondence sent out by Clif was even more anonymous—no return address. Why the secrecy? The group didn't want to tip their hand to the opposition, that is, to any of the other potential candidates for the Republican nomination, a list that logically included three winners in the 1962 gubernatorial elections: New York's Nelson Rockefeller, Michigan's George Romney, and Pennsylvania's William Scranton. And the group didn't want to face the media until they had laid down a solid foundation for the effort and an agenda for the future.

The meeting at the Essex was the fourth and indeed was *the* important one, as it was decision time, go or no-go. We were about to launch the first successful presidential draft in U.S. history. Twenty months later we would head into the nominating convention with the winning votes already in hand.

Strangely, we were to be dubbed a bunch of amateurs by presidential campaign historian Theodore White and political journalist Bob Novak—even, at times, by Goldwater himself. If by that they meant "unpaid," some of us qualified. If they meant "inexperienced," I think the term applied to none of us. I may have been an idealistic thirty-seven-year-old, soon to be caught up in the glamour of presidential politics, but I had been walking the political streets since 1948. The group we joined in Chicago that day included one governor, one senator, three members of Congress, elected and appointed state and federal officials, and a smattering of current and former Republican state committeemen, including Texas state chairman Peter O'Donnell, who would serve as chairman of our group. And the chief organizer—Clif White—was in my judgment the ultimate professional. Why do I say that? The politically unsophisticated think in terms of media exposure, headline-grabbing rallies and demonstrations. The tools of the professional's trade include state and county chairmen, precinct captains, fundraisers, poll watchers, phone bank volunteers, voter registration and petition drives, convention tactics, and Roberts Rules of Order. Clif White was a professional.

We had picked Goldwater as our candidate, although he had not yet picked us. We chose him because he was the conservative answer to the liberal policies of the Wilkie-Dewey-Rockefeller crowd who dominated the Party, armed with plenty of money, a solid political base in the populous Northeast, and—in our judgment—no sense of shame. Goldwater offered straight talk and blunt descriptions of what was wrong with America and challenged the EC (economically correct) thinking of the day: that the government was the solution to all ills. That only the government had enough money to tackle all problems, only the government had the collective wisdom to make the right decisions. "The Government," he liked to say, "does not have an unlimited claim on the earnings of individuals."

He found a ready audience, conservatives who felt locked out of the political process and who responded with an enthusiasm that at times slipped into adulation. He wrote a widely syndicated newspaper column, and a collection of his speeches—assembled and edited into the book *Conscience of a Conservative*—was selling at a rate of 50,000 copies a month. At one time thirteen national magazines were working on cover stories, including, in a bit of a stretch, *Popular Mechanics*. (The editors liked the fact that he was an inveterate "tinkerer.") The *Time* article, June 23, 1961, was not the predictable "Arizona cowboy goes to Washington," but took as its focus "the hottest political figure this side of Jack Kennedy."

Although, when *Time* asked Goldwater if he hoped to make a run for the presidency, he replied, "I have no plans for it. I have no staff for it, no program for it and no ambition for it." Our goal was to help him change his mind.

When Clif opened the Essex meeting he announced, "We're going to take over the Republican Party ..." (Those words were later to be widely quoted, and the citation was accurate—as far as it went. The media usually left out the second half of Clif's statement: "... and make it the conservative instrument in American politics.")

Then someone else stood up and added, "We're here to establish the National Draft Goldwater Committee." Why a "Draft" and not a "Campaign" committee? Because when Clif sometime earlier had introduced himself to the senator and had presented a summary of the group's intentions, Goldwater was cautious, even skeptical (who *are* these people?), and had not agreed to cooperate in, or even to endorse, the effort. At the same time, he did not ask Clif to cease and desist, which was encouragement enough.

Clif's game plan: There were 1,308 delegate votes, 655 needed for a win. The delegates were selected either by primaries (16 states, 541 delegates) or caucus (all the rest, 767 delegates). Thus, a candidate could lose every primary but still win the nomination by controlling the caucus process. How to do that? Get the right people into positions of authority. Clif had discovered that a great many GOP precinct committee posts were vacant—in some states, as many as half. Fill those jobs with supporters, conservatives, and you'd have a pipeline for filling the seats at meetings and state conventions and, eventually, the national convention. Some might call it stacking the deck. I call it sheer genius. Anyone, any candidate, could have tried to do the same thing. No one other than Clif seems to have figured it out.

Clif estimated that we would need about $3 million to cover rent, staff salaries, expenses of the primaries, and the convention. He asked if anyone wanted to be finance chairman—the one who beats the bushes for money; no hands were raised. Selection of a finance chairman would come later; however, I offered to be treasurer, the man who spends and keeps track of the money. Some of Austen Colgate's careful back-room mentality had rubbed off on me: establish controls and maintain an impeccable audit trail.

I was, in fact, later to submit the first-ever—of any party, any election—fully audited account of a presidential campaign.

We briefly agonized over the challenge of raising $3 million, but Chicago entrepreneur (Fannie May Candies) and philanthropist J. D. Stetson ("Stets") Coleman got things moving when he declared, "Look, everybody's been talking about how we need all this money, but who's going to put some up? I pledge $25,000." I added $10,000 of my own, and within an hour we all had pledged to a total of $285,000. We were in business.

We were also about to be exposed. Yes, the Essex meeting, just like the others, was held in secret. Or so we thought. It turns out there was a spy in our midst—unidentified to this day, although we had our suspicions—with his own agenda and a hidden tape recorder. By the next afternoon (December 3), the wire services had the story and by that evening *CBS Evening News with Walter Cronkite* featured some hastily grabbed footage of the Essex where "a group of prominent Republicans had met to plot a presidential campaign for Barry Goldwater."

That was accurate and pretty benign, as was the headline in the December 4 San Francisco *Examiner:* "Secret Move to Push Goldwater in 1964." The same day, the New York *Herald Tribune* localized the story as a "Move to Block Rocky," and the *New York Times* scolded that we were "splintering" the Republican Party. This was a theme picked up in a December 5 *Herald Tribune* editorial under the headline "The Folly of Factionalism, or, How to Fail Without Even Trying": "The latest Republican drama, that somewhat secret meeting of conservatives in Chicago, should be appropriately titled, 'How to Fail in Politics Without Even Trying.' Neither the plotting to promote Sen. Goldwater for the Presidential candidacy nor the conspiracy to block Gov. Rockefeller contributes to the health or harmony of the party. . . .Whatever the exact details, the conservatives are guilty of bad timing, narrow motives and poor politics."

However, a few lines later, the editor made a prescient case: "We don't blame the conservatives for dreaming of Barry Goldwater for President. The Rockefeller people are working with understandable zeal for their man, and the same can be said for supporters of Michigan's Romney and Pennsylvania's Scranton. But the point is, none of these men will have a chance and all their preparations will be purely academic if every faction pursues its own fractious way and the main goal of a party victory is submerged by the lesser goals of personal victory."

How true. . . .

When Clif went down to Washington to brief Barry on the meeting, he expected a cordial welcome—he was met with hostility. Barry almost exploded, "I have no intention of running for president!" Clif, perhaps a bit too defiant, offered, "Well, we thought we might have to draft you," and Barry lashed out, "Draft nothin', I told you I'm not going to run! And I'm telling you now. Don't paint me into a corner. It's my political neck and I intend to have something to say about what happens to it."

We later learned that someone—we think it may have been the Essex spy—told Barry that Clif was only in it to boost his political consulting business and for the "big salary." In truth, Clif was drawing so little money that he had to raid his kids' college funds just to pay his bills. We couldn't leave it at that, and Charlie Barr, an old friend of Barry's and one of the earliest boosters for a Goldwater candidacy, set up another meeting to include himself, Clif, and me. I was included, ostensibly, to discuss any funding issues that might arise, but it was really to introduce me as an alternative point of contact with the group, taking Clif out of the line of fire. (In fact, it would be some nine months before Barry and Clif would have another conversation.) Barry and I had met a few times in the past and he knew me as a contributor to some of his pet causes. At this meeting, Barry was certainly more relaxed with two people he knew better than he knew Clif, and he admitted that he didn't mind if the committee continued to work on his behalf, suggesting that perhaps it could even be expanded. He understood one important value of his candidacy: Even if he didn't win, the conservative movement would be nurtured and the voters would be exposed for the first time in thirty years to a clear choice. However, he would not commit "at this time" and reserved the right to call a halt at any time.

So the door was left ajar, and two weeks later I marched through to keep the dialogue open, to provide an update on our fundraising efforts. Barry was almost enthusiastic: "That's great, really a good start . . . for whoever will be our candidate." But he emphasized it was only a start. "A campaign is like a stool with three legs," he explained. "A good message, a good candidate, and someone to pay for it. Most campaigns do well on the first two, but without the third, the cash, the stool falls over."

Another two weeks, another visit (this time, at his home in Phoenix) where Barry shared his assessment of the major political figures of the day—the competition, if you will. JFK: good friend, poor president. LBJ: a "son of a bitch," a wheeler-dealer without scruples. Nixon: hard worker, insecure. Rockefeller: good friend, big spender of other folks' money. Scranton: good friend, entered the Pennsylvania governor's race at Barry's urging. Romney: didn't know him very well, didn't know much about him. Hubert

Humphrey: salt of the earth, stand-up guy, you could always trust him to keep his word, a truly nice fellow, but way too liberal.

Then Barry probed me a bit. Who was I? Where did I come from? Where did I think I might be going with this Goldwater for President thing? My story was easy to tell: Harvard, Navy, the banking business, a seat on the NYSE, some experience in political campaigns. "And," I emphasized, "it's not just me . . . it's Jerry Milbank and a team of experts from all over the country dedicated to the cause." When I told him that the committee would be going public within a few days, he gave me a look—perhaps of surprise, perhaps one of those inscrutable expressions that could mean anything you wanted it to mean—but then he made sure I understood his position: "I'm not a candidate at this time and won't become one unless I'm convinced that I have widespread support and the backing of a strong, well-financed organization." This was nothing I didn't already know.

On April 8, 1963, Peter O'Donnell launched the National Draft Goldwater Committee with a press conference at Washington's Mayflower Hotel, "to mobilize the tremendous, spontaneous enthusiasm for Senator Goldwater that is sweeping the country . . . and to encourage and channel the efforts of all volunteers who want to help Senator Goldwater."

A full-scale committee meeting came next. Clif, on his way to logging about a million miles flying around the country, reported on progress in filling those empty party slots, state by state. But we all had a more immediate concern, and the suspense was palpable: How would Goldwater react to the announcement?

That afternoon, some reporters tracked him down and pressed him for a comment. He said, "I'm not taking any position on this draft movement. It's their time and their money. But they are going to have to get along without any help from me."[1] A week later, we were able to really relax when he told the New York Times: "I don't want the nomination. I'm not looking for it. I haven't authorized anybody to look at it for me. But who can tell what will happen a year from now? A man would be a damn fool to predict with finality what he would do in this unpredictable world."[2]

An article in the March 26, 1963 Chicago Tribune was headlined: "Kennedys Fear One Man in 1964 Election—Goldwater." In truth, the Democrats hoped that no one noticed, because their strategy, then and for the near term, was to publicly downplay any threat from Goldwater and build up Rockefeller as the man to beat in 1964—and they were doing a pretty good job of it. When delegates to the 1960 Republican convention were asked by Congressional Quarterly (April 3, 1963) who was most likely to get the 1964 nomination, Rockefeller or Goldwater, better than 2 to 1 said "Rockefeller." (When asked whom they *preferred*, the score was about 4 to 3 in favor of Goldwater.) A Gallup poll taken at the end of April had Rockefeller the front runner among Republican voters at 43 percent; Goldwater had 26 percent, and the other potential candidates, Michigan governor George Romney and Pennsylvania governor William Scranton, had 13 percent and 7 percent, respectively. "Richard Nixon" was not included in the poll, although he was considered a possibility.

However, three things happened during the first week of May to change the Republican landscape: Richard Nixon announced that he was moving from California to New York, thus abandoning whatever political base he still had. George Romney's nascent presidential aspirations were dashed by Michigan's largest newspaper, the *Detroit News* ("Come home, George," the editor wrote on May 3, "and let's get on with the chores"). And Nelson Rockefeller got married.

When Rockefeller divorced his wife of thirty-one years and the mother of his five children late in 1961, most political insiders gave it little significance. But when the fifty-four-year-old Rockefeller was remarried May 4, 1963, to a thirty-six-year-old woman whose own divorce had just become final—and who appeared to be abandoning her four children in the process—things changed. There had been rumors of "another woman" for some time, and now suspicions were confirmed. There were rumblings in the press: In the eyes of many church leaders, the new Mrs. Rockefeller should have waited for a year. In the eyes of mothers everywhere, he was a homewrecker. Rockefeller's pre-marital Gallup poll standing of 43 percent dropped, almost overnight, to 29 percent, and Barry's rose from 26 percent to 40 percent. Bill Rusher put it in perspective: "Rockefeller is the only candidate who has turned motherhood into a liability!"[3]

By the middle of June, things were clearly swinging our way. Dick Nixon told a reporter from the *New York Times* (June 13, 1963) that "Among professional politicians, Senator Goldwater has the lead, and they have more influence on nominations than anyone else." Three days later the paper reported "Goldwater Gaining in Northeast, Republican State Chairmen Say." The *Washington Star* noted that, among a group of Eastern Republican party workers: "A surprising number—considering the scarcity of strong conservatives in the group—indicated a willingness, if not an eagerness, to see the nomination go to Senator Goldwater."[4] The June 14 edition of *Time* noted, "If the Republican national convention were to be held today, Goldwater would almost certainly be its presidential nominee."

And, from the Rowland Evans–Robert Novak newspaper column of June 24: "The fact that Senator Barry Goldwater is so far in front for the Republican Presidential nomination is proof of a little-understood transformation in the party's power structure. This transformation . . . is nothing less than a quiet revolt. The aggressive post-war club of conservative young Republicans from the small states of the West and South are seizing power, displacing the Eastern party chiefs who have dictated Republican policy and candidates for a generation."

Note well: "conservative young Republicans." We were indeed harnessing the energy of such groups as the Young Republicans . . . part social club, part political incubator. Clif White had long been involved, and John Ashbrook, one of the founders of Draft Goldwater went from chairmanship of the Young Republicans to a seat in Congress. Toward the end of June, I attended the 1963 annual meeting as a delegate from Connecticut. (Yes, in this crowd, thirty-seven counted as "young.") Goldwater, Rockefeller, Scranton, and Romney had been invited to address the convention; Goldwater was the only one who came, and he gave us a fighting conservative speech. "The old, respectable, sometimes noble liberalism of fifty years ago is gone for good." Don't be fooled, he said, by the phony liberals "with corrupt big-city machines whose job it is to deliver the bloc votes in the big Northern cities." Modern liberalism, he said, "is only a form of rigor mortis." The liberal Democrats "have not had a new idea in thirty years."

A fighting speech that foreshadowed a bit—okay, a lot—of fighting among the delegates, Goldwater conservatives against Rockefeller liberals. There was some pushing and shoving, wrestling over control of the microphones, attempts to rig the voting for a new chairman, and tempers were running high. As I recall, columnist Bob Novak was up in the balcony covering this, and when one of our guys found out he was with the media, he punched *him*, not realizing he could be an ally!

Novak was really upset. In his post-convention narrative, he wrote of "hard-faced, implacable young men with crew cuts and buttoned-down collars, shrieking into floor microphones and chanting and stamping their feet in union in a systematic effort to disrupt the convention."[5]

I don't believe I have ever had a crew cut, and I certainly am not hard-faced. I may on occasion have worn buttoned-down collars, but is that a sin? From my perspective, people were shouting into microphones because the microphones had been switched off by a Rockefeller man trying to control the debate, and our folks were stamping to show their disapproval. The outgoing (defeated) Rockefeller chairman told the *St. Paul Pioneer Press*, on July 6, that we "were using the exact same techniques used by the Communists," and he told the *Minneapolis Sunday Tribune* the next day that Goldwater's speech was like pouring "gasoline on the flames" of the conservatives. Other papers played a more accurate "Goldwater Takes Control of Young Republicans" theme, a theme we welcomed as demonstrating Goldwater's appeal among young voters.

Rockefeller was unwilling—nay, he was *unable*—to see the drop in his standing as a result of his own actions, and fumed at what he saw as a conservative vendetta. On July 14, he lashed out; there was "real danger," he said, from "extremist elements" trying to take over the Republican Party. He cited the Young Republican convention, where "the radical right lunatic fringe" resorted to the "tactics of totalitarianism." He claimed that "every objective observer . . . has reported that the proceedings there were dominated by extremist groups, catrefully organized, well-financed and operated through the tactics of ruthless, rough-shod intimidation. [Those] who successfully engineered this disgraceful subversion of a great and responsible auxiliary of the Republican Party are the same people who are now moving to subvert the Republican Party itself."[6] He was talking about me and my friends.

The July 15 "Rocky Declares War on Goldwater" headline in the *New York Journal-American* was predictable. But Rockefeller's strategy—if there was any—soon backfired. *Time* (July 26, 1963) suggested the outburst was a reaction to his precipitous drop in the polls and embarrassment over Barry's "well-publicized personal triumph" at the Young Republican convention. On the floor of the Senate, Nebraska's Carl Curtis offered, "It is my considered judgment that a man who would take such desperate and destructive measures against his own party in a gamble to gain some temporary personal advantage has already forfeited any claim to loyalty from any part of the party organization."[7] Goldwater's mailbags began filling with letters, as many as a thousand a day, urging him to run for president.

I thought it might be useful for Barry to make a foray into the liberal fortress of the Northeast and, through my contacts with the Hartford-based insurance industry, arranged for him to be guest of honor and dinner speaker at a convention of insurance agents. At a press conference in the afternoon, Barry was asked what he thought of the competition from Rockefeller for the Republican nomination. He answered, "I'm not sure he's a Republican."

It was around this time that I was to learn, to my distress but not discouragement, that the straight talk and blunt descriptions for which Goldwater was so admired could be severe liabilities in a presidential campaign. He had, I think, a constitutional inability to not answer a question, no matter how controversial the subject or unprepared his response. Such candor had always been his hallmark; it served him well in the Senate and when addressing adoring crowds of conservative supporters, but it was a disaster with reporters who could—and often did—emphasize the sensational or take his comments out of context, or both. Too late, he learned that such openness was an unaffordable luxury at the level of national politics. I would later learn that no less an authority than President John F. Kennedy, talking with journalist Ben Bradlee about a possible Goldwater candidacy, had suggested, "People will start asking him questions, and he's so damn quick on the trigger that he will answer them. And when he does, it will be all over."[8]

Wherever he went, Barry kept handing fat, juicy sound bites to the media. They were vintage Goldwater, as when he said that government couldn't stop depressions, it only starts them, or that he had voted against federal aid to education because he didn't think educators could spend the amount of money they were seeking. To a group of bankers at an Economics Club meeting, he said, "We are told that many people lack skills and cannot find jobs because they did not have an education. It's like saying that people have big feet because they wear big shoes. The fact is that most people who have no skills have no education for the same reason—low intelligence or ambition."[9]

Throughout the summer, he played reluctant debutante. He didn't say "no," but he wouldn't commit, either. An AP poll of GOP state and county leaders, released November 2, asked, in essence, who would be the strongest candidate against Kennedy. More than 85 percent said "Goldwater." Rockefeller came in at just under 4 percent. The governor was not deterred; he formally announced his candidacy on November 6. To show that he really knew how to play this game, he sent an announcement telegram and a bunch of red roses to every female delegate to all previous conventions. When told of this, Barry was not much impressed; that was not *his* style. He told us—more than once—that he would not be packaged "by some Madison Avenue agency." He later would tell the brilliant campaign PR man Lee Edwards that if anyone tried to create "puff pieces" about hobbies and habits, Edwards would be out of a job. Nothing about Barry's years-long passion for Ham radio. Nothing about his tinkering with autos (even though that had been a focus of the earlier *Popular Mechanics* profile). Nothing about his great skill as a photographer. By trying to force the campaign to stick with the issues, and only the issues, Goldwater the politician shut the public off from getting to know Goldwater the man.

By the middle of November, when we felt that we had lined up sufficient delegate strength, Jerry Milbank and I went down to Washington and asked for Goldwater's commitment. Barry was very gracious, but not yet ready. He reminded me of the third leg of the campaign stool: "I'm not going to go," he said, "unless I see a big chunk of change in the kitty." To this point, fund-raising during the "Draft Barry" period had been focused on raising work-ing capital; our finance team had been fairly successful, and we had brought in about $750,000, but much of it had been spent and, to Barry's point, we were going to need a lot more. Barry did try to be helpful. He said, "I have a buddy out in Washington who said he'd give me half a million dollars, and I have another friend who can raise a million bucks." So I called Barry's half-million-dollar buddy out in Washington—no dice; he would contribute maybe $12,000. The million-dollar guy was astonished: "I don't know how Barry got that idea!" Discouraging, to say the least, but Jerry, Stets, and I kept plugging away, and eventually we had a respectable treasury. The three of us went back to Barry with the numbers, and he said all right, he'd declare, but probably not until January; otherwise, media coverage would disappear into the deep well of holiday indifference.

At almost the same moment, *Time* got in a quick interview; to the point "What next?" Barry said, "God knows I haven't sought this position. I'm still wishing that something would happen to get me out of all of this. It's all a little frightening." The interview was published in the November 22, 1963, issue—the date on which "something" did indeed happen . . . something beyond comprehension.

I had known the young Jack Kennedy, slightly; I'd attended his wedding reception in Newport and once dated Jackie Kennedy's sister, Lee Bouvier. Call it a semi–blind date arranged by two of my old Owl Club friends, Bev Corbin and Steve Spencer. But our paths diverged and I didn't see Kennedy at all after he became president. On November 22, when the alarm bell on the stock ticker in my office began the urgent clanging that signaled "Bulletin, read immediately," the shock of the news was so great that I had to read it three times, thinking I was misreading some simple item. The pres-ident had been shot in Dallas.

At first, the assassination was blamed on the "radical right," especially the rabid right of Texas; even some on Goldwater's staff suspected as much. The Draft Goldwater office in Washington was closed because of threats, and death threats forced Texas senator John Tower's family to move into a hotel. Even the discovery of assassin Lee Harvey Oswald's connections to the Soviets and Cubans did not entirely quell the suspicions. The radical right was deemed capable of anything.

Now, with his friend John Kennedy dead and replaced by a man he did not admire, Barry was ready to give up even before declaring his candidacy. He wasn't interested in competing with a man he knew to be "a dirty fighter . . . a wheeler-dealer . . . and treacherous to boot. He'd slap you on the back today and stab you in the back tomorrow."[10] However, after a couple of days for serious reflection, he said okay—to us. But in private, he told his wife that he really didn't want to run, that he didn't want to be president, but that he did want to give conservatives a cause and a voice. "Lose the election," he said, "but win the Party."[11]

Barry made the formal announcement from his home in Phoenix on January 3, 1964. We suggested that he announce from one of the nation's media centers, Washington or New York, but no matter. January 3 was a Friday—a day of the week best suited to burying, not encouraging, media coverage, but no matter. Barry wanted to show that he was his own man.

> I will seek the Republican Presidential nomination. I have decided to do this because of the principles in which I believe and because I am convinced that millions of Americans share my belief in these principles. . . . I have been spelling out my position now for ten years in the Senate and for years before that here in my own state. I will spell it out even further in the months to come. I was once asked, what kind of Republican I was. I replied that I was *not* a "me-too" Republican. That still holds. I will not change my beliefs to win votes. I will offer a choice, not an echo. This will not be an engagement of personalities. It will be an engagement of principles.[12]

"A choice, not an echo." This was a play on the then-typical Republican approach to American politics; the Eastern Establishment more or less agreed with most Democrat positions and proposals, but suggested that "they" would be better able to carry them out because they all had MBAs from Harvard. Goldwater proposed to lead us out of that wilderness.

But there was a hint of what was to come: No members of the Draft Committee were invited to attend the event. We had expected that, effective with Barry' announcement, he would also announce a campaign organization that would fold in our team. We had assumed, not unreasonably, that we would simply change the name of the Draft movement to something like "Goldwater for President" and soldier on. It was not to be.

Goldwater was uncomfortable with people he didn't know and—perhaps in part because of the misinformation he had been given about Clif's motives—he was suspicious of Draft Goldwater. This all was made quite clear in his selections for top campaign staff, a close-knit palace guard that came to be known as the "Arizona Mafia." I find the term to be too pejorative; there is no question but that they ran protective interference for Goldwater, and at times made decisions for him that they were not qualified to make—but I found them all to be men of honor and goodwill.

Phoenix lawyer and Barry's longtime friend Denison Kitchel was campaign manager; Dean Burch, another Arizona lawyer who had once been his Senate office administrative assistant, was number two; and Dick Kleindienst (a Harvard classmate of mine, although we didn't know each other at school) was director of field operations. The immediate staff was to include speechwriter Karl Hess, generally acknowledged to be one of the best in the business, and Bill Baroody, president of the proto-conservative Washington think tank the American Enterprise Institute. Baroody had worked with Goldwater since the election of 1958, as sort of an intellectual mentor—a role to which, staffers told me, he brought a large measure of arrogance, which would get in the way later in the campaign. Baroody did not seem to suffer fools, foolishness, or anyone who disagreed with his judgment or advice.

For example, at one point *National Review* editors Bill Buckley and Brent Bozell had a meeting with Kitchel, Baroody, and another staffer. They proposed, among other things, to provide academic credibility to the campaign by assembling a team of well-known educators and other credentialed experts. However, each suggestion they offered was turned aside by Baroody. He apparently viewed "intellectual" as his territory; he wanted no help or interference from outsiders. As a result, Buckley, who practically created the conservative movement, was effectively shut out of the campaign.

Where the Draft Committee had built a solid infrastructure and established personal connections with Republican leaders throughout the nation, Kitchel and Kleindeinst were largely unknown and without political influence—except with Barry. In what I can only characterize as an astonishing blunder, key members of the Draft Committee were shunted aside, some to be given subordinate roles, others ignored. While there were hurt feelings aplenty, and friction galore, the Draft rejectees continued, nonetheless, to work on Barry's behalf throughout the primaries, the convention, and the campaign. As for me, I don't think Barry had any close friends who understood the duties and responsibilities of a campaign treasurer, so I was kept on in that capacity. I was the only member of the Draft group to be included in the immediate campaign staff.

Later, during a meeting of the campaign finance committee in Chicago, Barry did at least acknowledge our collective role, our contribution to the effort. "I thank the group that met here in Chicago at that *secret* meeting that the whole world heard about. There were times when I wished that Peter O'Donnell, White, Middendorf, Milbank and their group would go home and run their cattle ranches but now I'm grateful to them. Now, I want this job. And when I want something, I go after it."

Our fervor, he said, reminded him of a religious movement, and he admitted that he had not yet been doing a very good job. "I'm a clumsy idiot," he said, "with five feet and six hands." He pledged: "This is a campaign I intend to win. I have never lost a campaign and I'm too old to go back to work and too young to quit politics." He added, "My tail's too big to put between my legs."

And, he laughed, "Reporters throw up at the thought of me being nominated."

Chapter 4

Presidential Politics: Goldwater, the Nomination

Irst up on the campaign trail: the New Hampshire primary. In total, Barry was to spend twenty-three days clumping through the snow with a cast on a foot painfully sore from an operation, eighteen-hour days often wasted on the wrong audiences. How wrong? He was scheduled to talk with a group of eight-year-olds at a primary school. It was a campaign so disorganized that the very term "campaign" is seriously out of place. As social historian Theodore White noted, "For mismanagement, blundering and sheer naiveté, Goldwater's New Hampshire campaign was unique."[1]

At the beginning of this campaign, Clif put together a briefing book—itinerary, names of officials and people he would be meeting—but Kitchel and friends had not passed it on to Barry. On March 5, five days before the primary, Mary McGrory of the *Washington Star* wrote, "Senator Goldwater has yet to give a statistic about New Hampshire. He does not even trouble to mention the town in which he finds himself."

Was he unprepared? Or, maybe, he didn't much care. Barry's core message should have had resonance where the state motto was "Live Free or Die," but on the trail he was impatient, irritable. His speeches were dull and his delivery was flat. He made it crystal clear that he would rather be elsewhere. As he told one audience, "I'm not one of these baby-kissing, hand-shaking, blintz-eating candidates. I don't like to insult the American intelligence by thinking that slapping people on the back is going to win you votes."[2]

By contrast, chief opponent Rockefeller knew how to play this game; he shook hands, kissed babies, slapped backs, and charmed everyone. Where Barry was driven around in a Cadillac, Rockefeller rode on a bus with the press. Peggy Goldwater wore mink; Happy Rockefeller wore tweedy cloth. People in New Hampshire noticed.

On his first day in New Hampshire, Barry's truthful but blunt talk triggered the two most contentious issues of the entire campaign. At a press conference in Concord, he was asked whether or not he was in favor of continuing Social Security. His views on Social Security were no secret: He long had believed it to be an underfunded pseudo-insurance program, originally developed as a barely adequate safety net for elder citizens, many of whom in the depth of the Depression had no savings and little hope. Now, the Depression long past, the wages of every worker were being taxed to fund the program, but not every worker would likely need the program. Therefore, he responded, he would offer "one change," by making participation in the program voluntary. "If a person can provide better for himself, let him do it. But if he prefers the government to do it, let him." There were many better ways to invest the payroll tax, he suggested, and "get a better Social Security program."

Headline writing is an art, not a science; the people who write headlines try to boil a story down to an attention-getting essence. The people who write headlines, however, are not the people who write the stories. Thus, above a January 8 story that was largely accurate, was the *Concord Monitor* headline of the day: "Goldwater Sets Goals: End Social Security. . ." Copies of the article were soon distributed by the Rockefeller team to every Social Security beneficiary in the state. They knew that people who read headlines don't necessarily read the articles.

Later in the day, Goldwater set up what became the other key issue of the campaign. He was asked by a *Washington Post* reporter about President Eisenhower's recent suggestion that the six American divisions in NATO could be cut to one. Goldwater did not fully agree, but said that the number could indeed be cut, perhaps by one-third, if NATO commanders in Europe had the power to use tactical nuclear weapons on their own authority in an emergency. At another meeting with the press a short time later, he was asked about nuclear weapons in Europe and gave about the same answer: "I have said, the commander should have the ability to use nuclear weapons. . . . Former commanders have told me that NATO troops should be equipped with nuclear weapons, but the use should remain only with the commander."[3]

He meant, of course, *the* commander of NATO, not unit commanders in the field. He meant, of course, tactical nuclear weapons of limited reach— with a yield equal to perhaps forty metric tons of dynamite over a radius of about one mile (sub-microscopic compared with the fifty-*million*-ton weapons of the day). No matter, his comment was interpreted to mean that any hot-headed major could start a nuclear holocaust. No matter that NATO was already equipped with tactical nukes. No matter, also, that the policy he suggested was the policy, actual, of both presidents Eisenhower and Kennedy.

These two issues—or, rather, a willful and widespread misunderstanding of these issues—dogged him to the very end of the campaign, when a touring Lyndon Johnson would exhort the crowds: "Vote Democratic on November 3. Vote to save your Social Security from going down the drain. Vote to keep a prudent hand which will not mash that nuclear button."

But again I am getting ahead of the story.

By the middle of February, our estimated delegate count was 425 firm, 124 leaning. We were bringing some political leaders on board, but our greatest strength remained with the grass roots. We had pretty good control of fund-raising and were reasonably on target toward Clif's original budget estimate of $3.2 million. However, the campaign leaders—Kitchel and the others—seemed to have no plan and were spending money in scattershot fashion. Too much advertising money was spent in some places, not enough in others. They were spending too much money on charter aircraft. They were spending money on polls in areas where we didn't need the information, such as the District of Columbia.

This latter point sent my brother Harry (then president of the Conservative Party of New York City) off on a moderate tirade. "What on earth," he said, "is the reason for wasting money on polls?" Barry, he suggested—a creative politician with fresh new ideas—should create opinion, not try to conform with the popular notions of the day. "When moving into an uncharted sea, polls are useless." Harry had a point, but he was fixated on the Edsel debacle, the failed Ford product that had been designed by polls. He didn't understand the tactical value of political polling.

Barry wasn't concerned about the budget (or lack thereof), but he had some issues of his own, largely centered on the media's focus on his irrelevant off-the-cuff comments. "I have never in my life seen such nonsense," he told me; but he added, "I don't intend to butter up the press. . . . I've made one hundred and twenty-five speeches in Los Angeles, one hundred and twenty-five in San Francisco, two hundred and fifty in New York. If I'm not well known now, I never will be." Where my brother didn't understand the tactical value of polls, Barry was blind to the tactical value of working with the media.

His first trips into New Hampshire were met by record-breaking, cheering crowds, the largest in the history of many towns. Along the way, though, Barry lost some voters to his own missteps, and aggressive attacks by Rockefeller cost him more. Goldwater and Rockefeller tried to outdo each other with public meetings and purchased media, succeeding only in pushing the "undecided" vote as high as 50 percent. A team pushing a write-in vote for Nixon's 1960 running mate, Henry Cabot Lodge—who, as our then-ambassador to Vietnam, did no campaigning and wasn't even in the country—spent their time and money rounding up supporters and sending out sample ballots, on which they clearly demonstrated how to vote for a write-in candidate. The man who had not set foot in the state captured "undecided" and won the race going away, 33,007 votes. Goldwater was second at 20,692, with Rockefeller only about a thousand votes behind.[4]

We watched the returns on TV in a room at the Madison Hotel in Washington, while a bunch of reporters waited downstairs. Not more than eighteen minutes after the polls had closed, the networks announced the results. Barry took the news quietly, went down to face the cameras, and offered one of the most honest comments ever spoken by a politician: "I goofed."

Kitchel—the lawyer dabbling in public affairs—issued a press release: "It is most gratifying that a candidate from the far west, Senator Barry Goldwater, could do so well in the New England state of New Hampshire."[5] No one was fooled.

We began to enjoy victories: South Carolina, Wisconsin, North Dakota, Kentucky, and Illinois—although press coverage of the Illinois primary was bizarre. Goldwater had a big win against six candidates, but, "It was the first contest I have ever been involved in," Clif said, "where the candidate got 62 percent of the vote and still came out a loser in the press." As columnist David Lawrence, *Washington Star* (April 16, 1964), offered: "Maybe two and two don't make four, after all, in national politics. Judging by some of the TV and radio broadcasts on Tuesday night and subsequent comments in the press, Senator Goldwater got the highest number of votes . . . but nonetheless suffered a 'setback.'"

Arizona, Louisiana, New Jersey, Iowa, Texas, Ohio, Indiana, District of Columbia. Clif's unofficial reckoning soon put the total of committed delegates at more than four hundred. *Time* magazine, May 8, wondered at Goldwater's momentum: "It seemed hardly possible. Here was Arizona's Barry Goldwater, who only a few weeks ago appeared to be flat on his back in his quest for the GOP Presidential nomination. . . . Yet, as of last week, Goldwater was clearly the man to beat [at the Republican convention] in San Francisco." *Time* ascribed his come-out-of-nowhere to "the national preoccupation with primaries, which usually make more headlines than delegates," and to an "obsession with the polls. But no pollster ever nominated a Presidential candidate." Slow and steady, *Time* noted, "Goldwater kept collecting delegates while the unavowed and disavowed collected press clippings."

Clif White may have been pushed off the main stage by the boys from Arizona, but, aided by a throng of coordinators in the field, he continued to quietly work his strategy—fill the seats, grow the delegates—all unimpeded by the mismanagement of the campaign leadership or the missteps of our candidate.

On May 12, 1964, to show voters in the rest of the nation that even in Rockefeller's hometown Barry had pull, we held a "monster" rally in Madison Square Garden. The *Daily News*, the tabloid with the trademarked slogan "New York's Picture Newspaper," carried the banner headline "18,000 Cheer Barry In Garden" and filled the rest of the front page with a marvelous shot of the band playing, the crowd applauding, balloons dropping, Barry and his wife Peggy at the podium—and, standing with them and looking quite happy, yours truly.

May 24, during an ABC television interview, Howard K. Smith asked Barry about interdicting enemy supplies headed south along the Ho Chi Minh trail in Vietnam. Barry replied, "Well, it's not as easy as it sounds because these aren't trails that are out in the open. . . .There have been several suggestions made. I don't think we would use any of them. But defoliation of the forests by low-yield atomic weapons could well be done. When you remove the foliage, you remove the cover. . . ." The wire services ignored the "I don't think we would use any of them" part and reported that Barry—who was only discussing possibilities—had advocated the use of nuclear weapons in Vietnam. UPI later issued a retraction, but it was too late. They had already dumped gasoline on the "Goldwater is trigger happy" fire. With the California primary fast approaching, Rockefeller jumped on the story and spent $120,000 to distribute a pamphlet to California's three million registered Republicans: "Who Do You Want in the Room with the H-Bomb?"

In truth, most polls showed Rockefeller running a bit ahead in California when his sins—so to speak—caught up with him. Three days before the June 2 primary, Happy Rockefeller gave birth to a son. "Only Rockefeller," as Bill Rusher had said almost exactly a year earlier, "could turn motherhood into a liability."

Goldwater squeaked through by about 68,000 votes out of 2.1 million cast—in an election with an astonishing 72 percent turnout. It was not much, but enough.

Clif's three years and a million miles had been well spent in lining up key local support throughout the nation. Goldwater won all but two of the primaries he entered (he ran behind Rockefeller in Oregon) and piled up 2,150,000 votes—more votes than all other candidates put together.

About now in the time line, one non-campaign event merits brief discussion. The Senate passed the Civil Rights Act of 1964 by a vote of seventy-three to twenty-seven. Barry Goldwater was one of the twenty-seven. It made no political sense for a soon-to-be candidate for president to vote against a controversial but popular social issue on the very eve of a national campaign. Barry did a lot of things that made no political sense but that he believed were right. On this measure, he was not alone. He was joined in dissent by a number of legislators of some stature: Albert Gore Sr. of Tennessee, Sam Irvin of North Carolina, J. William Fullbright of Arkansas, Norris Cotton of New Hampshire, Bourke Hickenlooper of Iowa, Edwin L. Mecham of New Mexico, Millard L. Simpson of Wyoming, and John Tower of Texas, and George H. W. Bush, candidate for the Senate from Texas.

Goldwater voted against the 1964 Civil Rights Bill because he questioned the constitutionality of two sections, relating to fair employment and public accommodation. The latter—the so-called Mrs. Murphy clause—held that a person couldn't refuse to rent their home or a room in their boardinghouse to anyone. The goal was to ensure that African American or other ethnic minorities could not arbitrarily be excluded, but as written the law forbade discrimination against drunks, felons, wife abusers, and people who smoke in bed.

"I am unalterably opposed to discrimination of any sort," Goldwater said from the floor of the Senate. "I believe that, though the problem is fundamentally one of the heart, some law can help; but not law that embodies features like these, provisions which fly in the face of the Constitution." Goldwater argued that states have all the rights not specifically reserved to the federal government by the Constitution, and that employment and accommodation were local, not national, issues.

He was swimming against the current and knew it, but he stood on principle. "If my vote is misconstrued," he said, "let it be, and let me suffer its consequences." In hindsight his vote put a larger hit on his legacy, an unfair tarnish on his reputation today ("He voted against the Civil Rights Act of 1964!"), than on his election prospects then. It matters not that he had voted for the Civil Rights Acts of 1957 and 1960, that he approved of the other nine Titles of the Act of 1964, or that he had offered four amendments to the Youth Employment Act of 1963 to forbid discrimination because of race, color, creed, or national origin. It matters not that Goldwater had integrated the employees of his family department store before World War II. It matters not that as organizer of the Arizona Air National Guard after the war he ensured and enforced integration, this, two years before President Truman ordered desegregation of the armed forces. It matters not that he had been active in desegregating the lunch counters of Phoenix, or that he had been a member of the NAACP and Urban League.

Based on no known evidence, the nation's best-known political pundit—Walter Lippman—took an egregious leap of judgment and wrote, for the *Newsweek* issue of June 22: "In his extreme views on states' rights, [Goldwater] is in fact one who would dissolve the Federal union into a mere confederation of the states . . . he would nullify if he could the central purpose of the Civil War amendments, and would take from the children of the emancipated slaves the protection of a national union."

At the same time, another media titan reacted, not to Goldwater's vote, but to the torrent of abuse being heaped upon him. Newspaper publisher John S. Knight offered an apology, of sorts, for his brethren:

> Barry Goldwater is not my candidate, and I have done nothing to promote his Presidential aspirations, but I do think the Arizona Senator is getting shabby treatment from most of the news media.
>
> Some of the television commentators discuss Goldwater with evident disdain and contempt. Editorial cartoonists portray him as belonging to the Neanderthal age, or as a relic of the 19th Century. It is the fashion of editorial writers to persuade themselves that Goldwater's followers are either "kooks" or Birchers. This simply is not so. The Goldwater movement represents a mass protest by conservatively minded people against foreign aid, excessive welfare, high taxes, foreign policy and the concentration of power in the federal government.[6]

While Rockefeller was licking his wounds, one of the earlier-mentioned candidates woke up, saw an opportunity, and started running for real. Until then, Governor Scranton had been a minor player and had entered only one contest—the Oregon primary, where he took a minuscule 2 percent of the vote. Now, he officially offered himself as a candidate for the nomination. In so doing, he took a broad swipe at Goldwater's supporters. Don't, he said, "let an exclusion-minded minority dominate our platform and chose our candidates."[7] He went out on what was left of the campaign trail, where he drew respectable crowds. Scranton gained the backing—moral and financial—of Rockefeller, who officially quit the race and turned his entire campaign staff over to the gentleman from Harrisburg.

A week later, Henry Cabot Lodge resigned his post in Vietnam and came home to join the Scranton effort. President Eisenhower's brother Milton agreed to place Scranton's name in nomination (Ike remained scrupulously neutral). Scranton began rising in the polls, as former Rockefeller, Lodge, and Nixon supporters saw him as the last hope of the "moderates."

The polls didn't count for much. Scranton couldn't make a dent in our numbers; delegates who were already pledged to Goldwater remained pledged to Goldwater. Scranton addressed the Illinois convention on June 30. Of the fifty-eight delegates, forty-eight announced for Goldwater, and the rest declined to commit for any candidate. At the Utah caucus a few days later, Scranton learned to his dismay that the Young Republicans had captured the delegates almost a year before. He went on to Washington State, and it was a similar story: Twenty-two of the twenty-four delegates had been committed for more than a year. Delaware: The favorite-son candidate gave Scranton a hearing, then dropped out, announcing support for Goldwater. If Goldwater's campaign was clinically disorganized, Scranton's was fatally uninformed.

Chapter 5

Presidential Politics: Goldwater, the Convention

T rue to plan, we went to San Francisco with the winning votes in our pocket; I think Kitchel at last understood that Clif White perhaps knew his business, and Clif was put in charge of running our part of the convention. A wise choice: Clif had been working Republican National Conventions for sixteen years. He knew all of the things that could go wrong—failed communications, disruptive demonstrations, efforts to get delegates to change their votes—and knew how to prepare: backups to the backup communications, a trained security detail, and a system for maintaining contact with all delegates, including a buddy system where they roomed together and any one would rarely be alone and open to, well, persuasion.

I was on double-duty at the convention—treasurer of the campaign, of course, but I was also an official delegate from Connecticut, courtesy of Governor John Davis Lodge who, at our own state convention, jammed me down the throats of the Rockefeller-leaning selection committee. "Middendorf goes in!" he shouted, and that was that. As it turned out, I was one of only four Goldwater delegates from all of New England.

There was a flurry of odd stuff in the media, including a specious report that Barry was linked with extreme right-wing elements in Germany—a not-so-thinly-veiled suggestion that he was courting neo-Nazis. The "proof" included a purported interview in a radical German newspaper with which Barry had never spoken; the editors had created a Q&A with bits and pieces from some of our campaign literature, tweaked to conform to their own editorial bent. Of course, not one American reporter had bothered to ask Barry for comment before the rush to judgment.

The Scranton for President Committee published a daily *Convention News* that out-hectored the worst of the professional media. "News" reports in the issue of July 12 included "Vicious Drive For Goldwater Opened By

Radical Backers," and "Goldwater's Post Convention Plans Raise Questions Of Nuclear Sanity," illustrated by a photo of an atomic explosion.

That evening, the Scranton team tried to force a debate with Goldwater. An open letter from the governor was delivered to the press, the delegates (slipped under hotel room doors), and a copy was handed to me to pass to our candidate. The letter began, "As we move rapidly towards the climax of this convention the Republican Party faces a continuing struggle on two counts. The first involves, of course, selection of a candidate. Will the convention choose a candidate overwhelmingly favored by the Republican voters, or will it choose you?" And continued:

> Your organization does not even argue the merits of the question. . . . They feel they have bought, beaten and compromised enough delegate support to make the result a foregone conclusion. With open contempt for the dignity, integrity and common sense of the convention, your managers say in effect that the delegates are little more than a flock of chickens whose necks will be wrung at will. . . . Certainly you should not fear a convention you claim to control, and I would hope that we have not reached the point where you fear to face the nation.

Stirring phrases, but directed at the wrong crowd. Those delegates—the "flock of chickens whose necks will be wrung at will"—were *our* delegates, Goldwater delegates, because that's who they wanted to be. As we quickly learned, Scranton didn't write the letter and apparently had not even read it. He tried to distance himself from the content while taking "full responsibility." A neat trick, but it didn't work.

The convention was staged in an overgrown Quonset hut in South San Francisco called the Cow Palace, usually home to rodeos and stock shows. The convention formally opened on Monday, July 13, with a program of ceremonial and procedural folderol, although to get into the Cow Palace we had to pass through a throng of the semi-professional demonstrators who even today turn Bay Area events into theater. They chanted, "Barry Goldwater must go!" and carried placards: "Defoliate Goldwater," "Vote for Goldwater—Courage, Integrity, Bigotry," and "Keep NATO Fingers Off the Nuclear Button." It was not clear who or what they were supporting.

Tuesday night, Eisenhower addressed the delegates assembled. He sounded a lot more like Barry Goldwater than either Rockefeller or Scranton. "Let us not be guilty," the general said, "of maudlin sympathy for the criminal who, roaming the streets with switchblade knife and illegal firearms seeking a helpless prey, suddenly becomes, upon apprehension, a poor, underprivileged person who counts upon the compassion of our society and the laxness or weakness of too many courts to forgive his offense." Ike ended with a few well-chosen words of his own, not from the speechwriter: "Let us particularly scorn the divisive efforts of those outside our family, including sensation-seeking columnists and commentators, because, my friends, I assure you that these are people who couldn't care less about the good of our party. . . . [Let us] renew our strength from the fountain of unity, not drown ourselves in a whirlpool of factional strife and divisive ambitions."[1] A consummation, devoutly to be wished—and not achieved.

The high point of Rockefeller's campaign—and by this I am being facetious—came with his podium plea for support of a Scranton-proposed amendment denouncing "extremism." Eisenhower may have entered a plea for unity, but Rockefeller was not in a conciliatory mood. He claimed that his headquarters had received more than one hundred bomb threats. "We repudiate the efforts," he said, "of irresponsible extremist groups—such as the Communists, Ku Klux Klan, the John Birch Society, and others—to discredit our party by their efforts to infiltrate positions of responsibility in the party or attach themselves to its candidates."[2]

His remarks were interrupted by a series of angry "boos" from the audience, twenty-two times in five minutes. He smiled, looking brave in the face of such humiliation from his own party. "This is still a free country, ladies and gentlemen," he said, and television carried the spectacle, live and in countless replays, across the nation. He repeated his earlier campaign critique of our movement, condemning "infiltration and takeover of established political parties by Communist and Nazi methods."[3]

The booing intensified. "Some of you don't like to hear it, ladies and gentlemen, but it's the truth." Television, focused on Rockefeller at the podium and on some frenzied dissidents, did not show all of what was really happening in the hall—it did not show that it was not in large part our delegates who were booing, but spectators in the gallery. Clif White and his team, operating from a communications trailer outside the convention hall, were in touch with all of their floor leaders; "Knock it off," they ordered. All floor leaders reported: "It's not our people."

Was this a put-up job, rigged by Rockefeller himself? Barry seemed to think so, but he had no hard evidence. Clif White thought so, too; otherwise, he wondered, how did they get so many highly coveted gallery tickets? But Theodore White later reported that the crowd was truly angry. "As he taunted them," he wrote, "they raged." But at what? They didn't seem to know, he wrote, whether they were raging at "the East; or New York; or Communists; or liberals."[4] That they were supporters, followers, worshipers of Barry Goldwater, he had no doubt. But he also knew that, unlike the majority of men and women associated with the campaign, the members of this angry group really were out on the fringe.

The "sensation-seeking columnists and commentators" were quick enough to pile on, although the Rockefeller story soon was replaced by the story of Goldwater's victory. However, in the long term—yea, unto the present day—the story of Rockefeller's humiliation is the story of the convention. That is, that part of the convention that went by before Barry's acceptance speech, which created a sensation of a different sort.

Eight names were placed in nomination (even though Rockefeller had withdrawn from competition, he held on to his pledged delegates, hoping to forestall a first-round Goldwater victory). The mandatory speeches took seven hours; the voting, twenty-four minutes for Barry to reach the magic number of 655; and six minutes later, the roll call was over. The result: Goldwater, 883; Scranton, 214; Rockefeller, 114; Romney, 41; Margaret Chase Smith, 27; Walter Judd, 22; Hawaii senator Hiram Fong, 5; Lodge, 2. Scranton made the *amende honorable* and called for the nomination to be made unanimous. I suppose that it was, but some delegates were seen walking out of the hall.

I stopped smoking at 3 AM, Thursday, July 16, 1964. This is easy for me to remember, because I was locked in a bathroom at the Mark Hopkins, assigned to interview the potential candidates for vice president. Sitting on the tub for several hours—we couldn't go out into the other room; the media was everywhere, trying to get an angle, trying to get interviews—the bathroom was the only place we could be alone. Well, "alone" is a relative term. There was me, another Goldwater staffer, and each potential candidate and his sponsors; two or three people were standing in the bathtub, someone was sitting on the edge, everyone talking loud in order to be heard—everyone smoking. In those days we all smoked. It was glamorous and made us feel mature. And we didn't just smoke—we held our cigarettes in a certain way, straight out of the movies. Sophisticated.

Stupid. The smoke was so thick you could hardly see across the tiny room. By midnight, I was coughing so badly I resolved that if I ever got out of that room alive, I would never smoke another cigarette. And I never have.

Barry had said, "Narrow down the list." I don't remember how many were on "the list" at the beginning, but in the end there was only one: Bill Miller, chairman of the Republican National Committee. The runner-up was Walter Judd, endorsed to us by seven Minnesota congressmen, led into the bathroom by Clark MacGregor (it got really crowded). They put in a strong pitch for Judd, a true icon of the Party. However, we picked Miller the way a Wall Street analyst picks a stock: run the numbers. In Miller's case, that included personality, religion, and home state. Miller was a genuinely nice guy, Catholic (to balance Barry's Protestant faith with semi-Jewish roots), and a New Yorker. Barry, the westerner branded as a "right-wing extremist," was out of the mainstream and Miller was smack in the middle of it. We figured that with Miller on the ticket, the New York vote would be locked up.

In hindsight, I think we should have gone with Judd. He stood for something more. As a medical missionary, Walter Judd had seen how the Japanese operated, firsthand, when they invaded China; following his return home in 1938, he gave more than a thousand speeches trying to warn the American people and Congress to stop trading with the Japanese, to stop giving them the sinews of war with which they may later fight us. You should give up silk stockings now, he warned, or you may be giving up your sons later. He was right, but few people listened. Powerful. After the war, as a ten-term congressman, he was a fervent anti-Communist. In a losing race for vice president, Walter Judd would not have gone quietly down to defeat, but would have remained a fiery voice on the national scene. Nice guy Bill Miller more or less disappeared.

Later in the morning, Peter O'Donnell, Republican National Committee member Ione Harrington, and I—a bit hungover from too much celebration and a bit groggy from lack of sleep—served as the totally unnecessary official notification committee to let our candidate know that he had won, and offered our recommendation for vice president. Barry accepted the notification with genial good grace, agreed with the recommendation, and called Bill Miller to give him his own good news.

Still later, at a meeting with the fifty Republican state chairmen, Barry explained the choice of Miller—a man who had once called JFK the "foundering father of the New Frontier," and had advised that if Lyndon Johnson were offering a "Better Deal," someone had better first cut the cards. "Miller," Barry said, "drives Lyndon Johnson nuts."

He announced that he wanted his "Middendorf-Milbank" team to run the financial show. I would be treasurer of the Republican National Committee, and Jerry would be treasurer of the Goldwater for President Finance Committee, a marvelous vote of confidence in two young guys. But then, something of a shocker: Dean Burch would be chairman of the Republican National Committee, and Denny Kitchel would be campaign manager. Even though Clif had played such a critical role, he would remain in a subordinate position as Dean's assistant with the title director of field operations. After practically having invented the "Draft" movement, after having validated that he really knew what he was doing, and after more than three years pulling the wagon for Barry, he had hoped to be put in the driver's seat as RNC chairman. Clif first heard that he had been passed over from someone in an elevator, who said, "Is this thing on Dean Burch a secret or can we let it out?"

That afternoon, we went back out to the Cow Palace for Goldwater's acceptance speech. Dick Nixon made the introduction; unity was okay with him. It was time, he declared, not for the New Deal or the Fair Deal or the "Fast Deal of Lyndon Johnson, but for the Honest Deal of Barry Goldwater."

Barry Goldwater took "freedom" as the theme of his acceptance speech. "This party," he declaimed, "with its every action, every word, every breath, and every heartbeat has but a single resolve, and that is *freedom*—freedom made orderly for this Nation by our constitutional government; *freedom* under a government limited by the laws of nature and of nature's God; *freedom—balanced* so that . . . liberty, lacking order, will not become the license of the mob and the jungle."

He invited support, "Anyone who joins us in all sincerity we welcome," and clear thinking: "And let our Republicanism, so focused and so dedicated, not be made fuzzy by unthinking and stupid labels. . . ." And then, as he came to the end of his speech and in one of the most-quoted phrases of any political convention, Goldwater took on the major theme of the opposition's pre-convention debate: that he and his supporters were "extremists" and the Rockefellers and Scrantons of the party were the voices of moderation. "I would remind you," he said, "that extremism in the defense of liberty is no vice. And let me remind you also that moderation in the pursuit of justice is no virtue!"

At some point, a newsman in the press section exclaimed, "My God, he's going to run as Barry Goldwater!" The offending words had been written for Barry by political science professor Henry Jaffe, but they became his own. In the firestorm that erupted among Democrats and liberal Republicans, he maintained that the sentiment was accurate, although widely misunderstood.

Barry and Denny parsed the phrase for Eisenhower and his brother Milton. At first, the general was angry with Barry for having given the "right-wing kooks" a leg up and everyone else a punch in the nose. The conversation was touch-and-go, with our side losing, when Barry had an inspiration. "There's no more extreme action than war," he said. "General, in June 1944 when you led the Allied Forces across the English Channel, you were an 'extremist,' and you did it in defense of liberty." The general thought about that for a moment, then exclaimed to his brother, "By golly, Milton, I'm an extremist—and damn proud of it!"

Most media reaction to the nomination was negative, and, I suppose, predictable. Walter Lippmann claimed that Goldwater's election would lead to "a global, nuclear, anti-Communist crusade." Drew Pearson wrote that "The smell of fascism has been in the air at this convention." The *New York Times*: Goldwater's nomination was "a disaster for the Republican Party, and a blow to the prestige and to the domestic and international interests of the United States." The *Chicago Daily News:* Goldwater "has the invaluable ability to give a latent, fear-born prejudice a patina of respectability and plausibility." The *New York Post*: "the Birchers and racists have never before enjoyed so big a night under such respectable auspices." The *Louisville Courier-Journal* predicted: "This will be a campaign to sicken decent and thoughtful people."

Time—which reprinted the above comments in the post-Convention issue of July 24, 1964—injected some balance: "Who are the Goldwaterites? They wear tennis shoes only on tennis courts. They don't read Robert Welch or hate Negroes. They aren't nuclear-bomb throwers, and they don't write obscene letters to editors who disagree with them. They are reasonably well educated and informed. They are, in fact, nuts about Barry Goldwater without being nutty in the process."

In *their* post-Convention issue of July 27, 1964, *Newsweek* editors also offered a portrait of the Draft Goldwater movement: "Jack Kennedy wanted the nomination, recruited his cadres, planned his own strategy, his eye always on victory. Goldwater had a nationwide organization handed to him while he remained aloof, longing to remain in the Senate. Kennedy captured his supporters; Goldwater's supporters captured him."

The magazine defined these people who had "captured" the candidate: "Mostly obscure, humorlessly efficient, faintly Puritanical, they were propelled by motives as mixed as any revolutionary's. Some thirsted for authority, others delighted in the IBM technology of the new politics, still others yearned for a Free Enterprise Eden."

As for me—obscure, yes; I much preferred *Newsweek's* description of "An eager young giant of a man (6 feet 4, 215 pounds)." The magazine was properly fascinated with our fundraising success—"300,000 individual contributions, most of them \$1, \$2, and \$3,"—but overlooked Jerry Milbank, Frank Kovac, and others, to give me inaccurate (and unwarranted) credit as head of the fundraising effort.

Overall, *Newsweek* let two young members of Congress speak to our effort: John Ashbrook said, "Most older politicians are afraid to make decisions. 'Well, son,' they always say, 'I've been that route before.' We haven't had that inbreeding"; and Bob Dole stated, "We're not trying to turn back the clock, we're just trying to sound the alarm."

Chapter 6

Presidential Politics: Goldwater, the Campaign

H eading into the presidential campaign, Johnson had momentum; Barry took a vacation. Rather than capitalize on whatever public interest had been generated in his candidacy, the public campaign went on hiatus for almost six weeks. I suppose this was traditional—wait until Labor Day, it did not seem inappropriate at the time—but, while we were getting organized, LBJ was grabbing headlines, beginning with his acceptance speech at the Democratic National Convention that condemned the tactics of "fear and smear" and warned that "one rash act, one thoughtless decision, one unchecked action" could leave the world in ashes.

I still had a job in New York, of course, but also an understanding partner, and I was able to devote an increasing amount of time to the cause. The duties of RNC treasurer occupied some, but not all, of my time, and I was more than happy to be involved in a variety of other campaign-related activities, from helping with advertising to going out on the road with Barry. (On my own account, and out of my own pocket, I hired a photographer to document Barry's travels around the nation. The photographer was responsible for some of the best photos of the campaign.)

I directly coordinated the finances of the Republican National Committee, the Republican National Finance Operations Committee, the Republican Campaign Committee, Citizens for Goldwater-Miller, the Citizens' Campaign Committee for Goldwater-Miller, T.V. for Goldwater-Miller, the National T.V. for Goldwater-Miller Committee, and Women Voters for Goldwater-Miller. Overall, there may have been thirty committees with similar titles, set up to avoid limits on individual contributions to, and spending by, any one group. Under the law of the day, no individual could contribute more than $5,000 to any one committee, nor could any committee collect more than $3 million.

We laid down the finance and accounting procedures and established controls over expenditures. Our new finance chairman was the former chairman of the board of General Electric, Ralph Cordiner. Ralph was a businessman, not a politician, and in a departure from the usual campaign financing, he insisted that we run on a purely cash basis, not spending—or committing, which is about the same thing—any money we did not have in the bank. That made it difficult to plan for an uncertain future. Since radio and TV companies wanted funds in hand at least forty-eight hours before broadcast, our advertising agencies needed the money seventy-two hours before. That was for one-minute or thirty-second "commercials," which often could be booked at the last minute. For a longer program, sched- ules were set at least a month in advance; we couldn't book a half-hour slot unless we already had the money, roughly $130,000, kept in a sort of escrow account. Welcome to "Ralph's Rules," which sharply reduced flexibility to confront fast-changing events.

The RNC had a lot of work to do, adding space, rearranging offices, install- ing new equipment, taking the staff from about one hundred people to more than seven hundred. Staffers came in like a whirlwind, scrambling for office space like children playing musical chairs. One man introduced himself to another, adding "I'm the finance director of Committee X. What's your job?" The other man was greatly upset, because he thought that *he* was slated for that job. In the event, neither man became finance director. When an incompetent national committee holdover was fired for what was deemed to be good and sufficient reason, he triggered a telephone daisy chain through George Humphrey to Kitchel to Dean Burch to me—all within thirty min- utes. George (at home in Cleveland) was the eight-hundred-pound gorilla, and I immediately called him, only to be treated to vituperation for another thirty minutes; we were "Stupid, youthful, unlegal." And those were the nice things he said. When he finally calmed down, I explained what was at issue; he listened, and came on board.

Our fundraising effort was exceptional; in truth, the techniques we pio- neered during the primaries and the campaign set the standard for all who came after. Big money is usually easy to get, especially from lobbyists (usually, but in this election, they were betting on LBJ), but this gets very few peo- ple involved with the candidate. I pushed what I believe to have been some revolutionary fundraising tactics: charging petition-signers a dollar for the privilege, charging everyone a dollar for attending some rallies, and empha- sizing our willingness—nay, eagerness—to accept small donations through the mail. Call it, "A buck for Barry." "But," someone complained, "it costs nearly that much for the mailing." Yes; but each mailing that brought in a contribution, no matter how small (our average was less than $10), added a member of the campaign who was not only likely to vote for Goldwater, but also likely to convince their friends and neighbors to do so as well.

Frank Kovac assembled mailing lists of known conservatives and the 500,000 who had volunteered for Barry. Overall, we generated some 1.5 million contributions for the primaries and the campaign, an astonishing increase over the 50,000 supporters who contributed to the 1960 Nixon campaign, and providing a tremendous base for the next election. Was this emphasis on small-dollar donors a breakthrough in political fundraising? I can't say for certain—history is long and details are often obscure—but *Newsweek* was kind enough to give me credit for a "new money-raising technique."[1] After the election, Richard Viguerie, who already had cut his fundraising teeth on telephone appeals, turned lists of Goldwater contributors into a national direct-mail network of conservative donors . . . and political fundraising was never the same.

We hired the Opinion Research Corporation (ORC) for bi-weekly surveys; we learned—no surprises—that Goldwater "had strong convictions" and "spoke his own mind" and would likely hold down government spending. LBJ was seen as an unethical "deal maker" who would "promise anything to get votes," but on the whole he had been doing a good job as president.

The PR staff began to churn out brochures, advertising clip art, campaign "Guidelines" for local organizations. Our main advertising agency, Leo Burnett, came up with the punning slogan, "In your heart you know he's right," and PR man Lee Edwards managed one early coup: He leased a 106-foot-long billboard—just down the street from the Atlantic City convention center, then playing host to the Democrats—which he filled with the slogan and a photo of Barry.

The campaign assembled the usual trinkets. The "usual" included gold-colored elephant cuff links, earrings, and pins; campaign buttons, with the gold-colored elephant wearing Barry's black-framed glasses; inflatable elephants (in three sizes); clocks, boxes, and playing cards adorned with pictures of the candidates. There was "Goldwater Taffy," touted as a "Golden Opportunity to sweeten your campaign fund . . . a delicious confection, made with fine ingredients [that] will never require an apology for its quality." As a fundraiser, buy it for sixty-three cents a bag, sell it for a buck and a quarter. And, of course, there was a beverage called "Gold Water," an "orange-flavored soft drink for conservative tastes." Barry was induced to take a sip. "Tastes like warm piss," he said. "I wouldn't drink it with gin."

The not-quite-so usual: elephant-print boxer shorts. And the really unusual: glow-in-the-dark campaign portraits, available in two sizes, 8 x 10 inches and 16 x 20 inches. These probably had most utility as a surprise gag gift, surreptitiously hung in someone's bedroom.

I should note, of course, that the Democrats had their fair share of campaign dreck. Let one stanza of "Hello, Lyndon!" suffice; words and music by Jerry Herman, set to the tune of his Broadway hit, "Hello, Dolly!"

> We hear the band playin'
> And the folks sayin'
> "Let's all rally 'round the one who knows the score" . . . so
> Be our guide, Lyndon,
> Ladybird at your side, Lyndon,
> Promise you'll stay with us in '64.

The basic campaign strategy was, in Barry's words, "Let's go hunting where the ducks are"—where we could expect to win some votes. Except for a few token visits, forget New England, New York, and Pennsylvania. Concentrate on the Midwest (especially Ohio and Illinois, with 52 electoral votes); the South (127 votes); a smattering of traditional Republican states (Oklahoma, Kentucky, Arizona, 22 votes); Nebraska, Kansas, Indiana, Wyoming, Colorado, the Dakotas, and the smaller mountain states (perhaps 50 or 60 votes)—and, of course, the big prize: California with ninety-two votes.

As he had in his senatorial campaigns (a good-luck talisman), Goldwater launched his presidential campaign schedule on the steps of the county courthouse in Prescott, Arizona (where his uncle Morris had been mayor for twenty-six years), and ended two months later in the Arizona hamlet of Fredonia, population three hundred. In between, he visited more than a hundred cities, covering 100,000 miles. During the first week, we saw gratifyingly large crowds: 53,000 in Los Angeles, 18,000 in Seattle, and 16,000 in Minneapolis, where Barry out-pulled the former two-term mayor and Democratic candidate for vice president, Hubert Humphrey.

But as with New Hampshire, things quickly started going downhill. The crowds were there, but if "all politics are local," the locals were getting the wrong messages. At a rally in the tobacco, cotton, and peanut center, Winston-Salem, North Carolina, on September 15, Barry never mentioned tobacco, cotton, or peanuts. He warned the citizens of the peaceful retirement community of St. Petersburg, Florida, about rising crime rates but did not discuss Social Security. In poverty-stricken West Virginia, he blasted Johnson's anti-poverty program. In Fargo, North Dakota, he reminded farmers that 17 percent of their income came from Federal subsidies and asked, "Do you want that to continue?" He did have a plan for a gradual phase-out of the program. He did not explain it.

The Draft Goldwater veterans were appalled; the Kitchel-Baroody crowd didn't seem to notice. We complained—not for the first time—about the lack of a cohesive message and about our candidate's tendency to shoot from the lip. The criticism was not well received, and nothing changed.

Someone among the thousands of intelligent, active people involved with the campaign suggested that we take our messages directly to the people, with, perhaps, some control over the content, and we arranged to produce three thirty-minute TV talkers. The idea was sound—witness Ross Perot's success with the format in 1992—but the execution was dismal. The first was an over-produced question-and-answer session, "Brunch with Barry." Barry sat in the middle of a group of seven women, which included Maine's senator Margaret Chase Smith, several generic "mothers," a Vietnam widow, an "Italian Nationalities Representative" (whatever that really means; I take that from the stage directions). They asked questions and he answered them.

The second was a filmed address in which Barry denied that he was impulsive, imprudent, and trigger-happy. The only bright spot was a highly successful fundraising appeal by actor Raymond Massey, tacked on to the end, which brought in $175,000. We had done this over the objections of both Kitchel and Baroody, who thought such public pleading for money was undignified.

The third program was a thirty-minute "Conversation at Gettysburg," Goldwater and Eisenhower at the Gettysburg farm. We wanted to show the two men in comfortable conversation, discussing the issues, the future of the country, whatever they wanted to talk about. Well, they didn't talk about much of anything. They might as well have been discussing the weather, all at $4,000 a minute (to my horror as the bean counter). The program started with an inane question from Ike: "Well, Barry, you've been campaigning now for two or three weeks, how do you like it? And how does it seem to be going for you?"

From that point on, the program was going nowhere. Dan Dornan—the photographer I had provided to the campaign—told me that there had been no focus; Eisenhower rambled along, it didn't seem as if there had been any advance discussion of goals or content, and no key questions were suggested by the on-scene campaign managers. Even Barry sensed that all was adrift and tried to get the managers to take charge, to do anything. He was told, "It's okay, don't worry about it." At the end of the program, Ike offered—I guess—an endorsement of Barry. To the charge that Goldwater was a "warmonger," Ike said, "Well, Barry, in this mind this is actual tommyrot." We had intended to close off with another Raymond Massey appeal, but Kitchel said no way. The dignity of the former president was more important than the money. At the time, I thought a fund appeal might bring in $1 million, but that was before I saw the audience numbers. In a time slot where *Petticoat Junction* pulled 27.4 percent of the viewers and 25 percent watched *Peyton Place*, "Conversation at Gettysburg" was seen by 8.6 percent.

Opinion Research (ORC) reported that the audience for *any* of those thirty-minute programs was minuscule—conservative junkies looking for a fix and Johnson campaign workers looking for fodder. Almost everyone who tuned in out of curiosity quickly switched to something else. I would note, however, that despite the poor execution, of those voters who stayed the course, 67 percent of Republicans and 39 percent of Democrats came away with a more favorable impression of the candidate.

ORC also noted positive response to one of Barry's key messages: America was falling into a moral cesspool. Replaying one theme of his convention acceptance speech, and in one of his more successful approaches, our candidate charged that a lack of national leadership had "turned our streets into jungles, brought our public and private morals into the lowest state of our history," with climbing divorce rates, juvenile delinquency, and street violence. "When morals collapse," he said, "they don't collapse upward."

Clif saw an opportunity to confront the issue head-on with a thirty-minute TV documentary. "Agree completely with you on morality issue," Barry said in a memo to Clif. "Believe it is the most effective we have come up with. Also agree with your program. Please get it launched immediately."

The program was called "Choice." It was filled with images of immorality (women in topless bathing suits), depravity (drunken college students on a spree), anti-social behavior (rioting and looting in the streets), and failed leadership (a tall man in a cowboy hat driving a Lincoln convertible remarkably similar to LBJ's personal car, throwing out beer cans as he careened down the road). The stated goal of "Choice" was "to portray and remind the people of something they already know exists, and that is the moral crisis in America, the rising crime rate, rising juvenile delinquency, narcotics, pornography, filthy magazines. . . . [The American people] will see all this on television, and there is only one way they can go, and that is with Goldwater."

I saw a screening of the show on October 14, and I thought it was outstanding. I had been working most of the day on the budget; income was projected at $11.6 million, outgo $12.2 million—not too encouraging. Nonetheless, I scrambled around to find the $40,000 needed to purchase the air time.

We scheduled the broadcast for October 22, but the program never ran. The DNC obtained a print and showed it to a group of journalists, thereby triggering an avalanche of adverse comment. When Goldwater screened it (for the first time), he said, "It can't be used. Period. . . . It's nothing but a racist film." Although "Choice" gave equal time to black and white miscreants, on reflection, I had to agree that Barry was right.

How did the Democrats find out about, and get an advance copy of, "Choice"? For that matter, how did they know about forthcoming Goldwater press announcements in such timely fashion that they were able to make pre-emptive strikes with announcements of their own? How were they able to have pre-positioned "responses" to points Barry would make in a campaign speech—before he made the speech? A couple of such responses made it into newspapers printed before Barry was even in town.

None of us, of course, were aware then of what came to light later: Johnson had enlisted the assistance of both the FBI and the CIA. In 1971, FBI chief J. Edgar Hoover admitted to one member of our 1964 team, Bob Mardian, that the campaign plane was bugged and Goldwater staffers were investigated at the direct request of the president. The chief of covert action for CIA domestic operations—Howard Hunt—operated out of a phony news bureau in the National Press Building, collecting whatever he could about our campaign under the rubric, "Continental Press." Former White House press secretary George Reedy later confirmed that at least one hired spy was planted at our headquarters. We had been guarding against dirty tricks from our Republican opponents; how do you guard against espionage by the premier law enforcement and spy agencies in the world? Barry's initial reluctance to go up against an "unscrupulous" LBJ was not unjustified.

Since I wrote the checks that covered their expenses, I was in almost daily contact with surrogates in the field—notably, Dick Nixon and Ronald Reagan—and helped arrange their schedules. I discovered that they needed something to talk about. Barry's speechwriters were wrapped up with his needs, so I found myself also in the part-time speech-writing business, penning remarks for both Nixon and Reagan.

Nixon gave his all for Goldwater, 237 speeches in 36 states. Once, without mercy, I asked him to go to Hawaii, then to San Francisco, then to Los Angeles, then to Kansas, and back to Hawaii, all in a three-day period. He never complained, which didn't hurt his standing with the Party. Reagan, who didn't like to fly, was co-chair of the California Goldwater campaign and pretty much stayed in the state, but he gave about one hundred speeches and did terrific TV work, as well.

In fact, by all accounts, the best speech of the campaign, perhaps of *any* campaign, was Reagan's October 27 TV broadcast, dubbed "A Time for Choosing"—but it almost didn't happen because of objections by Kitchel and Baroody. They told Barry the speech was unacceptable, and instead proposed putting "Conversation at Gettysburg" into the booked time slot. I told Barry that was foolish, that Reagan would give us a great shot in the arm, but he called Reagan to ask him to cancel; Reagan said, "Well, it's not up to me, some other fellows are paying for the time out of their own pockets and, besides, what's wrong with the speech?" Barry said, "I don't know. I'll take a look." When finished looking at the program, he turned to Kitchel and Baroody and said, "What the hell's wrong with that?"

But Kitchel and Baroody would not give up—goaded, I believe, by our ad agency. Within three hours of air time they were still trying to plug in "Gettysburg." However, as Reagan said, the spot was being funded by a group of Californians, fellow members, with Barry and John Wayne, of the Sigma Chi fraternity. The Californians said Reagan gets the time or no one gets the time; having worked so closely with Reagan on the campaign, I was strongly on their side. The speech was an updated version of one that Reagan had made many times for his then-employer, General Electric. "A Time for Choosing" articulated Goldwater's positions better than Goldwater and launched Reagan's political career. The first "Reagan for President" club was established soon after, and he was elected governor of California in 1966 with a plurality of one million votes.

Our TV plan for the last couple of weeks before Election Tuesday included one fifteen-minute show, five thirty-minute visits with the candidate or his surrogates, and twenty-six five-minute spots inserted in some of the most popular shows on television, ranging from *Today* to *As the World Turns*. The final push would have been much greater, but for one thing. On this, there is confusion in the published record, so let me clarify.

It is true that under Ralph's Rules we had to run the campaign on a cash basis, spending no money that was not already in the bank. However, it is not true, as is often reported, that Ralph's Rules prevented us from buying extra TV and radio time in the hyper-critical final week. Then, our mailings were paying off and we had the money. One typical day in the middle of October, the post office delivered some 14,000 letters. A majority included checks, although many were empty. The senders were not forgetful: They wanted to make us pay the return postage. Why so many adversaries? Unlike the earlier mailings targeted to probable supporters, these went to lists purchased from commercial suppliers. But overall, during the last week of the campaign, almost $3 million came in from mail and TV solicitations.

As we entered the last week, Barry asked, "How are we doing?" I—ever the optimist—said, "Great!" and showed him the latest, revised, broadcast schedule. I told him we had the money. He put his hand on my arm and said, "Don't spend it." He told me to cancel the additional radio and TV spots and leave money in the bank to keep the Party alive after the election. Of course, he was right, and thus, perhaps $1 million was not wasted on the past, but passed along for the future.

We campaigned *for* Goldwater; the Democrats campaigned *against* Goldwater. Every charge lodged by Rockefeller and Scranton was picked up and integrated seamlessly into their campaign. They didn't need a big team of researchers digging into Barry's past positions; all they had to do was read the more recent press clippings. White House staffer Jack Valenti advised Johnson to treat Goldwater "not as an equal who has credentials to be President, but as a radical, a preposterous candidate who would ruin this country and our future," and to act as if Bill Miller was some sort of "April Fool's gag."[2]

In the Democrats' TV and radio commercials, produced under the direct supervision of the White House, Barry was a bomb-thrower who would ignite World War III and tear up Social Security along the way. The commercials were brilliant, devastating. The best-known hit was the infamous "Daisy" TV ad, which may have been broadcast—as a paid spot—only one time, on September 7. The scene: A pretty young girl playing "Loves me, Loves me not" with a daisy, picking off the petals as she counts, "One, two, three . . ." When she reaches "nine," a somber male voice cuts in and counts down, "Ten . . . nine . . . eight . . ." until the image explodes in the mushroom cloud of an atomic blast. We hear the voice of LBJ: "These are the stakes, to make a world in which all of God's children can live, or go into the dark. We must either love each other, or we must die." The voice-over announcer closes the spot: "Vote for President Johnson on November third. The stakes are too high for you to stay at home."

Goldwater was only four days into his campaign when the "Daisy" bomb was dropped—and from then until the end, he was on the defensive. By the middle of September, the Harris poll reported that 53 percent of women and 45 percent of men believed that Goldwater would take the country to war. I heard that LBJ's assistant, Bill Moyers, bragged that they hung the nuclear noose around Goldwater and finished him off. He was right.

Other Democratic commercials picked up where Nelson Rockefeller had left off. For TV, while a voice on the soundtrack declared that Goldwater would "destroy" Social Security, the video showed a pair of large, masculine hands searching for, and then tearing apart, a Social Security card. Some viewers swore that these had actually been the hands of Goldwater. On radio: "Barry Goldwater's plan means the end of Social Security, the end of widow's pensions, the end of the dignity that comes with being able to take care of yourself without depending on your children. On November 3, vote for keeping Social Security." And, of course, there was advertising of a different sort: the ubiquitous placards and signboards—"In your guts you know he's nuts"—that showed up everywhere Barry went. Johnson played "father of his country," campaigning with unabashed zest: eighteen-hour days, twenty speeches a week. He offered peaceful reassurance on the festering troubles in Vietnam—"We are not going to send American boys nine or ten thousand miles from home to do what Asian boys ought to be doing for themselves"—and offered a grave warning: "By a thumb on a button," he told a crowd in New Orleans, "you can wipe out three hundred million lives in a matter of moments." This was no time, he said, "to be rattling your rockets around or clicking your heels like a storm trooper. . . . Whose thumb do you want edging up that way?"

Ben Bradlee of the *Washington Post* told Goldwater that "Daisy" was "a fucking outrage," but C. L. Sulzberger of the *New York Times* fell for the gag, and wrote: "The possibility exists that, should [Goldwater] enter the White House, there might not be a day after tomorrow."[3] Barry said, as far as he could recall, he had never met, spoken to, or been interviewed by Sulzberger.

It may seem hard to believe, but most of the traveling press—especially those who had been with Barry throughout the campaign—liked the man, and some even tried to protect him from himself. When he gave one of his off-the-top-of-his-head answers to a tough question, they might ask, "Is that what you really want to say?" I think, of the fifty-three reporters on board for the last big swing, only three were really belligerent. Barry's big problem now was not with reporters, but with editors. Of all the major newspapers in the country, only three—three!—came out in support of his candidacy: the *Los Angeles Times*, the *Chicago Tribune*, and the *Cincinnati Enquirer*, which offered this perspective on September 29, 1964:

> Barry Goldwater has become the most slandered man in American political history. . . . He is portrayed as a poisoner of children, as a creature of the night-riders, as a pawn of the militarists and the warmongers. To see the viciousness of the vilification heaped upon him is to begin to understand the desperation with which his enemies are trying to cling to the perverted political order they have been foisting upon America. Their purpose is to do considerably more than defeat him at the polls: they seek literally to crush him lest any other muster the courage to ask them to account for their sordid works.

And, what of the broadcast media? It may be pure coincidence, but we saw a flood of documentary television shows on Truman, Roosevelt, and Kennedy. "The Young Man from Boston," an hour-long tribute to Kennedy, was run on some TV stations as many as four times during the campaign—all in prime time.

We began the final campaign swing on October 26 with another capacity audience at Madison Square Garden, and ended at sunset in Fredonia, Arizona, on November 2. In between, we made eighteen stops in seven days: Tennessee, Ohio, Iowa, Wisconsin, Illinois, Pennsylvania, Wyoming, Nevada, Arizona, California, Arizona again, Texas, South Carolina, back to California, and then on to Arizona. Air Force Reserve major general Goldwater frequently delighted in taking the controls of the campaign airplane, but his skills were, well, a bit rusty, if triple-bounce landings signify anything.

At the wrap-up in Fredonia, Barry thanked a lot of people but said nothing memorable. As we headed down to Phoenix for the vote and to await the returns, he gave me a weary smile and said, "Well, Bill, how are we going to do tomorrow?" The latest Gallup and Harris polls both had it at 64 percent for LBJ, 36 percent for Goldwater, but I, the team cheerleader, said, "Barry, it's in the bag. The silent majority will turn out in force." You may think my optimism was incredible, but lulled by the roar of the crowd everywhere we went, I believed it to be true. Any experienced politician will warn you: Don't see only what you want to see.

Just after Goldwater's nomination, James A. Farley, postmaster general in the Roosevelt administration, and therefore a Democrat whose opinion we might safely disregard, predicted that Goldwater would only carry six states. His view was challenged by Hamilton Fish, father of my Harvard classmate and a former Republican congressman with impeccable political credentials, and therefore a man to whom attention must be paid. In a July 20 letter to the *New York Times*, Fish opined that Farley "has been spending too much time traveling on business in Europe, where he must have absorbed some unfriendly news items in the English, French, and other European papers. . . . Every radical, left-winger, Socialist and Communist is against Senator Goldwater's courageous effort to stop the march of state socialism. . . . When this issue is presented clearly to the American people, Goldwater will carry *all* but six states."

On November 3, Barry Goldwater carried . . . just six states. Popular vote: Johnson, forty-two million; Goldwater, twenty-seven million. As the polls predicted, it was 64 percent to 36 percent.

NBC called the election for LBJ four hours *before* the polls closed in California. Barry was visibly stunned and went to bed.

The man who, in his heart of hearts, really didn't want to win, came off as a sore loser. He did not concede until the next morning. "Twenty-seven million votes is a lot of votes," he said with a touch of defiance, and, to many observers, the telegram he sent to LBJ was not a simple concession but a continuation of the campaign:

> Congratulations on your victory. I will help you in any way I can toward achieving a growing and better America and a secure and dignified peace. The role of the Republican Party will remain in that temper, but it also remains the party of opposition when opposition is called for. There is much to be done with Vietnam, Cuba, problems of law and order in this country and a productive economy. Communism remains our number one obstacle to peace, and I know that all Americans will join with you in honest solutions to these problems.[4]

Jimmy Breslin took a swipe in the *New York Herald Tribune* on November 5: "Among the many things Barry Goldwater knows nothing of is the way men are supposed to act when they lose the Presidency of the United States." Well, I think Barry was just reacting in his normal, un-political, tell-it-like-it-is fashion. Even though he expected to lose, he wasn't prepared for the magnitude of the loss. He was upset. He was embarrassed. I think, too, that he may have started regretting some of his choices during the campaign. He held a final campaign press conference. "I say to the President, as a fellow politician, that he did a wonderful job . . . and I have to congratulate him on it. . . . I want to thank all of you across this nation who turned out in those numbers to support my candidacy and that of Bill Miller and the Republican Party. I don't think that I have ever seen more dedicated people in my life who worked as long and produced the results that they did."

Privately, he gave the media a large share of the blame for his loss. Publicly—for a change—he chose his words with care: "I want to thank and again tell all of you fellows in the press, radio and TV that regardless of how you feel toward me I have a friendly warm feeling towards all of you, and I hope to see you again somewhere down the pike."

Other pundits piled on. The *New York Times* comment of James Reston, November 4, 1964, was typical: "Barry Goldwater not only lost the Presidential election yesterday but the conservative cause as well. He has wrecked his party for a long time to come and is not even likely to control the wreckage."

Reston, Teddy White, Bob Novak, and I don't know how many others had us down for the count. The Party in tatters. Leadership in the sewer. Well, at that point, I was part of that Party leadership, and we saw things a bit differently. Yes, there were problems within the Party. The Rockefeller-Scranton-Romney crowd was not happy with the conservative tilt; they wanted back in the driver's seat. They did not understand the sea change; that the center had shifted away from Philadelphia, New York, and Boston; that for the first time since 1932, power in the South was shifting back to Republicans; that more people had contributed to our campaign than had ever given financial support to the presidential campaign of any party—three times as many, actually, as contributed to the Democrats.

Not to put too fine a point on it, but the Republicans, "destroyed" by the Goldwater campaign, came back strong in the 1966 elections, adding four senators and forty-seven representatives, returning Goldwater to the Senate in 1968, and winning five of the following six presidential elections. But—again—that gets us ahead of our story.

A couple of days after the election, I stood alone in the shambles that had been RNC headquarters, 1625 Eye Street, NW, in Washington, D.C. The floor was littered with piles—great piles—of campaign literature, a mountain of those gold-elephant-with-glasses buttons. Phones were ringing off the hook; I answered a few. Creditors, screaming for their money. I tried to be reassuring: "Send in a letter," I said. I probably reassured no one. My secretary and my brother Harry came down from New York, and together we sorted through what seemed like thousands of bits of unfinished business; bills to pay, useless junk to be hauled away. We should have held on to the trinkets: Today, some are selling for hundreds of dollars each.

Jerry Milbank joined me for the political cleanup. The first order of business was to sign up Ernest and Young to do an audit. I wanted to account for every penny. Our numbers were precise and, for the first time in U.S. election history, I believe, we submitted a completely verified national audit, not just a certification of the balance sheet. For the political historians among you (or curious CPAs), I summarize: the Republican National Finance Committee (RNFC) supervised the spending of $14,416,324. About half—a bit more than $7.3 million—went for "publicity" and the overwhelming share of that—$5,606,635—was for radio and TV time and production. Other major items: salaries, $1,586,672; postage and express, $955,827; travel, $909,632, plus $807,997 for chartered airplanes and railroad cars; printing and reproduction, $555,252; telephone service, $389,113.

Dean Burch, Jerry Milbank, Stets Coleman, and I met with Barry to discuss the future. He said, "You are now the guardians and have to keep the flame alive." He was more open, I think, than he had been at any time during the campaign. "We made all of the mistakes in the book," he said, "but that's behind us. Seven and a half million Republicans lost faith in us because the damn fool Rockefeller and his tribe cast seeds of doubt." Barry said, "LBJ never laid a glove on me compared to the destruction of these men." Barry said, "Our job should have been to win the battle of image." Barry said, "We lost."

As it turned out, many of things we (the Draft crowd) saw as unwitting blunders—blasting the anti-poverty program in poverty-stricken West Virginia, for example—were things that Barry did on purpose, believing that voters would see him as an honest guy who didn't pander, didn't tell people what they wanted to hear but what they needed to hear, didn't promise things that didn't make sense, and wasn't afraid to tackle the big issues—a guy who would be an honest president and therefore worthy of their vote.

He may have been right, if only he had more time to prove it. According to our pollster Tom Benham, almost three times as many voters shifted their August preferences from LBJ to Goldwater as went the other way. Twice as many of the August "undecideds" voted for Goldwater as for Johnson. The problem was that only 20 percent of voters were undecided in August. In the middle of October, our pollster revealed that "defected" Republicans were coming back at a rate of 6 to 8 percent a week. He pointed out that if the trend continued at that rate, we would win the election . . . if the election were held in April.

Chapter 7

Presidential Politics: Nixon

I n a misguided effort to broaden the reach of conservative ideas, with the help of a few investors and after an informal discussion with the owners, the 3M Corporation, Jerry Milbank, and I bought the Mutual Broadcasting System for $1 million. How informal was the discussion? We sketched out the terms on the back of an envelope I had in my pocket. Our plan was to improve on the type of discourse then delivered by Fulton Lewis Jr. and later perfected by Rush Limbaugh. The plan faltered, because the five hundred or so affiliated radio stations under Mutual's management umbrella were independent entities, not owned by MBS. Some provided programming that could be used by the others—the name "mutual" was operative—but we found that it was simply impractical to get them all pulling on the same oar. As an investment, however, this wasn't a bad deal. The buyers turned a handsome profit when the Amway Corporation bought the network in 1977.

I settled back into the rhythms of Wall Street. Business was good, our best years ever, in which Austen and I put together ten of the largest insurance company acquisitions and mergers to that date, including the merger of Phoenix Insurance Company with Travelers; American General's purchase of Maryland Casualty (of which my grandfather had been one of the original financiers); and the acquisition of The Hartford by the prototypical conglomerate-builder, Harold Geneen for ITT. Geneen didn't worry about core-competencies or synergy or a "good fit"; he looked for a good business. He believed that companies that did well on their own would, as part of a greater whole, protect the parent company from cycles or downturn in one business segment or another. During his tenure, from 1959 to 1977, Geneen added about three hundred companies to the ITT portfolio, taking sales from $765 million to nearly $28 billion. He wanted The Hartford because it was a good, solid company, and once he had control he made it an even better, solid company. The cost of the Hartford deal was around $2.2 billion, and within fifteen years the Hartford had revenues of $11 billion and accounted for more than half of ITT's earnings.

Our services earned substantial fees—some in the seven figures. I must admit, however, that this thirty-nine-year-old missed the excitement of the political stage, even if, as treasurer of the RNC, I was at least involved. I would soon become more so, courtesy of Dick Nixon

Nixon had never stopped working for the party, and, maybe, for himself. Newspaper columnist Andrew Tully—not a fan—wrote, "Dick Nixon is wandering around the country like a salesman, running for president but refusing to admit it, and to the professional politician watcher he is unimpressive. . . . He is too much the new Dick Nixon. The Old Dick Nixon was infinitely to be preferred. . . . He at least had a personality. . . . Dick Nixon, circa 1965, is not so much a politician as he is a lodge-joiner.[1]

To that point, we had not cast our lot with Nixon but had been giving it some serious thought. Over lunch, November 10, 1965, Dean Burch, Jerry Milbank, and I agreed that Nixon was probably the front runner for the 1968 nomination; his efforts for Barry and other candidates had earned a lot of goodwill, but we knew that other credible players might emerge after the 1966 midterm elections. Our consensus, as recorded in my notes of the meeting: "Nixon is all we have at the present time and makes good speeches to boot. He suffers only from a lack of television personality and the fact that he has been licked a couple of times in other elections."

Someone must have been peeking over the transom. A few months later (in a February 14, 1966, *New York Times* column), David Broder quoted one of those anonymous political advisers so often favored by columnists: "Dick Nixon is in for a terrible shock. . . . [He] is trying to take the remnants of the Goldwater thing and give it some responsibility but it won't work."

Well, perhaps. We—what was left of the Goldwater inner circle—were those "remnants" and, despite the shattering loss at the polls, continued to enjoy the loyalty of a large number of probable Convention delegates. The leaders at the top may change, but the grassroots locals, the precinct and district workers, endure. Like the grass.

Toward the end of April, four Goldwater veterans (Peter O'Donnell, John Grenier, Fred Agnich, and me) and one new Republican insider (Fred LaRue) spent a weekend at Peter's Dallas office to launch "Project X." The label was more in fun than an effort at secrecy, as with the initial "Draft Goldwater" meetings, but our goal was serious: Did we think Dick Nixon was the best hope to win back the presidency—or, if not, to whom should we offer our support?

LaRue was a valuable addition. Personally close to Nixon, he in fact had just attended a strategy session in Chicago with Nixon and some of his advisers. Fred offered one cogent bit of intelligence: Nixon was spooked by the thought of having too many Goldwater supporters. However, we could bring a lot to the table. We could deliver delegates. We could deliver cash. We also—hardened by our experience with Goldwater—could deliver good advice. But would we be comfortable working with Nixon, and would he accept our support?

Nixon answered that last question without being asked. He invited Jerry Milbank and me to join him for a lunch and some friendly probing. We knew the real reason for the lunch, and both thought he was pandering, consciously or not, by constantly referring to "We conservatives." I could just picture him in different settings, each with a handy "We." Moderates, war veterans, fathers of two daughters. But when we got down to business, he was very direct: "Look, I gave my all for you guys, gave it everything I had, and I want you to give some thought to turning those delegates loose to support me in '68." After the lunch, I jotted down my overall impression: "A man of great energy, but not particularly prepossessing, a man of great devotion to the party, but perhaps motivated a touch by self interest, a man so much on the run . . . perhaps to obscure a shallowness that would show up if he slowed down and could be analyzed."

In the 1966 midterm elections, the Republicans picked up 700 seats in state legislatures, more than erasing the 529 seat loss of 1964. Where we lost 37 House seats in 1964, we had a net gain of 47 in 1966, plus 3 Senate seats and 8 governorships. The cover treatment of the post-election issues of *Time* and *Newsweek* featured the same six beaming Republican winners: Rockefeller, Romney, Reagan, and senators-elect Hatfield, Percy, and Brooke.

Romney's candidacy got a huge boost: Polls quickly put him as the front runner; Nixon and Percy tied for second; Ronald Reagan, fourth. The Harris poll (November 1966) had Romney winning fifty-four to forty-six over Johnson. Barry Goldwater was not thrilled: "Just where in the hell does he stand," Barry asked me in a personal letter, "on Vietnam? When he starts to level with the American people . . . then I think we can more studiously appraise Romney as a candidate but, up to now, I am backing Nixon and can't back anyone else."

Barry let his feelings boil over to unfriendly public comment, and the governor was quick to respond in kind. Well, before things really got out of control, and with memories of the warfare of 1964 so vivid, I exercised my position as an official of the RNC and stepped in with a bit of "shuttle diplomacy." I arranged to meet with Romney in his office in Lansing

(March 17, 1967) and prepared to endure a lecture on the true meaning of Republicanism—Romney often turned any conversation into a lecture—but he said, in essence, "OK, I'm willing to back off . . . but what about Goldwater?" So I called Barry; he agreed to drop the whole subject, and did.

Romney would soon enough blow his lead. Like Goldwater, he could not resist answering a question, even if he made up an answer as he went along. Goldwater was always forced into a discussion of things like the bomb or Social Security. With Romney, it was Vietnam. The fatal moment came in the middle of the summer of 1967; when questioned on Detroit TV about inconsistencies in his stated positions on Vietnam, Romney answered: "Well, you know when I came back from Vietnam, I just had the greatest *brainwashing* that anybody can get when you go over to Vietnam."

Soon enough the national media had noticed, and Romney, painted as a naïf wandering in international thickets, was accused of slandering two great Americans: Gen. William Westmoreland and Ambassador Lodge (back in Saigon for a second tour). Romney insisted on defending his statement wherever he went. Toward the end of the year he tried to recover his footing with another visit to Vietnam, which was roundly denounced as a shallow campaign trip, a desperate attempt to vault into office over the backs of dying men. In a private poll the RNC commissioned before the forthcoming New Hampshire primary, Nixon had the edge over Romney, five to one. After that, Romney's campaign sputtered along for a few weeks, until he dropped out.

The real winner of the 1966 election, virtually ignored, had been Dick Nixon. From the beginning of 1965 until election day, he helped raise $6.5 million, visited thirty-five states, and spoke on behalf of some one hundred candidates. He was building grassroots support by planting seeds. In the November 26, 1966, *New York Times* a statistician concluded that "a GOP House candidate for whom Nixon did not campaign stood only a 45 percent chance of winning while a man he embraced stood a 67 percent chance." Nixon's competition on the campaign trail included LBJ, Herbert Humphrey, and Ted and Robert Kennedy. The contrast? Robert Kennedy was usually followed by twenty or more reporters; Nixon's entourage, if thus it might be called, was maybe four but usually two. But, as the *Chicago Tribune* later would muse, "Bobby made a big hit with the teenagers. Richard Nixon put himself across with adults."[2]

While Romney was imploding, a "Nixon for President" committee opened a Washington office, headed by San Diego obstetrician Dr. Gaylord B. Parkinson. As GOP state chairman for California, Parky was author of the so-called 11th Commandment ("Thou Shalt Not Speak Ill of Other

Republicans"), which later became a keystone of Reagan's political philosophy. Nixon himself went on a six-month "political moratorium," which included an extended overseas fact-finding tour: Bucharest, Prague, London, Paris, Berlin, Rome (where he met with the Pope), and Moscow (where Soviet officials declined an invitation to meet). The main topic of interest, everywhere, was Vietnam, followed by East-West tensions and Chinese hostility.

When he opened his New Hampshire campaign on February 2, 1968, the uptight Nixon of 1960 had bloomed into a relaxed, jovial master of the press conference. A newsman asked why he wanted to be president. He parried; why would anyone want to be a reporter? "I think," he said, "covering a presidential campaign is worse than running one."

Nixon's strategy from the beginning was to take on LBJ and not run against any of the Republican candidates. Well, he won New Hampshire with more votes than all other candidates—Democrat, Republican, write-ins—put together. He had more votes than any candidate in any New Hampshire primary, ever.

Rockefeller was more or less a non-candidate until, right in the middle of the New Hampshire campaigning, North Vietnam's Tet Offensive demonstrated that it still had considerable force, despite years of American efforts—and pronouncements—to the contrary. Tet was a military defeat for the North; they achieved no objectives and did not, myth to the contrary, "capture" the U.S. Embassy. But Tet was a morale buster of major proportions for America, and it would drive Lyndon Johnson out of office. On March 31, 1968, an overburdened LBJ announced: "I shall not seek and I will not accept the nomination of my party for another term as your President." And Rockefeller was back in the game.

He tried, but he seemed to have lost his rudder. At a meeting of editors and reporters, according to a friend who was there, Rockefeller fell flat on his face. He read a speech that seemed to have been put together by a committee; he did enter some primaries; he was pretty much ignored. Rockefeller twisted some arms in an effort to convert Nixon delegates: Perhaps he could keep Nixon below the magic number, 667, force a second ballot, and then go head-to-head with whoever was still standing.

Then, just as the convention was ramping up, another latecomer entered the race: Ron Reagan, also working from the Rockefeller playbook by trying to create a first ballot deadlock. And Clif White was back in the saddle, counting delegates for Reagan. He asked me to meet with Reagan; the reason was obvious, and Reagan made a strong but friendly pitch. Would I shift my vote and bring along as many of my friends as possible? I had to say no, that it was too late in the game and, while I truly believed Reagan to be the ideological successor to Goldwater, I was honor bound to stick with my commitment to Nixon.

At a gala on the eve of the Convention, John Wayne was working the tables, warning, "Look fellows, if you don't vote for Nixon, I'll break all your heads open." I guess most of them were listening: Nixon won with 692; Rockefeller got 287, and Reagan, 182. I could not help but recall the "consultant" quoted in David Broder's column: "Nixon is trying to take the remnants of the Goldwater team and give it some responsibility but it won't work." But, that is exactly what he did, and the grassroots "remnants of the Goldwater team" were behind Nixon all the way. Along the way, in every poll that had been taken of Republican local officials and potential delegates, Nixon came out ahead. He had earned that support.

Here's a small, little-known footnote to political history: Jerry Milbank and I had decided, early on, to push George Bush for VP. We thought he could run well with any of the three leading candidates, no matter which got the nomination. Granted, he was a first-term congressman and not well known, but I felt that his relaxed personality was a natural for television and he would quickly make his mark as the ideal candidate: young, with a fresh face, a mix of East Coast and Texas to balance Nixon's California background, and a politically well-connected father who could facilitate fundraising.

I tested this idea on some friends from New England and a few journalists from Texas. They were encouraging. I called Bush, told him I was nosing around, testing the waters, and oh, by the way, would he like to be vice president? He said, "Who wouldn't?"

Jerry and I worked the floor at the convention, lining up what were probably sufficient votes to put him over. We obtained letters of support from delegations from seven states. And, as noted in the August 5, 1968, San Antonio *Light*: "Houston Congressman George (Poppy) Bush's vice presidential stock went up this weekend, with the national Republican treasurer pushing his candidacy for the GOP No. 2 spot."

Well, I was not pushing for Bush in my official RNC capacity, but as a friend and member of the Connecticut delegation. I had a "Bush for VP" banner hung in the lobby of his hotel. I spoke up at a press conference, encouraging support. I think Poppy was taken by surprise by the number of reporters who met his plane when he arrived in Miami a few hours later.

In any event, as soon as Nixon had the nomination, Milbank and I made an appointment to make the pitch: "Mr. President, we'd like to put forward the name of George Bush for vice president." We assured Nixon that we had lined up the votes.

"Oh, gosh, fellows," he said. "Gee, that's too bad. We're not going that way. I've already decided to put Agnew on the ticket." Spiro T. Agnew, governor of Maryland, was little known to the rest of the country, but that didn't seem to matter. "Agnew," Nixon explained, "will unite the Party with Rockefeller, and besides, he made a terrific nominating speech on my behalf."

I think we both blurted out, "Who?" We tried to talk about it, but Nixon was adamant. "This is my man! My man! Sorry fellows, you've really done great work, but Agnew's my man!"

The night of the election Nixon's secretary, Rosemary Woods, called and invited a few of us—Strom Thurmond, Fred LaRue, Jerry Milbank, me, and a couple of others—to come over to campaign headquarters at the Waldorf-Astoria and help count the votes, so to speak. We were stationed in the hall by the elevators, outside Nixon's suite, with some chairs and a TV set. Every now and then, Rosemary would come out of the suite and assure us that Nixon wanted to thank us, first of any, for our great support; we were "his team."

At about 12:30 AM, Herbert Brownell and some other Rockefeller types stepped out of the elevator and went past us to Nixon's suite; the door opened, they went in, the door shut. Perhaps an hour or so later, the door opened, they came out, got back in the elevator, and went down. I don't remember if they said anything to us, going or coming. As I later learned, they had been invited over by Nixon himself to discuss cabinet positions.

At about 2 AM, Rosemary came out and apologized. The boss had gone to bed, she said; he'd have to see us in the morning. I later found out that Nixon actually didn't go to bed until about 8 AM, and that, as soon as we had left, he called in his campaign manager, H. R. Haldeman, and they began working the phones. Then he brought in the rest of the immediate campaign staff for an impromptu celebration that went on for several hours.

Gratitude—at least, in politics—may be among the most fleeting of human emotions. Oh, well. I grant that Nixon was busy, and in the event, he had not really forgotten us . . . the acknowledgement was simply delayed.

Chapter 8

Ambassador: Netherlands, One

J ust after the election, Nixon staffer Peter Flanigan asked me, "Bill, if you were to come work in Washington, what would you like to do?" I told him there was only one position that interested me: secretary of the navy. Well, word came back that Mr. Nixon would be pleased to have me in that post; however, a few weeks later, I got another call from Flanigan. "The boss sends his apologies, but he feels that he has to give the Navy job to John Chafee." Chafee had been governor of Rhode Island but was now out of a job. He was not a Nixon loyalist—far from it—but Nixon wanted to reach out to the Rockefeller camp, and Chafee wanted the Navy job. "Would you mind," Flanigan asked, "stepping aside for the time being?" I would be next in line, he said, but in the meantime, would I mind picking some other post? Anything I wanted.

I was disappointed but not surprised, and I asked Peter for a day or two to think it over. But picking another post wasn't hard: ambassador to the Netherlands. I had been close to the Netherlands for many years; in fact, Austen Colgate and I owned the Van Waverin Tulip Bulb Company. It was the second-largest in Holland and, dating from 1665—Rembrandt's time— one of the oldest in the world. Thus, I already knew a fair number of businessmen and community leaders there. I did have some competition for the post, I would later learn: the actress Shirley Temple. Ms. Temple eventually was appointed a delegate to the United Nations General Assembly.

Isabelle and I were still living in Greenwich with the children, and Isabelle and the older kids, teenagers, were taken off-guard, and not at all happy, when I announced that we were all moving to Europe. Isabelle wanted to be a stay-at-home mother, not a diplomatic hostess. She agonized about following me with the kids until, quite literally, she had a conversion. A friend invited her to Bible study, and another friend suggested that in the Christian tradition, she, too, should focus on "service." It was as if, she told me, "the Holy Spirit touched my heart." Since that time—not just with me in the Netherlands but in her life—she has been a dedicated follower of Jesus Christ and thoroughly committed to the work of the Lord. In the Netherlands she found a compatible Anglican church just a five-minute bike ride from the residence, and she became a regular attendee at morning Matins and Sunday worship.

I know now, but was not sensitive to the fact then, that it was unfair to negotiate such a major change without fully discussing all the implications with my family, but I was caught up in the moment. My father was furious, but for another reason. When I told him about my new job, he said, "What? That's the most ridiculous thing I've ever heard, giving up a seven-figure income for a job that only pays forty thousand a year." Father's Depression era–generated opinion of the federal government probably had something to do with his attitude.

The rest of my family grudgingly accepted my decision, but I don't think any of them believed it would be for four years. I stayed with it because I loved it, and pitched in with great enthusiasm. I was bitten by the bug called public service, which transmitted a disease that would overwhelm my immune system off and on over the next eighteen years. I called it Potomac Fever.

I must say, however, that my first exposure to government service was . . . interesting. Someone passed me a copy of the State Department's official instructions for processing ambassadorial nominees. Let one section stand for all: "*Initial Contact.* After the President has announced either his intention to nominate a new Ambassador or has announced the appointment of a new Ambassador, the Assistant Secretary or a Deputy Assistant Secretary for EUR [Europe] will telephone the new appointee to offer his congratulations. . . . It is the responsibility of the Country Director to furnish the Assistant Secretary with the telephone number of the new appointee."

That's your friendly federal government at work.

As part of the processing, of course, I had to be acceptable to the host government, but the name Middendorf was a plus; my business ties with the Netherlands (which, of course, I now had to sever) were certainly helpful; and my longtime interest in the paintings and accomplishments of Dutch and Flemish masters of the "Golden Age" was warmly noted in the press.

To prepare, I made arrangements with the partnership to cover any contingencies that might arise. I made arrangements to cover my family's needs until they could join me. I took a Foreign Service Institute course in the Dutch language. I was briefed on Soviet techniques for gathering information (and warned of bugging equipment that might be concealed, even in a shoe. This was not a TV-inspired joke).

My processing was coordinated by the State Department country director for France/Benelux, Charles Tanguy. Let me say, right up front, that I was so impressed with Charles then—and later, as we worked various trans-Atlantic issues—that I brought him over as deputy chief of mission when that post came open.

Under Charles' guiding hand, I had more than 125 preparatory meetings with officials at the departments of State, Treasury, and Commerce; the CIA, USIA, scores of senior officials at the White House and other government agencies; and the leaders of such major international businesses as IBM, Chase Bank, National City Bank, and Chemical Bank. One of those White House officials was the national security adviser, Henry Kissinger. Henry said, "Bill, stay close to me. . . . The president and I would like to have you communicate, on the major issues, directly with us."

Of course, on major issues, I did report often to the president or the National Security Council (NSC), but as I quickly learned, it is impossible to operate an embassy on the other end of thirty or forty telegrams a day, some of great magnitude and on every issue imaginable—agriculture, trade relations, military—without the support of a very competent desk officer and others at the State Department. There was no way any ambassador could channel routine communications through a White House official with barely any support staff at all. In truth, I think Henry's primary foci of Russia, China, and Vietnam kept his attention, and he really didn't have much time to deal with issues concerning the Netherlands. Once in the job, I dealt more often with Henry's deputy, Helmut Sonnenfeldt—but only within the established chain of command.

The intensive schedule paid off. I got to know almost everyone at State with whom my office would ever likely have any dealings, and they got to know me. I was not a faceless bureaucrat at the other end of the communications chain. When I had a request or needed support, I got it. In fact, during my first year, I think I made fourteen trips back to the States so that, as often as not, instead of a cable, I was there in person, standing at the desk to present and discuss my needs. Fourteen trips—all but one, I would add, at my own expense.

Finally, anointed by the Dutch and crammed full of data, it was time to demonstrate my fitness for the post, first, privately to a handful of senators, and then through a full hearing before the Senate Foreign Relations Committee.

In this, I was pretty confident. I wrote out responses to anticipated questions: Why do you want the job? What are your qualifications? How long do you intend to stay in the post? How do you see the job of ambassador? In truth, I was prepared to discuss geography—character and size of the population, voting patterns, GNP, major imports and exports, nature of the host government, the names and backgrounds of leading government officials, and our modest military presence in the country.

Looking back at my notes, I find four items strongly underlined:

- Answer only the question asked.
- Do not volunteer info on matters not being asked.
- Don't show off knowledge.
- Do not prolong argument.

That's pretty good guidance for almost any situation.

Up for confirmation at the same time was my friend, former Connecticut governor John Lodge, who had been nominated as ambassador to Argentina. Because we were both from Connecticut and had one sponsor in common (my neighbor, Sen. Prescott Bush), we shared the same hearing. My other sponsor was a man who had been at Harvard with my father and uncle, former Massachusetts senator Leverett Saltonstall.

The confirmation hearing should have been a breeze for John, who had been ambassador to Spain in the Eisenhower administration. However, after some routine questions, the committee chairman invited him to make a closing comment, if he wished. He did so wish, and replied, somewhat along the lines of, "Yes I do, Mr. Chairman. I want you to know that Mr. Franco is a fine fellow who has gotten a bum rap in the media." But Franco's unsavory connections with Hitler, before and during World War II, were not media hype, and the committee exploded with hostile questions.

Forewarned is forearmed. When the senator asked me much the same question, I replied, "I am deeply honored by the president's nomination, and, if confirmed by the Senate, I look forward to serving in this challenging assignment." I was approved within minutes; Lodge's confirmation was held up for months.

Senator Bush gave me a parting bit of advice: "It's not important how many friends you make when you're in the job, any important job—you'll have lots of them. What's important: How many of them you have after you leave." I was also cautioned by a long-term State Department hand, "Don't take the side of the host country in an argument with your own." Good advice, but fortunately, this was never an issue in my posting. (And were I, today, to offer an admonishment of my own to an incoming ambassador: For God's sake, don't go native. Too many do. Well I recall one of my contemporaries who adopted a very fake upper-class accent, trying to appear, I suppose, as if he "belonged.")

I was nominated in April, confirmed in June, and enjoyed my first diplomatic success before actually leaving to take the post. The Dutch prime minister and the foreign minister were on a swing through the United States, and I was included in some of the official and social functions.

Well, I sensed an opportunity. As I had learned during my briefings, two long-standing Dutch requests were hanging in the air, unresolved. One was for a nuclear-powered submarine, and the other was for the national airline, KLM, to have landing rights in Chicago.

The Dutch argued that their responsibilities within NATO would better be served if they had a nuclear submarine; they believed that Eisenhower's secretary of state, John Foster Dulles, had promised them one. However, the issue was much too complicated. The Defense Department and the CIA were opposed; the infrastructure needed to support a nuclear boat was almost beyond belief, and there was some concern that Soviet spies could worm their way into the crew and steal secrets. I knew that there was no way I could engineer a deal.

But landing rights? Ah, good old American politics.

I asked for a quick meeting with Nixon. "Mr. President," I said, "I have a favor to ask, something to get me off to a good start with the Dutch." Nixon sat there, his feet up on the desk, writing down everything I said on a big yellow legal pad. I finished my pitch, he said he'd take care of it, and he did.

The Dutch were delighted, but I did not make any points with fellow ambassador John Eisenhower, Ike's son, over in Brussels. He got me on the phone and said, only half joking, "Bill, you S.O.B.! Now the Belgians are on my case. They want landing rights for Sabena." I don't think they ever got them, at least not during his tenure.

I arrived at my post the first week of July, taking over from a great career Foreign Service officer, William Tyler, who became head of the prestigious Washington museum and conference center, the Dumbarton Oaks Foundation. I must say, as with the pre-confirmation processing back in Washington, nothing in my arrival was left to chance, or imagination. *Vide* the following advice, sent by cable from the deputy chief of mission, who had reviewed my draft of a brief arrival speech: "Suggest that last sentence arrival statement would sound more spontaneous as follows: Finally I am grateful to President Nixon for having assigned me as his personal representative to the country of my choice—*en ik zie er verlandend naar uit mijn uiterste best te doen in Nederland.*"

Yes, I had studied the language, but I have little doubt that my rendition of the Dutch equivalent of "I look forward to doing my utmost in the Netherlands" did not sound very spontaneous. To that point: My first public speech was a few days later, to some business council. I was giving it in Dutch, and, in spite of diligent rehearsal, I was stumbling all over the place. The subject matter, something about agricultural subsidies, was far from lively. Glancing around an audience desperately fighting to stay awake, I could tell that they were losing the battle. At last, Foreign Minister Joseph Luns stood up and said, "Mr. Ambassador—with all due respect—we would be greatly thrilled if you would speak English here." It was, needless to say, the last time I tried discussing any highly technical matters in Dutch. I did, however, use the language in general discourse, for social courtesies, and so forth.

The whirlwind of official contacts did not end when I left Washington: In my first few weeks in The Hague, I made forty-one formal calls on Dutch officials and fifty-five on resident ambassadors. And, of course, I quickly became acquainted with the key members and inner workings of my post, spread over three sites: the Embassy, and consulates in Rotterdam and Amsterdam, employing some 226 people, of whom more than half were local, non-American staff.

I presented my credentials to Queen Juliana on July 14. I don't know how this may be done in most countries, but at The Hague, it is done *right*. I was togged out in full formal diplomatic kit: top hat, white tie and tails, and white gloves. ("Not worn," I was advised by very detailed memoranda provided by the embassy staff, "but carried in the left hand.") I was picked up by an astonishingly ornate gilded carriage, pulled by four of the best-matched horses I or anyone else had ever seen.

More guidance from the Embassy: "On arrival at the Palace, the Queen's Chamberlain and the Ambassador alight and, with their top hats held at their left breasts, acknowledge the playing of the American and possibly also the Dutch National Anthem."[1]

On arrival, I was met by—and reviewed—the Queen's Guard. ("The Ambassador thanks the Commander and congratulates him on his fine guard.") The pomp and circumstance was real, not artificial, and walking into the Queen's palace, Huis Ten Bosch, was like walking into the seventeenth century, the walls covered with great paintings of the Golden Age. Things in The Hague don't change very much or very often; in truth, there is a Dutch saying: When you die, try to do it in The Hague because, in The Hague, everything happens ten years later than in the rest of Europe.

The queen was about sixty and had been the reigning monarch since 1947. ("The initial form of address is Your Majesty; then, Madame is used.") She was very gracious, of course, and our conversation ("Approximately ten minutes") was very general—although she did drop a personal note. She told me how much she enjoyed playing the violin; she did not, however, then or later, offer a demonstration.

Chapter 9

Ambassador: Netherlands, Two

H ow can I best describe the job of ambassador for anyone who may someday wish for a similar role? In the public mind, I suppose, it conjures visions of international party time for political fat cats. There is some truth in that: A great deal of diplomacy involves breaking bread with friends and foes alike, and the average man in the street will likely not come to the attention of the president or White House staffers seeking to fill the jobs.

The underlying reality is that most people who are in a position to make useful contributions, whether in private industry, government service, or in a political campaign, are people who have been pretty successful—those who understand the nuance of negotiations and the value of alliance. This includes people with whom I had the honor to serve, such as publishing giant Walter Annenburg, posted to the UK; former Fed chairman Arthur Burns to West Germany; former Connecticut governor John Davis Lodge to Argentina; Curt Winsor (who had a PhD in International Studies) to Costa Rica; career Foreign Service officer Everett Ellis "Ted" Briggs in a number of Latin American posts (both Winsor and Briggs proved invaluable during my own posting at the Organization of American States); and two men I had the privilege of recommending to presidents Nixon and Reagan: banker Shelby Cullom Davis for Switzerland, and businessman/historian John Loeb for Denmark. In my Wall Street days, Davis had been Middendorf, Colgate's major competitor in the specialized field of insurance stocks, but he was an honest, fair, and worthy adversary; John Loeb had worked with me on Ronald Reagan's first election campaign (where I was chairman of the International Economic Advisory Committee). With Julian Gingold, John wrote three brilliant papers on the status and future of the U.S. dollar.

I soon learned—as I know it may come as a shock to many business types who take such an assignment—that the job of an ambassador is a vast departure from running almost any kind of business. The business world is vertical: One gathers and assesses information from below, makes decisions, and lives with the results. In business, I could measure success or failure, often day to day, by the movement of the securities I recommended, or the health of our balance sheet. Diplomacy, by contrast, is horizontal. You are not an individual performer; you're part of a vast team where your efforts are submerged to the collective. Gray is the color of diplomacy, compromise is the common currency, and there is no daily measuring stick for success.

As ambassador, one represents the president but often acts as the extension of one's State Department desk officer. A large part of the job is to gather information and forward what is learned along with recommendations. The desk officer passes the cable along to the assistant secretary of state for the region. He or she usually makes whatever decision seems appropriate. The assistant secretary may, on rare occasions, consult with the secretary of state. On even rarer occasions, the secretary may confer with the president. Whatever guidance is generated is then passed back through the chain to the ambassador: Deliver this note. Present this démarche. Take this position. Sign this treaty or agreement—and always, "Find out more."

I came into the job with twenty-plus years' experience as a hard-fighting, no-holds-barred executive. I was accustomed to making my own decisions—yes, in consort with my partner—and making them quickly. I had to make quite an adjustment, and this led to a permanent change in my personal style: Now, whenever government action is involved, I'm more collegial, checking with everyone in sight before I make a decision.

Most ambassadors not from the Foreign Service come to the top posts because of political affiliation, but that does not give them a license to be political. A few months after I arrived on the scene, the new chairman of the Republican National Committee, Rogers C. B. Morton, thought to revitalize RNC operations in Europe. There was an office in Paris, but I suspect it had not been very effective. Rog sent a representative to an ambassadors' meeting (in Italy, as I recall) looking for suggestions. Someone had a bright idea: Have the Republican-appointed ambassadors spread a Republican message, especially to Americans living abroad. Use federal employees to promote partisanship? The idea died a-borning.

There was a proper "political outreach" component of the job—for example, trying to help Europeans understand such matters as the U.S. two-party system. (Only two, they wondered? Why not seven or eight? Or twenty-eight, as competed in one Dutch legislative contest?) And, of course, things only tangentially political were certainly within bounds. We held regular, three-times-a-year briefings for anyone or everyone in the American business community.

Rog Morton did put his finger on one problem: The European image of Nixon was rather fuzzy. Little wonder—the presidential portrait hanging in the Rotterdam Consulate was a bit out of date; I made sure that JFK was replaced by RN. Over time, I tried pretty hard to get the president to stop by on any of his European trips ("They're really looking forward to seeing you and Pat in the Netherlands") without success. To my knowledge, no U.S. president had ever visited the Netherlands while in office. (Two of them, of course—John Adams and his son, John Quincy—had been to Holland as ministers plenipotentiary before serving as president.) George H. W. Bush, who had visited at least twice while I was in the Hague, later became the first man to visit the country as president.

On the surface, the Netherlands of 1969 had the look of a happy fairy tale. Clean and scrubbed, the country and the people; unfailingly friendly; industrious. This general reputation of the Dutch is not of late invention. Teenager John Quincy lived in Holland when his father was posted there. Young John's mother, Abigail, in a letter sent from her home in Massachusetts, hoped "that the universal neatness and cleanliness of the people where you reside will cure you of all your slovenly tricks, and that you will learn from them industry, economy, and frugality."[1] She was right on the mark.

Everyone, even the queen, rode around on bicycles, and I quickly followed suit. When Barend Biesheuvel was appointed prime minister soon after my arrival, I pedaled over to his office for my courtesy call. Of course, having lived and worked for so long in New York City, I wasn't quite sure about the safety of unattended bicycles, so I asked the security guard who opened the door if I might bring the bike inside.

I should not have worried about my bicycle, but there were plenty of other things of concern in the Netherlands—under the surface, the fairy tale was often dark. The Dutch economy was bedeviled by wage and price controls, rising taxes, and inflation (the cost of living in 1971 was 21 percent higher than the year before). The Dutch government was in perpetual turmoil. There were five major political parties, always forming, dissolving, and re-forming coalitions. During my four-year tenure, they went through four prime ministers and one eight- or nine-month period without any prime minister at all.

When I arrived, Piet de Jong had the watch, quite literally, as he was a former submarine commander. He soon was followed by Barend Biesheuvel, then Norbert Schmeltzer—whose government may not even have been accorded full recognition, it was so tenuous—and then the hiatus, followed by the laborite (Socialist) Joop den Uyl heading a coalition of all five parties.

When he was merely a member of Parliament, Joop would often drop by my residence and share some of my wine and cigars. Once he became PM, he declined all invitations. "I can't come anymore," he said, "because of your country's involvement in the Vietnam War." My country had been just as much involved in the war when he enjoyed my hospitality, but I guess he then felt obliged to make a statement.

Joop's political hero, his idol, was the Social Democrat Willy Brandt, chancellor of West Germany. "You have to understand," Joop told me, "that the only people who can deal effectively with the Communists are the Socialists, because we understand each other. We wouldn't have all of these problems with the Soviet Union if people like Willy Brandt and I were in charge of Europe." Brandt even was awarded the 1971 Nobel Peace Prize for his efforts at improving East-West relations. I refrained from passing along Kerensky's contrary experience; Joop wouldn't have believed me, anyway. Not long after I left my post to move on to another assignment, the world learned that the Stasi—the East German secret police—had an agent posted as a personal assistant to Brandt. So much for his ability to deal with the Communists.

Foreign Minister Joseph Luns (he, who had so graciously acknowledged my clumsy attempts with the language) was a remarkable man. I believe he had served as a foreign minister longer than any other European since Tallyrand (who served in that capacity in France, 1792–1807). Joseph was a habitual joke teller . . . but always of the same seventeen jokes, half of them at the expense of Charles de Gaulle. The joke telling followed a predictable routine: He would recite them in a set order, joke number one, then number two, on to seventeen, and back again to one. Picture this scene: a dinner party, time set for eight o'clock. Everyone arrives at precisely three minutes before eight (the Dutch are very punctual). At some time during the evening, Joseph begins the routine, but at eleven on the nose, the party is over. He might be in the middle of joke number seven—his audience, of course, enthralled—but when the clock chimes the hour, Joseph checks his watch and makes a gracious exit without even finishing the joke. At the next affair, wherever it might be, I swear he would pick right up at joke number eight. He was generally so well liked that this bit of boorishness was accepted with a sort of amused tolerance. I must have heard and, of course, laughed at each of those jokes about twenty times—and can't remember a single one.

I had been in the post for about two years when Joseph came to ask a favor. "I would like," he said, "to be secretary general of NATO." At that time, many of the top international agency jobs in Europe already were held by Dutchmen, and it seemed like uphill work to plug in another; but I was willing to try. I learned that Secretary of Defense Melvin Laird had not yet given any thought to the topic, so I called Mel and asked if the U.S. would consider supporting Joseph Luns as secretary general of NATO? Mel said, offhand, that he didn't have a problem with it, but was anyone else in the running? I didn't know, but only half in jest I suggested that a German, so close to the end of the war, would be fearful of his own shadow; the British don't want it; the French aren't eligible because DeGaulle did not want France to be on the NATO Military Committee; and the Italians can't have it because the outgoing incumbent is Italian. I told Mel that Joseph was not only a first-rate guy, but he was pretty much on our side. Mel called back about a week later and said, "I think we can go with your man." With our support, Joseph won the appointment—a job that he held for nineteen years, and in which he was superb.

The senior Communist in the Netherlands—Soviet ambassador Lavrov—was a pleasant fellow who followed the rules. Part of his job was to harangue me about supposed U.S. crimes in Vietnam and elsewhere. I suspect that it was important for him to let his superiors back in Moscow know that he was doing his job. One time, he invited me over to the residence for a chat. After the usual pleasantries—Would I like to join him in a vodka? No, but thank you—we sat down on the couch and he launched into a carefully rehearsed peroration. How do I know it was carefully rehearsed? About three minutes into the diatribe, his chauffeur came into the room, whispered something into the ambassador's ear, and left. With no sign of shame, Lavrov reached up under an ugly painting hanging on the wall behind the couch. I heard an audible click, whereupon he started his little speech all over again, letter perfect, from the beginning. I interrupted for a moment, to ask if I might have a vodka after all.

This was a period of much diplomatic ferment for the United States, and Vietnam was the point around which everything seemed to revolve, a running undercurrent to everything we did. This was the period of the "Cambodian incursion," the shootings at Kent State, the publication of the Pentagon Papers. TV coverage in the Netherlands was brutal, and we became targets of left-wing anger. I got an urgent call from the consul general in Amsterdam, Gene Braderman. He wanted some Marines to go up and protect his office from protesting anti-American mobs, then ranging in the streets, breaking things. "The Dutch can't help," he said. There were not many Marines on the embassy detail, but give a Marine something to do, and he will *do* it. We got through that incident with some damage to his office, but none to personnel.

Another time, a small crowd had gathered outside the embassy; however, television news was happy to participate, and, every time the TV showed placard-waving people tramping around outside the embassy, even more people would show up. The crowd had grown to perhaps three hundred, all chanting, "Ambassador, come out," or words, some not quite so bland, to that effect. My security people wanted me to slip out through the back door, where my driver Charles would be waiting to spirit me away. I said, "We're going out the front," and told the driver to bring the car around.

Was I brave or foolish? Maybe I was just reacting without much thought. In any event, I said, "Open the door," and walked out, alone, into the crowd. Sudden silence. People stepped back to let me pass. I got in the car, closed and locked the door, and said, "Charles, let's go!"

Not a moment too soon. The crowd recovered from its momentary relapse into natural Dutch *politesse* and started banging on the car and shouting.

From time to time, there were personal threats. Once, an anonymous caller recited the exact itinerary of a trip later in the day, and told me at which point I could expect to be killed. We didn't cancel the trip, but we changed the route. Another time, after some particularly strong anti-American threats, I asked one of the Marine guards to spend a few hours at the residence. I wasn't so much worried about myself, but the house was full of my kids, the youngest four. Baby-sitting was not in the security guard job description—protection of people was the responsibility of the local police, and the Marines were assigned to protect U.S. government property. Well as far as I was concerned, the residence qualified. I felt a lot better when a Marine was close at hand.

Clearly, not every moment was given over to serious issues. One evening, we had a diverse group of friends to the embassy, including Soviet ambassador Lavrov and the eighty-year-old Christian evangelist Corrie Ten Boom. Perhaps you have not heard of her; during the war, she and her family saved hundreds of Jews from the concentration camps—until they were betrayed by an informant, arrested, and sent to the camps where all but she died. After the war she lectured and wrote several books, telling her story and carrying the message of "God's forgiveness." Corrie gave Lavrov a copy of her own memoir, the international best-seller *The Hiding Place*, which he graciously accepted (and, perhaps just forgetful, left behind; I had it delivered to him the next day). Corrie and Isabelle became fast friends.

Shortly after the 1969 *Apollo 11* landing on the moon, I hosted a visit by the astronauts, who brought with them two small pieces of moon rock. We presented these to the Dutch government, and they were put on public display. Recently, the Associated Press reported that Willem Drees (who had been prime minster some eleven years before my tour and who is now deceased) had given a museum what everyone seems to have thought was one of the moon rocks—it had been insured for half a million dollars until it turned out to be a piece of petrified wood. There was a flurry in the media until AP checked around; no one in the embassy or the State Department had any record of a gift to Drees, and the Dutch government verified that they still had both moon rocks safely under lock and key, in the permanent collection of the Rijksmuseum.

I tried to get out and around. I think I visited every major town in the Netherlands and, whenever possible, undertook some ceremonial task often with my whole family in tow. We opened the Cheese Market in Alkmaar, for example—the first day of the new season—rather like the symbolic guest opening the NYSE by banging on a bell. Cheese vendors waved their fragrant wares under the noses of passersby, basket makers wove their baskets, and clog makers carved their clogs, all under the watchful eyes of a throng of camera-wielding tourists.

I should tell you, however, about one of those ceremonial affairs, gone awry. By tradition, the ruling monarch goes down to the port to welcome the herring fleet on the first day of the catch. By tradition, the monarch takes up a wriggling, live herring . . . and swallows it whole! The crowd then looks to the honored guest—me—to do likewise. Honored guest screws up his courage, discovers that it is not as easy as the queen made it look . . . and chokes. The queen, a wise and gracious woman, was most polite, and did not join in the general laughter.

Any ambassador receives a large number of visitors, some of whom are asking for favors, some of whom are offering favors, some both at the same time. As, for example, a certain Dutch-born Swiss citizen whose family steel company had dealt with both sides during World War II. They had a large operation in Rotterdam, but his visits, I think, were not to check on his business but to curry favor with the Americans. For a big-time industrialist, he was an odd dresser, with lederhosen and an open shirt, carefully arranged to highlight the hair on his chest—rather like a male bird sporting his plumage. I think he had five wives, favoring models and beauty queens, each five or ten years younger than the wife he was leaving, and he always gave each, as a going-away present, a valuable painting. During one visit, looking around the residence that I had decorated with some Classic-era Dutch paintings from my own collection, he said, "You don't have any Impressionists; you really should have at least one. I gave a nice Monet to my last wife; she lives in Switzerland; she might loan it to you—give her a call." I did call. She said, "You want to borrow the Monet? Come pick it up, fine."

I drove over to Switzerland. The ex-wife was very gracious if a bit vague "Let me see . . . if we can find the painting. It was of what? Oh, wait, yes, the one from my ex-husband." Her sour expression told me what she thought of her ex-husband; we found the painting behind a couch—which told me what she thought of it—and she said, with a wave of her hand, "Please, take it." I'm not sure if she had any idea just who I was or where it was going.

I hung it in the embassy, three women in a blue boat, but it was too much of an off note compared with the old masters on display, and it was not on my list of favorites, either. I found it to be superficial, lacking technical skill and emotion—but I guess that's why they called Monet and friends "impression-ists." I tolerated it for maybe six months, and then took it back. The owner seemed as disinterested with the return as she had been with the leaving.

Armand Hammer (usually identified as "the millionaire Chairman of Occidental Petroleum") was an acquaintance of some years standing, grow-ing out of his own passion for art (he and his brother owned New York's Hammer Galleries). Armand visited me at the embassy and, I guess, assumed that I owned the Monet, because soon after my tour had ended he called to offer me $10 million for the painting. I gave him the name of the owner, and have no idea whether or not he followed through.

I don't want to dwell overmuch on my adventures in art—an important part of my life but not necessarily of my memoir—but I can't resist men-tioning a few. I was once offered the chance to buy an old Master painting from a church in Spain, where it had been hanging over the altar for almost four hundred years; the church needed the money to fix a roof badly in need of repair. Well, I asked "Old Masters" art expert Daan Cevat to join me to take a look. The chancel was dark (they used candles to light the services) and filled with the gentle sound of the nuns, hidden behind a screen, pray-ing for the new roof. We had a flashlight, and when Daan saw just the bot-tom of the painting, he said, "We must leave."

When we were out of the building, he elaborated: "That's a copy. The original is in a museum in America." But how could this be? I had been told the painting had been owned by the church since it was painted in 1577. As it turned out, the painting had been sent to a restorer in the 1870s, and, yes, came back as a copy while the original was quietly passed through a series of owners, finally to come to rest some forty years later.

An "art" adventure of a more pleasant sort: Early in my tour, before Isabelle and the kids came over and I had some spare time on weekends, I took the opportunity to study stained-glass-window making with one of the world's leading experts, Joep Niclaus, and helped him create an enormous window for the William of Orange Church in Delft. Joep allowed me to paint some small areas near the top; satisfied that I had some skill, he allowed me to make more than a dozen much smaller windows, including a baptismal window for the American Anglican church in The Hague. I also learned to make "Delft" plates, commemorating something or another and illustrated in a characteristic blue paint. I presented them to various friends and associates, including President Nixon. (For Joseph Luns, a plate in which I portrayed him making his final speech before Parliament. I later learned that, upon his death in 2002, he bequeathed the plate to the Rijksmuseum.)

The most significant non-official and non-family event of my tour was my discovery of music. Not in performance (I studied piano as a child, without distinction) but in composition. In the spring of 1971, I was most fortunate to meet an absolute musical genius, Somtow Sucharitkul, son of the Thai ambassador to the Netherlands. When he discovered that I had always been interested in composing but had no idea how to go about it, he volunteered to be my teacher and, more important, my collaborator. We started with a few hymns for my church, then a small piano concerto, and some other minor pieces; I worked out the melodies, and Somtow helped me develop the orchestration.

And then, the bold move. With Somtow's invaluable assistance, I composed a symphony to commemorate Queen Juliana's twenty-fifth year on the throne. I was most flattered when Philips recorded a performance of my *Holland Symphony* for release during the Jubilee Year celebrations, and was doubly honored by its broadcast, along with an extended interview of yours truly, on Dutch national television. I presented the score to Her Majesty during a farewell lunch she held in my honor.

In the meantime, encouraged by modest success, I turned the residence into a miniature cultural center, with a special focus on music. On several occasions I invited Dutch composers to create something new, to be played during one or another soirée. I think perhaps fifteen took up the challenge, including, notably, Princess Margriet's husband Peter van Vollenhoven.

One dinner, in honor of the pianist Artur Rubenstein, was not so successful. Oh, the dinner was fine, the company, gregarious, but the music ended on a different note. There was a marvelous Bösendoerfer in the residence, my own piano, and I asked Mr. Rubenstein if he would care to play something for the guests, anything at all. He said, "Oh, I have to tell you, I am under contract with Steinway and I am not permitted to touch another instrument." Not even in a private party at the ambassador's residence!

Over the years since, and always with the technical collaboration of Somtow and others, I've put together a fair number of compositions, ranging from nocturne to opera. Many, if not most, have been in commemoration of something: a visit to a foreign country or celebrating the launching of a new Navy ship. I've put a special focus on marches, and a few years ago,

I was most gratified to receive the Edwin Franko Goldman Award from the American Bandmasters Association.

I have been honored when my compositions have been played by such stellar orchestras as the National Symphony and the St. Louis Symphony, and when I have served as guest conductor at a number of orchestral and band performances, at home and abroad, usually playing one of my own works. I make no claim whatever to any skill as a conductor; my style, if you will, has been described as enthusiastic, but stiff—what might be called the "Al Gore School of Conducting." And, while over the years I gained some confidence in making music, I was not at all grounded in the conducting thereof. Not to worry; as I was preparing to conduct the Boston Pops in one of my compositions, maestro Arthur Fiedler told me everything I needed to know: "The secret of conducting? When the band stops playing, stop waving."

Chapter 10

Ambassador: Netherlands, Three

I came to the post as a businessman, and I was determined to add whatever value that experience might offer. At that time, top management at the State Department did not emphasize matters of trade, as if the business of statesmen did not include, well, business.

By contrast, the Dutch were all business. Dutchmen headed or held key positions at such international trade organizations as the Bank of International Settlement, European Economic Community (EEC), Organization for Economic Cooperation and Development (OECD), and the International Monetary Fund (IMF). The Netherlands was the largest investor in the United States; the Dutch had more money invested in our country than we had in theirs, well over $2.2 billion, compared with $1.7 billion U.S. investment there. Much of the Dutch investment, of course, was concentrated in a few firms—Shell, Unilever, Philips—then among the largest non-American concerns in the world.

The Netherlands was already one of our best customers, where about nine hundred American firms had operations of one sort or another; but I knew that there was room for many, many more. The Netherlands was a free market, with minimal barriers to trade. In fact, Dutch foreign trade for 1972 was equivalent to 76 percent of GNP, compared with only 9 percent in the United States.

The Embassy staff could help U.S. exporters explore the market and help line up competent local agents or distributors; we would not act as salesmen, but only as trade facilitators. I must say, when I suggested this project to the staff, they jumped at the chance. We started by assessing the marketplace and analyzing opportunities, targeting industries for which we believed there was a large potential market. We didn't bother with computer hardware, vehicles, and aircraft because such companies as IBM, Ford, and Boeing were already well established in the marketplace. We concentrated our efforts on software, environmental controls, cargo handling systems, pumps and valves, printing and graphics, food processing, franchising.

We appointed a staff national campaign manager for each target line, a remarkable team. Bob Jelley, in Amsterdam, concentrated on the computer and printing industries; Gene Griffiths in Rotterdam followed electronics and test equipment, and encouraged Dutch companies to invest in the U.S. In The Hague, Ralph Griffin took on materials handling and environmental systems; Carlos Moore worked with health care industries and ran our Visit USA program. Ben Kennedy focused on American plant investment and product manufacture in the Netherlands.

Commercial attaché Harold C. Voorhees was in overall charge, and John Blodgett developed a clear plan of action: Identify the products and producers; research the markets; identify all importers, dealers, and agents in the target industry; identify and appraise the quality of upcoming trade events (in the Netherlands and elsewhere). For instance, when we learned that American trade centers in Europe were mounting trade shows in some of our target industries, we arranged charter flights and invited Dutch merchants and potential customers to join us, at their own expense. Over time, there were six such missions, each sold out, which carried more than four hundred top-drawer Dutch customers to visit American exhibits in Oslo, London, Frankfurt, and Paris.

Our program incorporated all logical marketing techniques: direct mail ("Take advantage of one of the largest and fastest growing markets for American products"), visits to potential customers, reverse trade missions, charter flights, negotiations over trade barriers—notably, gaining favorable treatment for U.S. citrus exports. We coordinated with the American Chamber of Commerce and the Visit USA offices in Paris and Brussels.

The embassy staff developed and ran the program; I played cheerleader, adviser, and activated my personal network in support. On one of my visits home (May 1970), I sat down with Nixon, gave him a full briefing on our effort, and urged him to spread the word. As before, he sat there, feet propped up on the desk and a yellow legal pad in his lap; he took notes. I followed through with a letter to Maurice Stans at Commerce, in July, on the same subject.

Dutch businessmen were concerned about the U.S. recession; I arranged for Fed chairman Arthur F. Burns to meet with investment bankers and government officials for freewheeling discussions. An innovative export tax–relief program, proposed by the administration, was hung up in Congress; I became a lobbyist without portfolio to Congress for the Domestic International Sales Corporation (DISC). This would permit an American corporation to defer federal corporate income taxes if the money was invested in new exports.

My lobbying tactic? Not complicated: I won the support of a key chairman, Arkansas congressman Wilbur Mills, who bragged that he had never been outside the United States, with a simple reminder that his state was a major exporter of soy beans and would be a major beneficiary of the program. The legislation did pass, although there were some inadvertent conflicts with international compacts that had to be worked through. As a result, DISC was replaced in 1985 by the Foreign Sales Corporation (FSC) and—apparently still flawed—in 2000 by the Extraterritorial Income Exclusion (EIE) act. Maybe we'll get it right.

The road to expanded opportunities was not always smooth. As one of our first initiatives, I wanted to send a letter to the CEO of every company on the Fortune 500 list, inviting each to come over for a visit and to explore export opportunities with the Dutch. I asked the Commerce Department—simple-minded me—for a mailing list of the CEOs. I waited months; it never came. Eventually, we copied the information from a business magazine and sent out the letters, which we should have done in the first place, but I was trying to touch what I thought were all of the proper bases.

Response to those invitations was, I'm afraid, tepid. A lot of American CEOs seemed uninterested in developing European markets; that was uphill work, and, even with the slowdown in the U.S. economy in the early '70s, it was still a lot easier to deal within the vast and homogeneous U.S. market. We persevered. I sent similar invitations to the governors of our fifty states; I well recall one delegation of some twenty Georgia businessmen, led by then-governor Jimmy Carter, looking for opportunities to sell goods and services to the Dutch. Carter was a magnificent tour leader, making a powerful presentation at the many meetings we had arranged with the Dutch. He was also a gracious guest, repaying my efforts by appointing me an admiral in the Georgia Navy. Pretty heady stuff for this former lieutenant (jg).

And, to be fair, I must note that—mailing lists aside—the Commerce Department was indeed involved in overseas business promotion, providing, among other services, outstanding "Buy American" exhibits at major European trade shows and expos. We just knew that more could be done.

Our embassy's small but potent Military Assistance Advisory Group, the MAAG, was pursuing opportunities in their own sphere, especially an open competition launched by the Dutch government to replace a fleet of aging Royal Dutch Air Force Lockheed F-104G Starfighters. The candidates included the Swedish Saab Viggen, the French Mirage F-1, the Northrop P-530 Cobra, the Lockheed CL1200 Lancer, and the McDonnell-Douglas F-4 Phantom.

Ours was a tough balancing act, to put forward the interests of the U.S. competitors in general without favoring one over the other. However, I was not constrained from passing along an unclassified U.S. Air Force analysis—using sophisticated techniques perhaps not available to the Dutch—that showed that the F-1 "would be a disaster in combat" (for the Dutch, that is) with the newest-version Soviet MiG, and that the Viggen was not even in the same league.

One issue, in this sort of international deal, was the "offset." How much business would the winning company put in the Netherlands, either in co-production or totally unrelated business? The general manager of a Dutch electronics company told me he favored the Viggen because the Swedes were offering to buy other military hardware from his company; I told him, "You know, Northrop is offering a minimum of $350 million worth of direct aircraft work." He said, "Ahh. . . ."

Lockheed was pushing hard for their candidate: the CL-1200 Lancer (Air Force designator X-27). This was, essentially, an updated version of the F-104 with increased fuel capacity and a new engine. For Lockheed, it was a cost-effective proposal—they already had the tooling and hoped that the Dutch would see familiarity as an advantage. Lockheed designer Clarence "Kelley" Johnson, head of the famed Skunk Works, wrote to tell me that Secretary of Defense David Packard told him that the CL-1200 was a project he wanted to do very much. But then, noting a dark cloud on the horizon, Kelley added, "There is much talk here of the so-called 'lightweight fighter' for which there may be competition for a prototype soon. This aircraft makes use of one F-15 engine and is the size of the original XF-104." He was not enthusiastic: "Its range and endurance are very short and the ability to carry external stores very poor in my view."

In March 1972 I escorted Dutch defense minister Hans de Koster on a ten-day swing through the United States that included visits to both Lockheed and Northrop—not to mention visits to Army, Navy, and Air Force bases and meetings with the secretaries of defense and air force.

At just this point in time, the Norwegian air force bought twenty-two *used* F-104s from the Canadian air force. Dutch Socialists, opposed to any major weapons purchase, were delighted and put some pressure on the government. If old F-104s were still good enough for the Norwegians, why not also the Dutch? The Dutch air force was not persuaded. By July, the field had been narrowed to one competitor and an invitation for offer was sent to Northrop.

However, as Kelley Johnson had predicted, there indeed was a new USAF competition that, in effect, put all other competitions on hold. One month after de Koster's trip, the Air Force issued development contracts to

Northrop and General Dynamics. These led to a 1974 fly-off between a single-engine General Dynamics YF-16 and the twin-engine Northrop P-530 Cobra, now dubbed YF-17. Lockheed's CL-1200 had been evaluated and was not in the running.

In the event, the YF-16 won. The so-called lightweight fighter is today the F-16, of which more than four thousand have been put into service worldwide. In June 1975 a NATO consortium of the Netherlands, Belgium, Norway, and Denmark selected the F-16 in a head-to-head competition with the French Mirage. As for offset, most of the aircraft and engine components came to be manufactured in five NATO countries, with complete aircraft assembled in Belgium and the Netherlands. In a small irony, Lockheed—cut out of that competition—purchased the General Dynamics aircraft business in 1992. Thus, the grand winner is now certifiably a Lockheed product. YF-17 lived on to see another day: In fact, during my tenure as secretary of the navy, it was transmogrified into the F/A-18 Hornet.

Outside the "target industry" envelope, but great fun nonetheless, we arranged for what I believe to have been the first California wine tasting and display in Europe. Just before he headed off to his new job in Washington, Ambassador Tyler had taken me down to the cellar of the residence and waved his hand over rows and rows of dusty bottles of wine. "I can't very well take it with me," he said, "and it may be some value to you." He offered to sell all to me for a very modest fee, which is how I came to be the proud owner of what may have been the best collection of first-rate wine in the neighborhood. I put much of it to good use, entertaining diplomats, of course, especially after I had joined a wine-tasting club that rotated events among the homes of the members. I could almost pretend that I really knew something about wine.

Thus emboldened, I convinced some California winemakers to bring samples of their wares to The Hague, there to discuss the California approach. The French community was furious; some of our friends thought the idea was hilarious. What a great joke: Everyone thought that California wines were called something like Mountain Red, came in gallon jugs, and sold for less than a buck.

"Everyone" was surprised. Even some of the French (who came to the event, disdain at the ready) admitted that, well, you may have something here. I don't think the California wine industry made any quick killings on the European market, but it was a start.

Our greatest success—not a specific trade deal, but a confirmation, if you will, that we had been on the right track—came in the middle of my tour, when the State and Commerce departments launched a study on "assistance to American business overseas." I do believe that Nixon had paid attention. The Senate Commerce Committee convened a hearing in Brussels, at which I was pleased to testify. Teams of investigators were sent around the world, studying existing programs—all embassies promoted trade to some degree, of course—and gathering suggestions. The result: a State-Commerce coordinated "target industry" program involving all over-seas missions, beginning in fiscal year 1974. The effort was remarkably simi-lar to ours, although, where we had focused on eight product categories, they narrowed the field to five—which were more or less identical to five of ours. To conform, we dropped two of our lines but kept environmental controls, because this seemed to be a natural for the Netherlands.

And the State Department made a change that I found particularly grat-ifying: When reporting on the fitness of the foreign service professionals, "henceforth, all officers will be evaluated on the basis of their concerns for U.S. business."

Toward the end of my tour, *Business Week* (December 16, 1972) explained the administration's new "business promotion" effort, in a focus on our pro-gram under the headline, "World Trade: A U.S. Ambassador's New Business Role." They went into pretty good detail: our eight product areas, the direct involvement of as many as twenty-two members of the embassy staff, our saturation bombing of Dutch business prospects, banks, and airline offices with brochures "designed to induce visiting U.S. businessmen—whether on vacation or business—into considering the Netherlands as a potential mar-ket." Tongue firmly in cheek, the author noted that "it does not appear that Middendorf's pushiness has sparked any resentment among the Dutch" and suggested that, because of my business background and this focus on trade issues, I was one of the more effective ambassadors in Europe.

Another affirmation: A State Department inspection team declared The Hague to be "one of the most professionally run [embassies] of any in the Foreign Service." I was most proud to later receive the State Department Superior Honor Award and, in 1985, from the Netherlands, the Grand Master in Order of Orange Nassau.

I had set a limit on my ambassadorial tour; four years was enough. Isabelle had been playing ambassador's wife since 1970—except it wasn't play, for her; it was hard work. There was an event practically every night: dinners at the residence, receptions, formal and informal parties. I got all the glory, rubbing shoulders with the high and mighty. It fell to Isabelle to be the con-stant hostess, to make sure everything was in order, and to deal with the frus-tration of not having enough time to spend with our children. And so, in March 1973, I submitted my letter of resignation and prepared for my return to the States. Charley Tanguy became chargé d'affairs, until Kingdon Gould Jr., our ambassador to Luxembourg, was shifted to The Hague.

On my last day as ambassador, June 9, I was sitting in my office. One of the Marines called on the intercom and said that there was a gentleman at the entrance with a bicycle, and he wanted to come up. Well, I said fine and went over to wait at the elevator, and who should appear but former prime minister Biesheuvel, with his bicycle. His gesture—returning my call in kind, so to speak—was most gracious and fully representative of the best qualities of the Dutch.

Chapter 11

Secretary of the Navy: One

I n May 1972 John Chafee left the job of secretary of the navy to make an unsuccessful run for the U.S. Senate (he had better luck four years later). I was busy in the Netherlands, and if this was an opportunity to call in my chips, I did not recognize it, nor would I have tried to exercise it. In the 1968 campaign, John Warner had headed up "Citizens for Nixon," and his reward had been assignment as undersecretary of the navy. Now, he appropriately moved up to secretary.

However, I got a visit from Nixon's attorney, Herb Kalmbach, with a different job offer. Herb told me that Secretary of Commerce Maurice Stans had been asked to run the finance committee for the Committee to Re-Elect the President (known by the strangest acronym ever: CREEP), and he wondered if I could come back to serve as treasurer. I declined; I felt as if I had done my share, and besides, I was enjoying my post—who wouldn't?—and I was delighted to be supporting American interests in such a great country.

At about this time, and to my dismay—in a revelation unconnected with my current or future employment—I learned that economic tinkering had not been limited to the New Deal. A few months earlier, in a misguided effort to control inflation, Nixon imposed wage and price controls for a period, it was announced, of ninety days (which, truth to tell, stretched out for almost one thousand days and was a monumental failure). Over at the Fed, chairman Arthur Burns elected to take the costs of food and energy out of an inflation index. The expressed rationale was that prices of those items were too volatile and therefore contributed to long-term inaccuracy, but to my knowledge the real reason was to help Nixon get re-elected by keeping "visible" inflation under control (and much lower than it actually was). In fact, the planned inflation rate of 2 to 3 percent rose, over time, to 14 percent.

In any event, my four-year tour had ended but out in the rest of the world the Cold War was still raging, and there were important challenges to be faced. Peter Flanigan said that Nixon's "promise" of the secretary of the navy job could be kept, in a manner of speaking. If I were still interested, they would bring me down to be undersecretary, with every expectation that the top job would at some point open up and be mine.

Yes, I was still interested. Undersecretary of the navy, on its own merits, is an important job. It had been held, for example, by both Roosevelts: Theodore in 1898 and Franklin D. from 1913–20, although at the time the title was assistant secretary of the navy. I was sworn in on August 3, 1973.

Adm. Elmo Zumwalt Jr. was chief of naval operations (CNO). I had met Zumwalt several years earlier—I was still ambassador to the Netherlands—after he had been featured in the December 21, 1970, *Time* magazine under the headline, "The Military Goes Mod." Nice portrait on the cover, scary article: It implied that there were going to be big social changes in the Navy, which some critics had summarized with a slogan: "Beer, Beards and Broads." Beer machines in the barracks, beards for the sailors, and women eligible for almost any assignment. The article quoted a just-retired admiral: "How far can we permit absolute freedom of speech, deportment and dress—and still hang on to the indispensable element of discipline?"

Zumwalt, at age forty-nine, was the youngest man ever appointed CNO, over the heads of some thirty senior three- and four-star officers. Was he too young, too much in tune with the hippie movement of the day? I was not opposed to changes designed to make life better for the sailors, but the Netherlands had just been going through what looked like a similar experiment, a relaxation of some military standards. Salutes were not required, and recruits could wear their hair long, in ponytails. You might call it the Socialist approach: "We're all just people, together." In my judgment, it was a dangerous approach. The salute—a custom going back to the Middle Ages—is a sign of recognition and mutual respect, not of slavish subordination. The liabilities of long hair should be obvious to anyone who has ever worked around machinery.

I learned that Admiral Zumwalt was going to be in London the following week. I felt it was important—ego to the fore!—to warn him that he was sailing into shoal waters. I called his office at the Pentagon to ask for an appointment, and he got on the phone. "I'll be glad to see you," he said, and we set a time. So I flew over from Amsterdam to London at my own expense, went to Navy headquarters at Grosvenor Square, was offered a cup of coffee and a chair, and immediately began to feel a bit foolish. I had been expecting some sort of wild-eyed kook, and here was one of the most gracious men I had ever met.

Well, I was there with a purpose, so I began telling him about my concerns. He listened, thoughtfully, nodded his head, seemed to care about what I had to say. But after about three minutes I was thinking to myself, What am I doing here? He probably knows all of this stuff already. And I was right. At some appropriate point, he said, "Mr. Ambassador, don't believe everything you see in the media. Sure, I'm trying to make some changes in the Navy, make it a better place for all of our sailors, but I'm not going to do any of this stuff I hear they're doing in the Netherlands." In summary, he said it would be a great Navy and we'd all be proud of it.

Little did I realize that in three years, I'd be his boss.

When I came on board, Zumwalt had less than a year to go as CNO, and the personnel changes he had engineered, for good or ill, had been made. On balance, he did help make it a better Navy. But Zumwalt's tour was difficult, and controversial. He started with a handicap: His elevation was not welcomed among much of the senior officer community, especially those dozen or so who might have expected to get the job themselves. He wanted to eliminate discrimination—racial, gender, and class—because he saw such issues as tearing at the fabric of morale. In so doing, he intruded on what some officers saw as the prerogatives of command, and many, including many among the retired community, derided or encouraged resistance to many of the changes. Some of them were quite happy to roll back the clock after he retired. No more beards!

Let me put Zumwalt and his famous (or infamous) "Z-Gram" messages to the fleet in perspective, with one example. Before Zumwalt, a commissioned officer could cash a personal check up to $50 at the Navy Exchange, a limit imposed as much to ensure an adequate supply of cash on hand as for any reasons of distrust. An officer's word was his bond.

Before Zumwalt, an enlisted sailor could cash a check, on base, up to $10. He might have several thousand dollars in his bank account, but the Navy chose not to believe him, prima facie. A $10 limit, period; Zumwalt changed that. Everyone was equal in the eyes of the cashier. This was not Socialism; it was not "interfering" in the chain of command; it was fairness.

Zumwalt moved the marker forward in a number of areas; the Navy accepted the idea of a black flag officer, and the first was my friend Sam Gravely (who retired as a vice admiral in 1980). A nurse, Alene Duerk, was promoted to rear admiral in 1972—the first-ever female naval officer of flag rank. In the same year, the Navy experimented with a mixed-gender crew on a non-combatant ship, the USS *Sanctuary*; it seemed to work. Just before I came on board, Zumwalt announced additional efforts to "eliminate any disadvantage to women resulting from either legal or attitudinal restrictions." Women were thenceforth granted limited entry into all ratings, accepted into the NROTC program, and, for the first time, female line officers were eligible for promotion to flag rank.

The most difficult issues were yet to be resolved, and they were perhaps more symbolic or emotional than practical. Should women be admitted to the Naval Academy? The real issue with admitting women to the service academies was not the cost of adding bathrooms, but what to do with the new officers once they graduated. The law prohibited women from serving "in combat," which, for the Navy, meant on board any ship (or in any aircraft) that could be placed in an environment where hostile fire was exchanged. Narrowly defined, they could serve only on tugboats or hospital ships. Therefore, a number of new female officers could—in theory—fill so many shore billets that there would be no place for many of the men to go. Some could be stuck at sea for their entire careers. Not a happy prospect, and certainly not much of an inducement to remain in the Navy for a career.

We did begin admitting women to the Naval Academy; 81 graduated with the class of 1980 (along with 1,212 men). Serve on warships? Fly combat aircraft? Those questions eventually were answered in favor of women, although I was more of a reluctant observer than an active participant. At a hearing before one congressional committee, I admitted that I wouldn't want my own daughters to be in combat. After, a woman rushed up and said, "How dare you?!" I was being honest; back in 1946, when LCS 53 stopped at Saipan for medical screening, I was told about several Army nurses who had wandered off into the night. Their bodies were found the next day, throats slit by holdout Japanese troops.

I was not alone in my concern. Congress did not repeal the "combat exclusion" for another twenty years.

Admiral Zumwalt's successor was announced in late March 1974: Adm. James L. Holloway III, who came in as the vice chief of naval operations the month after I began my tour as undersecretary. Then in April, John Warner left to head up the Bicentennial Commission and I began filling in as "acting" secretary with every expectation of getting the job for real.

But something strange had happened on the way to my promotion. Because of the Watergate mess, Nixon was so preoccupied with keeping his own job that he was little concerned with employment issues at the Pentagon. James Schlesinger, the secretary of defense, had his own candidate for the Navy Department, a man in the shipping business. Some of my friends learned of this—Jim certainly never told me so—and we quickly mounted a small counteroffensive. Having been treasurer of the Republican

Party for so many years, I'd made a lot of friends on the Hill, and spoke with some people whom I knew would be supportive: Bob Wilson in the House, Barry Goldwater, John Tower, and John Stennis in the Senate. I didn't play sore loser (you know, "I was promised!"), but I let them all know that I was very much interested in the job, if they might be pleased to speak on my behalf. It wasn't too many days before they sent a petition over to the president, urging my appointment.

Nixon may not have been paying much attention before, but he certainly noticed this petition. He was then having problems with Congress and was likely to have a lot more, if the talk of "impeachment" moved past the talking stage. The president clearly decided that, if it would make some people on the Hill happy to see me as secretary of the navy, why, it was just fine. Nixon later told me a story, which I found hard to believe, that Barry Goldwater was not one of the people who supported my candidacy. According to Nixon, when my name finally came to his attention, he called Goldwater: "Your guy is up for secretary of the navy. Should I push it or let it go?" And (according to Nixon) Barry said, "Oh, Bill's had enough." That doesn't coordinate with Barry's warm support when the Senate Armed Services Committee held my confirmation hearing, which, according to Barry, may have been one of the shortest on record.

The full Senate vote came less than two hours later. I was back in my office at the Pentagon and, in fact, was just then meeting with legendary entertainer Bob Hope when I got the congratulatory phone call. (A staff officer later told me that when escorting Hope to my office, one of the Pentagon janitorial crew seemed to recognize him as someone important, but looked puzzled. When Hope passed the same person on the way back from my office, she broke out in a big smile: "I know who you are! You're Jack Benny!" Hope, I was told, did not appear to be amused.)

I was not the first secretary of the navy to have once been in wartime naval service; for the nearest examples, both John Chafee and John Warner had served as enlisted men (Marines and Navy) in World War II and both as Marine Corps officers in Korea. However, I certainly was the first who actually had a degree in naval science. I also, unknown to most people, had an unbeatable naval heritage: Baltimore mariner William Stone, an ancestor on my father's side, had been one of the first five or six captains appointed in the Continental Navy. In fact, in late 1775, Stone provided two merchant ships he owned—renamed *Wasp* and *Hornet*—to become warships in the cause of independence. This certainly gave me a sense of personal tradition for working with what I have always viewed as the most tradition-oriented of the armed services.

The job of secretary of the navy lost some caché—it certainly lost a seat in the president's cabinet—when the Defense Department was established in 1947; however, the job still had a lot of clout. The Navy was a massive organization: $33 billion annual budget; 526,000 men and women in the Navy; 196,000 in the Marines; operating more than 500 ships; 7,000 aircraft; and 215 major installations that were staffed by several hundred thousand civilian employees. Indeed, it is a large and complex organization, with in-place procedures, long-standing traditions, and strong-willed and independent-minded leadership.

I think the Navy has always been thus, from the very beginning: attracting a breed of mariner who quickly could earn the trust of superiors and thrive on the ability to make difficult decisions when well out of touch (measured in months, if not years) with headquarters. This is a useful trait when faced with sudden danger, but it may be a complicating factor when required to work within the headquarters itself. Complicating, that is, for the headquarters staff. I wouldn't have it any other way. The last thing our Navy needs is a bunch of "yes" men and women.

My Holy Cross degree in naval science and my stint in the Navy, of course, gave me a certain level of knowledge and understanding, but my 1940s Navy had more in common with the Phoenicians than with the Navy of nuclear engineering, computers, guided missiles, satellites, and lasers. More useful, I found, was my political, diplomatic, and business background. I also had to change my focus: The State Department tries to predict the actions of nations by divining intentions; the Defense Department analyzes capabilities. If the Soviets came up with a great new weapon or tactic, it didn't matter how peace-loving they might seem as guests at some Washington cocktail party. At the least, the Defense Department had to assume that, at some point, the new capability might come under the control of someone who was not so peace-loving. And the department had to plan for such an eventuality.

I made a vow, right at the start, that I was not going to try to be a supererogatory CNO; the primary job of the CNO is to operate the Navy. The primary job of secretary of the navy is to recruit, equip, train, and maintain the Navy and the Marine Corps—those things that for the most part require approval and funding from Congress and, therefore, the support of the American people.

Here, at the height of the Cold War, making the case for the Navy—to carry the message of "seapower" (which is just as vital today as it was then) to the public and Congress—was important, indeed. The United States is dependent on overseas supply of sixty-eight of seventy-one strategic materials, including oil, copper, zinc, lead, tin, rubber, titanium, and aluminum, almost all of which, around 98 percent, must come by ship. By comparison, the Soviets imported only two raw materials from overseas: tin and rubber. A key U.S. Navy mission (then, and now) is to keep the sea lanes open for our traffic; a key Soviet mission was to deny such transit. With enough submarines and minelayers, theirs was far the easier.

The secretary of the navy has broad opportunities to take the Navy story to the taxpayers in public meetings, by making speeches, and by sitting down for media interviews (all of the above coordinated, in my case, by my special assistant for public affairs, the exceptional Capt. Bob Sims). In just my first ten months as secretary of the navy, I traveled 35,000 miles and gave more than fifty speeches. I honed my skills as a pitchman—such skills as I have. As a public speaker, I hope that the importance of my message offsets a less-than-oratorical delivery. I added another tool to the public relations kit and established a Secretary of the Navy Luncheon program at the Pentagon. During my tour, three hundred of the nation's top business, financial, and labor leaders (including the chairmen of our largest steel and automobile companies, AFL-CIO leader George Meany, and mega-millionaire Naval Academy graduate H. Ross Perot, who later made a run for president) accepted my invitation, about twelve at a time, to sit down with senior Navy officials for a frank discussion of the issues of the day. It gave me a great audience to make my un-subtle pitch for more ships.

I made a special point to include our sailors and Marines in my outreach: Overall, I visited more than three hundred ships (including a few of those of our allies)—more, I was told, than any other person, military or civilian, in history. Since I had once been an engineer officer and knew, firsthand, how underappreciated were the men in the bowels of a ship, I created the Golden Snipe Award (the title was recommended by Adm. Hyman G. Rickover; "snipe" was current slang for what in World War II we called "the black gang," a term that was properly retired). This was presented to the engine room crew of pretty much every ship—foreign or domestic—that I visited. There were, however, two exceptions: One, the USS *Constitution*, the oldest ship in the Navy, had no real engine room; and two, the chief engineer of one ship had been relieved of his duties the morning before my visit and the skipper himself suggested that his ship should not be given the award.

However, the most important part of the job, the one with the greatest impact on both the present and the future, was to be the advocate for Navy and Marine Corps programs that were vital to the defense of our nation. The money to fund every multibillion-dollar program or buy every ten-cent lock nut; the money to train, equip, and pay every sailor and Marine; the money to create, repair, or rebuild every installation worldwide, comes from

Congress, the gatekeeper for the taxpayers. And this is where my active political experience really came into play. I knew a lot about the game, I knew a
lot of the players, and they knew me. Access is the first step.

Anyone in Congress may have his or her own idea as to what may or
may not be appropriate. Members vote for or against programs for a wide
range of reasons, none of them hard to understand. Some, too busy with
their own committee assignments or special interests, don't study all of the
issues and vote the party line. Most, regardless of the party line, believe in a
strong national defense. Some, regardless of the party line, take a far-left position, that the United States has no business being the world's policeman and
the monies can better be spent on social programs. Some, regardless of the
party line, are interested in programs in direct proportion to the amount of
money or jobs the programs will bring into their districts. When campaigning for support, we certainly played to each member's special interest.

In this, I learned an important lesson during one of my first visits to
Capitol Hill, a courtesy call on then–house majority leader Thomas P. "Tip"
O'Neill, a Democrat. I asked how I could get more ships for the Navy.

He said, "Let me tell you how this town works. Quincy Naval Shipyard
hasn't been getting any business lately; there are a lot of unemployed citizens
of Massachusetts up there." The message was clear. I managed to shift scheduled overhaul work on two destroyers from the Philadelphia Naval Shipyard
to Quincy. This may have infuriated the Pennsylvania delegation, but ever
after, I got a fair hearing from Tip. A note on O'Neill: He was a rabid partisan, would go to the mat on almost every issue in which Republicans were
somehow involved—but at the end of the day, quite literally at 5:00, he
might happily meet me for drinks and to swap lies. One Thanksgiving, he
invited Isabelle and me to join him at his home on Cape Cod for a ceremonial drink. Quite a guy.

New weapons systems, new aircraft, new ship types: Anytime you put
the word "new" in front of a program, be prepared for heated argument from
Congress. Why do you need a "new" program? What's wrong with the "old"
program, for which we so recently put up millions of dollars? Why can't
the old program be upgraded, at less cost? The questions are always fair; the
answers must be just.

In high season, Admiral Holloway and I—often joined by Marine Corps
commandant Gen. Louis H. Wilson (a Medal of Honor recipient who was
my choice for the job)—averaged at least one committee hearing a week,
covering pretty much the entire range of procurement and operational matters: shipbuilding, aircraft procurement and force readiness, USSR naval
capabilities and shipbuilding trends, our operational tempo, and personnel
matters. But day to day, my team and I worked the individual members and

staff. I prepared for every call I made, often holding a "murder board" practice session, with my own staff tossing me every difficult question they could think of, and helping me with the answers. Just before going into a member's office I mentally ran through the five points I wanted to cover. I took subject-area experts along, when appropriate. If I promised to get back with a copy of a report or an answer to a question, get back I did, as soon as possible and usually the next day.

I'm sure I've not told you anything that you don't already know. I always found strong support from members who represented Navy towns like San Diego, Norfolk, and Newport; members whose districts included major shipyards, like Bath, Maine, New London, Connecticut, and Pascagoula, Mississippi; members who owed a favor to an important constituent, with which we might be able to lend a hand.

Sometimes I called in old friendships, even though we had grown ideologically quite distant. A few of my toughest opponents were liberal politicians from my old stomping grounds of Connecticut, New York, or Rhode Island, but they also were friends of many years standing. Friends will at least listen to your argument, and often give you the benefit of the doubt. Sometimes we just stroked egos, gave a "Friend of the Navy" award or an invitation to speak at a shipbuilding event (of which there were always at least three: the keel laying, the launching, and the commissioning). For an extra touch we might invite a member's wife to be the ship's sponsor, an honorary appointment without responsibility beyond standing on a flag-draped platform, champagne bottle in hand, to say, "I christen thee USS *Whatever*," but an honor nonetheless, which forever would serve as a symbolic link between the lady and the ship.

And, since every member's career thrives on local publicity (and withers without it), we made sure to contribute our share. And in this, please understand: I wasn't supporting Republicans over Democrats, I was building support from both for our Navy programs. We might have a photographer on hand for a meeting, which quickly provided a photograph that could be used in a constituent newsletter: "The secretary of the navy called on me." If my legislative chief (initially Rear Adm. Edwin K. "Ted" Snyder, followed by Rear Adm. George E. R. "Gus" Kinnear Jr.; two absolutely brilliant officers both of whom went on to richly deserved promotion) said, "This is going to be a close vote," I might go out to an Armed Services Committee member's home district, give a speech, praise the congressman: "Greatest living American; stalwart in defense of the few precious moments of freedom we have left." My visit would almost always result in a front-page item in a local newspaper, often with a photo of the member and me shaking hands.

Does this seem shameless? Let me say, it was effective. We often got the vote, despite opposition from their congressional colleagues.

A few years ago, I was conducting the Navy Band in a public concert of one of my new marches, when I spotted a former Democratic member of the Senate Armed Services Committee, long retired, in the audience. From the podium I said, "It is my honor to introduce a great American, who helped keep the Navy as the final shield of freedom. Would you all please give him a well-deserved round of applause?" After, he came over and said, "That's the nicest thing that ever happened to me."

A committee staffer may at times be as important as a committee chairman, because the chairman, always overburdened, relies on the information and advice his staffers provide. The staffers do the research, assemble documents, arrange for testimony. If a staffer is opposed to your program, for whatever reason, your job has become more complicated, so you want to be very certain that the key staff members, at the least, understand everything. I know of some—more than a few—high-level appointees who would rarely, if ever, go to bat and fight for a program if it meant trooping up to the Hill to beg staffers for a hearing. Undignified, some might say. I say dignity be damned; I was after results. The overall military budget is limited and we were in constant competition with the Army and the Air Force—especially the latter, which was always being championed by Barry Goldwater. He once chided me for trying to be "too aggressive." I took that as a high compliment.

Some years after I left the Navy Department, I joined in establishing the Defense Forum Foundation. Several hundred congressional staffers are invited to monthly luncheon seminars on topics of significant national interest, featuring a key military, diplomatic, or political leader—up to and including secretaries of Defense. We always have a big crowd, still going strong after thirty years under president Suzanne Scholte. In fact, just as this manuscript was headed to the publisher, as chairman, I conducted our sixth seminar on the Chinese navy, which is embarked on a major expansion and is pursuing vital developments—new submarines, advanced antiship missiles, an electromagnetic pulse weapon that could knock out our computers, and cyber threats to our national defense. As I told the staffers, many of whom have no personal experience with or memory of the apocalyptic threats of the Cold War, we must be prepared to counter their capabilities—and, I warned, it can take ten or more years to bring new systems to operational capability. We can't wait until intentions become manifest before we start working the problem.

Nixon resigned as president on August 9, 1974, and Vice President Gerald Ford, appointed not quite a year before to replace the disgraced Spiro Agnew, was sworn in as chief executive. Gerry quickly let me know that he was a "Navy" president. (Well, in a manner of speaking, so too were the other Navy veterans: Kennedy, Johnson, Nixon, Carter, and Poppy Bush. Is there a pattern here?) "Consider me to be your contact at the White House," he said. I certainly was happy to know that someone over there was interested in our efforts; to that point, we had been getting no help from the White House on any of the programs we were working. I think I heard from the White House only one time during the period when Nixon was hunkered down in the bunker. I was alerted that a call would be coming through on the special secure phone. A staff officer escorted me to the secure room with the secure phone. As you may appreciate, this all made me a bit nervous; were we about to go to war? Had I been put on report by some angry politician? This was a period during which Nixon's inner circle—Chuck Colson, Bob Haldeman, and John Erlichman—was running a reign of terror and no one felt safe. The call was from Erlichman.

"Middendorf—you there?"

"Hi, John."

"I got a big request for you."

Big request? They wanted me to find a Navy Department job for someone they wanted to get rid of but, under civil service rules, couldn't fire.

Ford was an old friend, much more relaxed than Nixon ever had been. At one point, he said, "Bill, you've got a great job with more than a million men and women united in a common cause, the crew standing at attention and saluting as the carrier steams past with the band up on the bow playing one of your marches. I'm over here wrestling with our country's future with a staff of 350 people, some of whom are wrapped in a battle of ego, and I've got to try to keep everyone happy." He seemed to long for the days when, in Congress, he could bring people together; now he had to play referee.

Ford brought in Nelson Rockefeller as an appointed vice president, and while I was initially disturbed by that selection, I can only say, now, that Nelson became a staunch ally. Yes, you never know; Nelson Rockefeller had always been "the enemy." He may have been a Republican, but he seemed to stand for everything I didn't believe in. Well, one day, up at the Capitol, we literally bumped into each other and fell into conversation. In my eyes, he had always been a devious plotter, sitting in his castle on the river, finding ways to spend his vast fortune in support of liberal causes. In my circle of friends, he was known as "Old BOMFOG," for his frequent use in speeches of what seems to have been his favorite phrase: the "brotherhood of man, fatherhood of God." Yet, here was a most engaging fellow, very outgoing, who seemed to be sincerely interested in my efforts to boost the Navy. He said, "Bill, I'm underemployed here as vice president, I've always been fond of the Navy, and I want to help." I said, "Welcome aboard!"

Rockefeller became a strong supporter of our efforts; he made phone calls on our behalf, and went along with me on several congressional visits. He also accepted my invitations to be the graduation speaker at the Naval Academy, and the principal speaker at the commissioning of the nuclear aircraft carrier, USS *Dwight D. Eisenhower*. For reasons not clear at the time, the Party dumped Nelson and put in Bob Dole as vice-presidential candidate for the 1976 election. In a face-saving move, Nelson announced a full year ahead that he did not want to be the candidate.

Chapter 12

Secretary of the Navy: Two

I came on board at the height of the Cold War, at a time when nuclear-missile-equipped Soviet submarines, able to wipe out a third of our population in a matter of minutes, were lurking just off our coasts and the Navy was focused on rebuilding our own dangerously diminished fleet. While comparisons between the U.S. and Soviet navies are no longer of the greatest significance, they were a vital part of our efforts in the 1970s. Much of our fleet was World War II vintage, reaching the nominal thirty-year warship life all at the same time. We were retiring obsolescent ships to free up money for new construction but, in so doing, had reduced the fleet to a dangerously low level: down from 932 ships in 1968 to 587 in 1974 (of which only 325 were classified as "warships," the rest being patrol craft, mine sweepers, amphibious ships, and auxiliaries). A further overall reduction of 64 was scheduled through 1977.

The Soviets, on the other hand, never known for a blue-water fleet, were moving away from a traditional coastal defense and building a "new" navy from scratch, with almost two thousand ships in the water and gaining on the U.S. Navy at a rate of four to one. Granted, we knew that our ships and systems were better, but in any given confrontation numbers could prove vital, and (as a former Soviet admiral told me during a post–Cold War visit to the "new Russia") the Soviets operated on the assumption that quantity equaled quality. Ten marginally qualified ships could overwhelm one great ship. Nonetheless the Soviets were catching up in real quality. Their newest operational antiship guided missile, for example, had twice the warhead of our planned counterpart, *Harpoon*, which was still in development.

The primary missions of the U.S. Navy, sea control and power projection, call for a variety of capabilities, but not all ships can meet all mission requirements at all times. In the face of budget realities, Zumwalt backed a concept dubbed "High-Low." Fewer high-cost, 90,000-ton, big-deck carriers and guided-missile cruisers (nuclear powered) as a trade-off for many more ships of lesser capability.

Key elements of the "low" program were patrol frigates (which could handle many destroyer missions) and the sea-control ship (SCS)—a small, 17,000-ton aircraft carrier equipped with helicopters and some vertical and/or short takeoff and landing (VSTOL) aircraft. The SCS mission was to maintain control of sea lanes, and to provide protection of underway replenishment groups, mercantile convoys, amphibious assault forces, and task groups. The concept had been tested through some two years of operations of a modified amphibious assault ship, USS *Guam*. The SCS was priced out at about one-eighth the then-current cost of an attack carrier. Zumwalt was black-shoe Navy, a surface-warfare officer; there were senior brown-shoe (aviator) officers who saw SCS as an unacceptable compromise. (The distinction—black- or brown-shoe, grew out of the normal day-to-day uniform kit of the two factions: The traditional naval service dress blue uniform, worn by all officers on occasions of nominal ceremony and by ship drivers much of the time, came with black shoes; the day-to-day costume for aviators was green or khaki, with which brown shoes were appropriate.)

The nuclear Navy (for which shoes were not a talisman), as represented by one man, Adm. Hyman G. Rickover, was adamantly opposed. Rickover believed that all major surface combat ships should be nuclear powered: expensive to build, but perhaps less expensive over a lifetime and free from the need for constant fuel resupply when at sea. Many planners were opposed. They may have agreed with the cheaper-in-the-long-run arithmetic, but they pointed out that the annual shipbuilding budget is not amortized over thirty years. There was hardly enough money in the world, let alone the Defense budget, to build a two-ocean nuclear Navy all at once. There wasn't much of an argument when it came to a focus on nuclear-powered submarines, which could operate, submerged, for months at a time. The submerged operational capability of a diesel-powered boat was measured in hours.

John Warner was lukewarm on the SCS; on the other hand, Secretary of Defense Schlesinger was a fan and made sure that the first significant funds for construction were in the proposed budget for fiscal year '74.

Well, I came along just about the time the budget cleared the Armed Services Committees and was nearing the Appropriations Committees, and when we got word that the SCS was in trouble, Zumwalt asked for my help. He said, "I'll work the Democrats, you work the Republicans, and let's see what we can do." I went up the Hill, full of confidence; I was cordially welcomed, but I had a feeling that the road had become very steep, indeed. I didn't know that the fix was in, that Rickover and some heavyweights in the aviation community had greased the skids, to ease my way back down. I was caught in a tug-of-war between black shoes and brown.

Nonetheless, I may have been of some service: While the House Appropriations Committee cut SCS, the Senate Appropriations Committee did not, and left the money in the budget. The issue went to conference, and the Senate won.

Then, toward the end of the year, Rickover tried to move some money around in the *next* year's proposed budget—soon to be sent to Congress—to shift about $250 million of ship construction money from "low" ships to two nuclear-powered guided missile frigates. For the same money, the Navy could have as many as ten patrol frigates. Rickover made a pitch to Schlesinger, who asked Zumwalt for comment. Zumwalt said, in effect, let's make a deal. Give Rickover $100 million in new money, if he would pledge support of the sea-control ship and the frigates planned within the proposed budget.

Schlesinger made the proposal to Rickover. According to Zumwalt, Rickover said, "In other words, you are blackmailing me." Schlesinger said, "Yes"; Rickover said, "I accept." Except—according to Zumwalt—Rickover didn't exactly keep his end of the bargain. I certainly can attest to that. I went back on the Hill to start the next budget cycle, full of confidence; I came back down with polite "thanks" for my comments but no commitments. I would note: Despite the attempts to smother the program, the SCS concept survived, to a point, and a new class of amphibious assault carrier was given SCS capabilities through juggling the mix of aircraft on board—heavy emphasis on VSTOL and ASW (antisubmarine warfare) helicopters.

Like many folks in the Navy Department, I had mixed experience with, and mixed feelings about, Rickover. Two quick examples: One day, I overheard Rickover berating some poor junior admiral who had piped up at one of my staff meetings in response to a question I posed on some nuclear issue. Rickover seemed incensed: "Who are you to speak to the Secretary?" I invited Rick to come back to my office, later, and suggested he might exercise loyalty down as well as loyalty up. I told him I found his remark to that flag officer to be offensive, and that I wanted to hear from people with contrary views who were not afraid to voice them. The junior admiral was kind of like the honest little kid in *The Emperor's New Clothes*. Rick was not amused, but he may have softened his approach.

Another example: P. Takis Veliotis, chief executive of the company that was building our nuclear submarines, was known as a good businessman, a hard but fair negotiator whose company was turning out some very fine ships. Rickover said he was a crook. But Rickover applied the word "crook" to a lot of people, and since he was in effect Veliotis' boss and took no action, we gave the charge no credence. But Rickover was right: In 1983, Veliotis

My mother, Sarah Boone Kennedy, the day she was presented to King George V and Queen Mary, Buckingham Palace, 1935. (*Author's personal files*)

My grandfather and namesake, John William Middendorf, in a friendly caricature. One of the leading investment bankers of the day, with a portfolio of railroads and utility companies, he was soon to be hit by a 1903 market collapse. (*Author's personal files*)

Proud and happy: Ens. J. W. Middendorf II (USNR), 1945, engineer officer and navigator of LCS (L) 53. (*Author's personal files*)

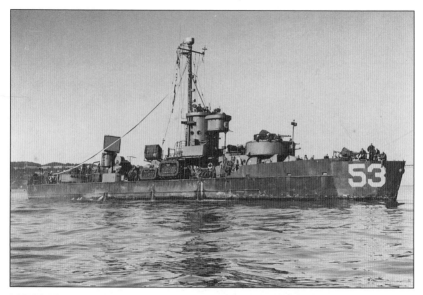

LCS (L) 53 as we entered San Francisco Bay, home from the war. I'm the taller officer on the bridge. (*U.S. Navy*)

Eventually, as other officers were detached, I became acting squadron commander, charged with putting the ships in mothballs at Portland, Oregon. We must have done a good job; twenty years later, some were reactivated and given to South Vietnam. My ship (third from right), which had been through some rough action before I reported on board, was not among them. It was sold for scrap in 1949. (*U.S. Navy*)

My first meeting with Robert Frost. I soon assembled a fine collection of original copies of his poems. (*Author's personal files*)

Goldwater for President campaign PR manager Lee Edwards managed to rent this billboard in Atlantic City, New Jersey, as a stunning display ("In your heart you know he's right") for delegates attending the nearby Democratic National Convention. (*Campaign photo of Goldwater and the billboard by Don Dornan*)

for those who think

Thinking is in the wind from coast to coast. People are on the lookout for peace and freedom – the right outlook for Goldwater. His principles and programs are so clean, so refreshing. Think . . . and vote Goldwater.

GOLDWATER DRINK AND NEWSBOOK FOR SALE AT GOLDWATER HDQ., 1493 POST ROAD, FAIRFIELD.

August 22, 1964

One example of campaign dreck: When Barry took a sip, he spat it out and exclaimed, "It tastes like warm piss!" (*Author's personal files*)

Escorting former president Dwight D. Eisenhower to a "Military Preparedness" meeting, 1964. (*Don Dornan*)

Barry Goldwater was met with adoring crowds everywhere he went, which I took as a positive omen. It was not. (*Campaign photo by Don Dornan*)

A study in body language: Former president Dwight Eisenhower and Senator Goldwater after filming the disastrous TV program, "A Conversation at Gettysburg." (*Campaign photo by Don Dornan*)

On the campaign trail with Barry and Peggy Goldwater. (*Campaign photo by Don Dornan*)

Inspecting the queen's honor guard the day I presented my credentials as ambassador to the Netherlands. (*U.S. Embassy photo*)

THE STATE OF GEORGIA

By His Excellency
Jimmy Carter
Governor of said State

Commander-in-Chief of the Army and Navy and the Militia thereof

To The Honorable   J. WILLIAM MIDDENDORF, II   Greeting:

Whereas, reposing especial trust in your patriotism, valor and fidelity,
I do, by these presents, constitute and appoint you

Admiral of the Georgia Navy

This former lieutenant (jg) is promoted to admiral, courtesy of Georgia governor Jimmy Carter, as he headed a delegation of businessmen on a tour of the Netherlands. (*Author's personal files*)

Dutch foreign minister Joseph Luns and me, July 1971. We had just been dropped from a helicopter to the deck of USS *Springfield* (CLG-7), flagship of the U.S. Sixth Fleet, on a visit to Vice Adm. Issac "Ike" Kidd. The United States later supported Luns' successful candidacy for secretary general of NATO. (*U.S. Navy*)

Boston Pops conductor Arthur Fiedler giving me a few pointers as I prepared to conduct the orchestra in a performance of my "Old Ironsides" march. (*Author's personal files*)

Discussing strategic issues with legendary entertainer Bob Hope, at the very moment the Senate was confirming my appointment as secretary of the navy. (*Author's personal files*)

I visited more than three hundred ships; here, receiving honors on board the oldest commissioned warship in the world, USS *Constitution*. (*U.S. Navy*)

Meeting with the crew of USS *Basilone* (DD 824), on deployment in the Mediterranean. Lurking in the background: a Soviet intelligence-gathering (i.e., "spy") ship, monitoring our communications. (*U.S. Navy*)

Presenting the Order of the Golden Snipe to the engineering crew of one ship—the name of which, I apologize, was not recorded. CNO Admiral Holloway told me that I visited more engine rooms than anyone in the history of the Navy. (*U.S. Navy*)

Adm. Hyman Rickover, "father" of the nuclear Navy; Adm. James L. Holloway III, CNO; me; and Arizona congressman John J. Rhodes with a model of the attack submarine USS *Phoenix* (SSN 702). (*U.S. Navy*)

Secretary of the navy immediate staff, 1975. From left: John Jenkins, Bob Sims, Chris Coon, Bill Kelly, Bob Ferneau, Les Palmer, Henry Vitali, Jerry Burke, me, and Doug Mow. (*U.S. Navy*)

The Defense Team, 1976. From left: Secretary of Defense Donald Rumsfeld, me, Secretary of the Air Force Thomas Reed, and Secretary of the Army Martin Hoffman. (*Defense Department*)

With John Warner, my predecessor as secretary of the navy, during his 1978 successful run for the Senate—the first of five. (*Author's personal files*)

Presenting a bicentennial "Don't Tread on Me" flag to President Gerald Ford. (*U.S. Navy*)

Isabelle, me, First Lady Nancy Reagan, and President Ronald Reagan. (*White House photo*)

As ambassador to the Organization of American States (OAS), listening, I'm sure, to a diatribe from one of our less friendly members. (*OAS photo*)

A power-packed meeting at the European Community. Foreground: EC president Jacques Delors. Back row, from left: U.S. trade representative Clayton Yeutter, Secretary of the Treasury James Baker, Secretary of State George Shultz, Secretary of Agriculture Richard Lyng, and the U.S. ambassador, yours truly. (*EC photo*)

Discussing the Heritage Foundation proposed constitution for Russia, with President Boris Yeltsin. The Communist-dominated Duma—parliament—refused at the time to adopt our version. (*Author's personal files*)

With British prime minister Margaret Thatcher, Tokyo, 1989, at a meeting of the International Democrat Union (of which, with Lord Jeffry Rippon, I was co-treasurer). IDU was founded in 1983 by Dame Thatcher, President Reagan, and others to promote democracy around the world. (*Author's personal files*)

fled to his native Greece—where he remains to this day—to escape federal indictment for racketeering and fraud. To my knowledge, this was a personal, not corporate crime and had no apparent impact on the quality of our submarines, which are today being built by the same company.

At each of our morning meetings, the briefer pinpointed the location of Soviet missile subs. Thanks to our secret underwater network of sensitive listening devices, dubbed SOSUS (for sound surveillance system), we could detect them as they slipped through the Faeroes-Iceland gap, then track them as they hid for a while behind the Mid-Atlantic ridge, before heading west to take up station a few hundred miles off our coast. Of course, we did not let them travel alone: One of our extremely quiet subs would be shadowing them, ready to retaliate in the event of attack. (One morning, while the grim subject of life or instant death was being discussed, I asked Rickover, "Rick, what the hell would we do if we got word right now that they had a couple of missiles headed our way?" We had no missile defense. He said, "We should tell the president, then go home and pull down the curtains.")

From the overall standpoint of national security, our most significant procurement was for the *Ohio*-class submarine, to be equipped with a new, long-range Trident nuclear-tipped ballistic missile. (A footnote of sorts: I wanted to call it the "Michigan" class, to honor President Ford's home state, but Gerry—among the most self-effacing men—told me, "Do not!"). There was heavy opposition to this newest missile: We already had the Polaris/Poseidon missile submarines, secure and almost undetectable, always at sea, carrying enough destructive power to obliterate the Soviet Union several times over. Why did we need to spend vast sums of money on a new model?

That argument did not address the rapidly growing Soviet blue-water fleet, steadily improving submarine detection technology, and if "Moscow" was the nominal target, the range of the Polaris/Poseidon missiles kept the boats on a tether that extended not too much west of Ireland and required operating bases in Scotland and Spain. Our national strategy was focused on "deterrence," having sufficient overwhelming force and capabilities to cause a potential enemy to back off. That meant having sufficient overwhelming force ready at hand. A Trident submarine might be parked in New York harbor—or, more to the point, almost anywhere in the Atlantic, greatly complicating the search factor—and hit Moscow and environs with twenty-four multiwarhead nuclear missiles that could be launched within minutes of a Soviet attack on the United States.

Negotiating points in our favor, in a manner of speaking: The USSR already had seventeen advanced Delta-class submarines, which could send missiles even from Soviet national waters to pretty much destroy any city in the United States. The earliest that Trident could enter service would be 1979, and by that time the Soviets would have twenty-five Deltas. Soviet defense spending overall was almost double ours—which, as a percentage of the federal budget, was the lowest since 1940.

We had the Republican votes for Trident but few among the Democrats. I went to Rhode Island senator Claiborne Pell—a very liberal Democrat, but a friend of mine from way back. "Claiborne, I need your help. First, large portions of our new submarines are going to be built up here in Rhode Island, and two, it's the final shield of America and I need your vote." The program won. Life is relationships; politics is compromise.

In my judgment, the second most important ship program in development was a potent combination of ship, radar tracking, and computer-controlled anti-missile system, to be called Aegis (after the shield of the Greek god Zeus). The Navy had known for some time that we had no defense against incoming antiship or land-attack missiles—but the solution was not clear or simple. These missiles do not fly in predictable trajectories but can maneuver all over the place. They can skim just above the surface to avoid traditional radar. They can be accompanied by a bunch of clever decoys, intended to overwhelm defenses. The Navy had proposed various combinations of radar, warship hull, and onboard antimissile missiles and had tested some, and a scheme was coming together when I had my first briefing on Aegis.

The radar—very large and very heavy—was to be installed in an oversized deckhouse on an existing hull design, and I recalled in a flash my terrifying moments trying to keep LCS 53 from capsizing. I asked, what is the nominal metacentric height? As it turned out, in the interim scheme I was shown, it was dangerously high, but to my relief I found that the Navy was working on the problem. In fact, the Navy had determined that Aegis was such a complex and challenging project that in a departure from the usual practice where the contractors pretty much ran the show, a special Aegis office was set up in the Naval Ship Systems Command, headed by the brilliant Rear Adm. Wayne E. Meyer. Meyer had been involved with the program for several years, knew the problems, knew the contractors, and knew—from exposure to some increasingly contentious members of Congress—the strength of the opposition.

Aegis joined Trident as one of the vital programs of the day, equally controversial, and one that occupied much of my time when, along with Meyer and others, I began working on Congress. I'm proud to say that, despite the mind-boggling cost of about $1 billion per ship, we got the program through Congress. Aegis—the system—has been installed on six different ship classes, all of which are known generically as Aegis cruisers or destroyers. This, I believe, has been the longest-running Navy shipbuilding project, ever, with upgrades and new components introduced as they become available. Aegis remains our main defense against antiship missiles (such as those just now being developed by the Chinese) and has been suggested by Secretary of Defense Robert Gates and President Barack Obama as an effective—and ready—alternative for the "missile shield" that former president George W. Bush proposed to develop and install in Poland and Czechoslovakia. They may have a case; I won't enter into that argument. The first Aegis ship, the cruiser *Ticonderoga* (CG 47) went to sea in 1983. The one-hundredth Aegis ship, a destroyer fittingly named USS *Wayne E. Meyer*, was delivered to the Navy in 2009.

I might note that our efforts to expand shipbuilding programs were given a hand by the Soviets themselves. During the Yom Kippur War (October 6, 1973)—during which Egypt and Syria attacked Israel—some ninety-six Soviet ships were lurking in the area. The State Department pondered "intent"—what, indeed, might they do with all of those ships? The assembled forces included some of the Soviet Navy's most potent, which goes to capabilities, and we had to know how to deal with each and every one of those ships, if and when an "intention" became manifest. If the Soviet intent simply had been intimidation, it surely backfired. By thus flexing their naval muscles in a geographic area outside of their normal zone of interest, the Soviets helped make our budget negotiations with Congress so successful.

One example: In June 1976, a House/Senate conference approved the largest shipbuilding bill in at least twenty-five years, $6.6 billion for new ships, including long-lead funds for a nuclear carrier, modernization of a nuclear cruiser, and overall plans to bring the fleet to six hundred ships—and keep it there.

It was about here that I found myself on opposite sides from my old friend Barry Goldwater, who saw his role with the Armed Services Committee as promoting planes for the Air Force. The Navy was getting a much bigger share of the budget than the Air Force and there wasn't too much he could do about it. As I noted earlier, I already had the votes lined up, working with the large number of Republican members whom the RNC helped get elected—along with those Democrats who represented communities where the Navy was a major force.

Another "aftermath" of the Yom Kippur War: Egypt was ready to re-open the Suez Canal, which had been closed since 1967, but was stymied by huge quantities of unexploded ordnance and damaged ships. The U.S. Navy trained more than 1,500 Egyptian military personnel in mine clearance, and in a year-long operation ending in June 1975, helped raise 10 sunken ships and clear more than 200 tons of unexploded ordinance and 686,000 land

and antipersonnel mines from the canal and its banks. In symbolic appreciation for the Navy support, Egyptian president Anwar Sadat awarded me the Order of the Arab Republic of Egypt (Rank A).

One of the more contentious issues—about which the Air Force was on our side—was the plan for a logistics base on the British Indian Ocean island of Diego Garcia. This would provide a strategically located refueling and replenishment stop for our carriers and long-range bombers. We had some important Democrats on our side—congressmen Melvin Price and F. Edward Hebert, and Sen. John Stennis—but some Democrats were bitterly opposed. At one hearing, one of them got so mad that I was certain he was about to take a swing at me; John Stennis had to intervene. We were desperate for funding, and Congress was playing games. They gave us money to build a bowling alley and a movie theater on the island, but not funds to dredge the harbor so that our carriers could come in and dock. Letting carriers anchor at Diego Garcia, they said, or letting long-range aircraft operate from the planned landing strip, would be violating the "Zone of Peace" of the Indian Ocean.

Whose zone of peace was that supposed to be? Diego Garcia is an island in the middle of the Indian Ocean: 1,800 miles from Saudi Arabia, 1,000 miles from India, 2,000 miles from Africa, and distantly confronted by Soviet naval facilities arrayed around the northern shores, in Aden, Mogadishu, Berbera, Socotra, and Iraq. Our critics argued that if we played "good guy" and pulled back, if we just left Diego Garcia to the seabirds and land crabs, the Soviets would match our good intentions. That argument didn't hold water. When the British earlier had pulled their military out of a small garrison on Diego Garcia, the Soviets expanded, not contracted, their influence into the littoral.

Senator Pell—strongly opposed, and here was an issue on which I could not call in any markers—asked the CIA to review the matter. CIA director William Colby, perhaps trying to curry favor with some in Congress, gave Pell a damning estimate, suggesting the Soviets would respond with force. Pell ran with it, passing copies out to all of his compatriots, but we were flying blind, as no one had bothered to share this bit of wisdom with the Navy. When we found out, Holloway and I went to Colby and asked for an explanation; he backed off a bit and more or less apologized. (I would note that, not too long after this incident, President Ford fired Colby and replaced him with George H. W. Bush.) It took great effort to get the program back on track, but we finally won. The facilities at Diego Garcia were there when we needed them, especially during Desert Shield/Desert Storm (1990–91) and the more recent operations in Afghanistan and Iraq.

Chapter 13

Secretary of the Navy: Three

During my first week or so as secretary of the navy, I called all the inter-agency people in for an important meeting: We were about to enlarge the scope of one of our most sensitive programs. The code name was Project Sanguine, the purpose of which was to communicate with our submerged submarines on station in the middle of the ocean. This would be more than just a "bell ringer" capability, that is, more than a one-way system to send a one-word alert or a launch message to the sub; we envisioned the possibility of establishing more effective communications.

Project Sanguine used an extremely low frequency (ELF) radio signal with a wavelength of some 2,500 miles. The key to ELF transmissions was the antenna, a grid of cables, laid just underground over widespread solid granite substrate. The radio energy would be directed up, thence to bounce back from the stratosphere and into the ocean to a depth of several hundred feet. The antenna grid would have to be laid over an area comparable in size to Rhode Island, and the Navy had located just such an area: solid granite just below the surface, in very rural, very undeveloped, upstate Wisconsin. But there was a problem; the residents of very rural upstate Wisconsin had been told by people who opposed Sanguine that exposure to ELF might cause anything from human sexual impotency to dried-up milk cows.

The operative word was "might"; no one really knew. The Navy calculated that the average energy received would be less than from lying under an electric blanket, or from sitting next to a sixty-watt light bulb. The Navy did not do a very good job of convincing the residents; the opposition did a wonderful job, and Congress was giving the Navy a very hard time. In truth, as one of his last official acts as secretary of defense, in January 1973 former Wisconsin congressman Melvin Laird directed the Navy to put the system pretty much anywhere *except* Wisconsin.

However, we had been granted sufficient real estate at a Navy facility at Clam Lake, Wisconsin, for a limited trial of the concept. For a really effective test, though, we needed more land. I explained the situation to the interagency group, expecting that all attendees would appreciate the need for the improved capability.

Someone asked a question: "What will we do if we don't get the extra land?"

I said, with my usual optimism, "Maybe we can ooze out a bit," implying, of course, that we would be able to acquire more land and expand the antenna field. Well, the next day I got a call from a congressman to ask if I would please explain what I meant by "oozing out"?

A lesson learned: Be careful about what you say, and how you say it—to anyone. No damage was done in this instance, but I learned that casual wishes were out of place and precise discretion had to be applied across the board. We later discovered that at least one man working in the CNO office was passing operational information along to North Vietnam—he was caught.

And a note: Science marched on, the design of the antenna was changed, the size of the antenna field was reduced, safety was demonstrated, and the system became operational—now officially called ELF—in 1989.

When I relieved John Warner (April 8, 1974), in one of the last bits of turnover he told me that the most classified mission of the day—so classified that I had not been brought in before—would be getting under way in about seven weeks. A combined CIA/Navy effort dubbed Project Jennifer was set to recover the remains of a Soviet Golf-class diesel-electric-powered ballistic-missile sub that sank exactly six years earlier and remained apparently intact on the ocean floor, a treasure trove of Soviet weapons technology and code books. Thanks to SOSUS and a search-and-photograph mission by one of our submarines, we knew where it was—the Soviets didn't have a clue. There was a problem, however: The wreck was three miles down in the middle of the Pacific, and nothing that size had ever been pulled from the ocean floor at anywhere near that depth.

Clearly, a special recovery platform would be needed, unlike anything ever seen before. The CIA cut a deal with movie producer and aerospace mogul Howard Hughes to provide cover. He would pretend that he was building a ship (for which we paid) designed to recover manganese modules from vast underwater fields, the prototype for a deep-sea mining business. Two key elements: a big claw for lifting, and a sophisticated positioning system to keep the ship exactly above the target. The manganese modules are real, and they have real value, so the cover story, especially involving one of the world's most eccentric billionaires, was believable. Although technically a U.S. naval ship (USNS AG 193), it was called the *Hughes Glomar Explorer.*

The ship arrived on station in July, ready to work. You can imagine—
here I was, breaking in to my new job, expanding my contacts, and working problems on the Hill, while staying in almost constant contact with my
office, waiting for any break in the news. My staff (most of whom didn't
know about the program) didn't have to give me details on the phone, just a
message along the lines of, "Jenny wants you back in the office." Well, things
did not go as well as we hoped. *Glomar Explorer* certainly pinpointed the
wreckage, lowered the big grappling claw down three miles, gently cradled
the sub, and on August 12 began the lift. Unfortunately, the hull broke in
two, with the part holding the coveted code books sinking back to the bottom, but I believe that several nuclear torpedoes were recovered, along with
the bodies of some Soviet crewmen who were buried at sea. That ceremony
was filmed, and at some point, after the effort had become public, we shared
the film with the Soviets.

Sure, we wanted to send the claw back down, but by the time the broken-
off half could be located and *Glomar* readied for a retry, winter was closing
in, the seas were far from calm, and "calm" was a condition of being able
to remain accurately positioned over the wreck. We would wait for spring,
except: On February 7, 1975, the *Los Angeles Times* broke the story, quickly
followed by a major story in the *New York Times*—our cover was blown and
the game was over.

There were efforts to sell or lease the ship, to recover some of the government's investment, but without success, and she was put into mothballs
in 1977. There is a happier ending to this story: At some point, some clever
soul realized that *Glomar*'s potential wasn't limited to hauling things up
from the bottom, but that it also could be converted into a deep-sea drilling ship for oil exploration. This was done, and it was put out on a thirty-
year lease to a consortium of oil companies.

Secretary of Defense Schlesinger—former head of the Atomic Energy Commission, and former director of the CIA—was a deep thinker, a pipe smoker
who, when asked a question, would take a puff or two, look up at the ceiling,
think about it, and then give a reasoned response. Schlesinger tended to focus
on strategic issues; Deputy Secretary Bill Clements worked on procurement.
Clements and I went back many years; he had been state chairman of the
Republican Party in Texas when I was treasurer of the RNC, and we were
comfortable working together on even the most controversial issues.

Clements was appalled at the cost of the Navy's new air-superiority
fighter, the F-14. Yes, it was a very effective weapon—armed with the Phoenix
air-to-air missile, an F-14 could simultaneously take on six enemy aircraft, as
far off as two hundred miles, and hit them all. However, Clements called me

and Admiral Holloway down to his office and said, in effect, that twenty-two million a copy was outrageous; we were to get those sharp-pencil boys of ours to come up with something a lot less expensive. Something like a seven-and-a-half-million-dollar airplane; maybe one that could also drop bombs? Thus was launched the VFAX program ("V" from the Navy's traditional code for "heavier-than-air," and "FAX" for fighter/attack/experimental).

As noted earlier, the prototype Northrop YF-17 had been in competition for the Air Force "lightweight fighter" contract, but lost out to the YF-16. With modifications—electronics, digitization, glass cockpit (and incorporating recent developments in modularization, such as rapid engine changes), F-17 could take on the attributes of both a fighter and attack aircraft and meet the demanding requirements for carrier operations. VFAX explorations began in August 1974; by the following May, the go-ahead was given to turn YF-17 into the F/A-18 (originally called just plain F-18).

Ah, here's another irrelevant but interesting footnote: YF-17 contractor Northrop, lacking experience with carrier-based aircraft, asked McDonnell-Douglas to join as the prime contractor for the Navy version. (Northrop planned to build a "land" version on its own for overseas sales; after some legal wrangling, the land version was shelved and Northrop became a subcontractor to McDonnell Douglas.) In 1997, McDonnell-Douglas was taken over by Boeing; thus, it is now properly called the Boeing F/A-18. Sometimes, you can't tell the players without a program.

There were some compromises: The original model didn't carry enough fuel for optimum mission requirements; it wasn't yet the perfect all-around airplane, but for the money, it was a pretty good start. And it got better, as every year passed.

"Here's your baby," I said as I gave Clements the package. I also handed him a list of nicknames from which he might choose. The F-14, for example, was called "Tomcat." On the list for the F/A-18 was "Hornet," to extend the Navy's two-hundred-year tradition with that name. I may have told him that my ancestor, Captain Stone, had provided the first of the seven warships named *Hornet* to the Navy. I was not disappointed when Clements picked "Hornet."

By the end of 1974, U.S. active participation in the Vietnam War had ended, and we were working with the South Vietnamese to develop a self-sufficient and democratic Vietnam. But by early spring 1975, things were not going well; two-thirds of the country was under control of the North Vietnamese and fighting was intensifying. When I made my last visit to Saigon, in the middle of April, I was amazed at the rosy report offered by our ambassador,

Graham Martin. The Vietnamese CNO, Commodore Chon, thanked me for authorizing $1 million to build a deperming dock. "This will keep our navy's future brilliant for years to come," he said.

Well, as the world knows, things were not rosy and the future was not brilliant. Two weeks later the North began a final offensive against Saigon, sixteen divisions pushing a bow wave of thousands of hopeful refugees toward the American Embassy. Ambassador Martin called for what became the largest airborne evacuation in history—in one day, April 29, helicopters took one thousand Americans and six thousand Vietnamese out to our waiting ships.

Down in the situation room at the Pentagon, I watched as Admiral Holloway took charge, trying to gauge results and assess remaining needs. "How many are left at the embassy; how many more lifts?" It was clear to me why this man had been chosen to be CNO; with calm authority, he called for a final nineteen sorties, and that was that. Ambassador Martin—carrying the embassy flag—and his Marine guard were the last to leave.

Well, we had ignominiously lost a war; our Vietnamese allies had lost a country. However, while the news focused on the helicopter lift, the South Vietnamese navy was taking bold corrective action. They loaded their ships with families and supplies and set sail en masse for the Philippines and a very uncertain future. There was at least one thing our Navy could do to help those men with whom we had worked for so many years: establish a program whereby these families would be welcomed in the United States, under the rubric of a voluntary "sponsorship" program. The sponsors would provide a temporary home and a guarantee that the Vietnamese families would not become burdens upon the taxpayer.

There were legal issues to be resolved, of course, but we first had to establish a framework, a method for soliciting volunteer American families and then matching them with Vietnamese families. This great humanitarian effort—the brainchild of one of my special assistants, Capt. Brayton Harris—began immediately, the day that Saigon fell. Within two days, Harris had arranged seed money funding through a Navy office originally created to provide in-country humanitarian assistance, and within a week we had an ongoing task force headed by naval reserve Capt. Charles Trieschmann, who volunteered for a six-month temporary-duty assignment.

When the Defense Department learned of our effort, they stepped in with a program to encompass all of the services. Call them Johnny-Come-Lately. Defense tried plugging data into a massive computer program that, because of problems with widely varied spelling of names and the reluctance of suspicious refugees to provide accurate information, was a mess. Captain Trieschmann had a work-around. He sent former Vietnamese officers out to the refugee camps armed with simple questionnaires; they verified the answers on the spot. We were seeking not just name, rank, and serial number, so to speak, but family preferences for location (warm climate, please; few were interested in, say, Minnesota), education, and job skills. For example, a former justice of the Vietnamese Supreme Court was found stacking boxes; he ended up with a major law firm.

The initial thought had been to find individual sponsors, and our first volunteer host was retired admiral Zumwalt, whose basement became the temporary home of a Vietnamese navy family of five. However, as the program got under way, we found that language and cultural issues intruded and made matches of one family to another difficult, so most of the effort was shifted to finding broader support from a range of government and private aid organizations. One example: The governor of Iowa came in with a simple proposal: The state would sponsor families with farming experience, and many of the navy veterans had grown up on, or their wives worked in, rice paddies and pig farms. Iowa was a winner.

In 1975, Mel Laird was chairman of Wolf Trap Farm Park for the Performing Arts (a cultural venue just outside of Washington), but he was thinking of dropping out and asked me, in the event, would I be willing to take on that responsibility? I said, "Sure, just let me know." Well, as it happened, I was visiting an aircraft carrier in the Mediterranean—which was being followed by one of the Soviet ships that typically shadowed every move of our major fleet units—when I was handed a radio message from Laird: "Operation Wolf Trap is on." Radio traffic to and from the Soviet ship—which was being monitored on the carrier—jumped many-fold, while, I am sure, they were trying to decode what this cryptic missive really meant. It was clearly important, addressed to the secretary of the navy and from a recent secretary of defense. Were they the "wolf" about to be trapped? (Incidentally, the day after Jimmy Carter was elected president I was replaced as chairman. The organization now wanted a Democrat in the post.)

Also in 1975, a group of Marine Corps Reservists asked me to endorse an effort to enhance morale, physical fitness, and perhaps encourage some young men and women to enlist: They wanted to stage a classic 26.5-mile marathon, to start and end at the Marines' Iwo Jima Memorial in Arlington, Virginia. I not only endorsed the idea but commissioned and paid for a scale model of the Memorial as a trophy for the winner. The first Marine Corps Marathon was run in 1976, with just more than one thousand finishers. These days, perhaps 30,000 may enter the race. In truth, the race has reached maximum capacity (as determined by the police and other safety forces) and online registration is usually filled within a few days of opening. It is, I believe, the fifth largest marathon in the United States. Each runner's time is calculated by a small computer on the shoe, which records when they cross the starting line and the finish line. Thus, a runner is not penalized by starting at the back of the pack. The race has been dubbed the "People's Marathon," because anyone can enter; there are no big cash prizes to attract elite runners—just the Middendorf Award for the winner—and it is not unusual for a first-timer to win. I have entered (and finished) eight times; my best time was 4:22, just about twice that of the typical winner.

I might note: I had better success, over the years, in my chosen sport. I started rowing as a teenager and remained active until I was eighty. I participated in perhaps twenty "Head of the Charles" races in Cambridge, won a national championship in Masters Sculling in 1979, and in 1985, New Zealand's Jay Limerick and I were presented the World Masters Rowing Championship Globe (Pairs) in Toronto.

Also on the fitness front, Holloway complained about the high percentage of senior officers and chief petty officers who were overweight and out of shape, and he wanted to do something to encourage physical fitness. For my part, I started the "Twenty-Minute Club." When I would visit a base in, say, Okinawa, I would invite everyone to run a three-mile course in twenty minutes—and I would hold the stopwatch. It was amazing how many actually made it, given the public embarrassment if they did not, although I do admit to a bit of fudging that I blamed on "a faulty stopwatch." If some struggling soul made it across in, say, twenty-four or twenty-five minutes, I called out the time as twenty. All told, many thousands received "Twenty-Minute Club" certificates.

Except for the most senior promotions and postings—such as service chiefs and fleet and area commanders, which largely are determined by the secretaries of navy and defense and the president—almost every officer promotion is handled through a selection-board process. One exception was choosing a new chief of chaplains, with the rank of rear admiral, which fell to me. I was presented with three outstanding candidates and sat down with each to try to discern which would be best for the job. My choice: Capt. John O'Connor. (The day after his promotion, he invited me to join him on a visit to the Pope, in Rome. This was not payback; the Pope was conferring sainthood on Mother Seaton, whose sons had served in the Navy.) Later, after retirement from twenty-eight years of Navy service, O'Connor went on to become a cardinal in the Catholic Church, assigned to the Archdiocese of New York.

On the subject of personnel assignments, I must make note of my personal staff. The quality of all of our professional sailors is high, and the folks assigned to work directly with the secretary of navy must be considered first among equals. Here's a list (also noting promotions or assignments that came after) and if I have left someone out—because there were staff changes from time to time that may have eluded my notes or escaped my aging memory— I ask forgiveness.

- *Executive Assistant:* Capt. (later, Rear Adm.) Doug Mow
- *Administrative Assistant:* Cdr. (later, Vice Adm.) John Poindexter
- *Judge Advocate:* Capt. (later, Rear Adm.) John Jenkins.
- *Marine Aid:* Col. (later, Lt. Gen.) D'Wayne Gray, followed by Col. Henry Vitali, followed by Col. (later, Brig. Gen.) William A. Bloomer.
- *Chief, Office of Legislative Affairs:* Rear Adm. (later, Vice Adm.) Edwin K. "Ted" Snyder, followed by Rear Adm. (later, Adm.) George E. R. "Gus" Kinnear Jr.
- *Special Assistant for Public Affairs:* Capt. Robert Sims (later, Assistant Secretary of Defense for Public Affairs).
- *Special Assistant for the Bicentennial:* Capt. Brayton Harris (later, Assistant Director of the Selective Service System).

I made so bold as to expand my staff by one, perhaps, unique addition. I wanted to have an experienced political operative close at hand to conduct intelligence sweeps and run interference with Congress, and the Navy Department chief of legislative affairs (noted above) and the House and Senate liaison officers—outstanding all, such as Capt. John McCain (who came in as Senate liaison just as I was leaving office)—could only, by law and common sense, do just so much. Since Congress controlled everything, it was vital to track every nuance and know where key members stood on every critical issue. I certainly didn't have the time, even though I had the personal contacts, to hang around Capitol Hill to tease out this vital information.

I brought in Bob Ferneau, a man I had worked with through the Republican Party, and gave him the title deputy undersecretary of the navy with the charge, "Keep me informed." I'm not sure if that job title had existed; I may have created it. Technically, Bob was one of my special assistants, but I had learned long before the value of a good title. It opens doors that might otherwise remain closed by status-conscious military professionals who wear their rank, their pay grade, and their status, on their sleeves and shoulders. That's useful if everyone is in a sinking boat, to identify the senior, and therefore most responsible, person; however, some military people are too concerned about their relative standing—some of them, perhaps, pathologically insecure—as with one relatively senior officer I know of, who, before taking a phone call from an officer of equal rank, would quickly check the Register of Officers that had every single officer in the Navy listed in order of seniority. If the caller was even one number, one place on the list, senior, the greeting was, "Yes, sir, (or ma'am); what can I do for you?" To a junior—even if only by one number—it was the more casual, "Hey Charlie (or Charlene), how's it going?"

To make my point: I had a staff assistant, Lt. Eric Berryman, a junior action officer with a PhD (along with a Purple Heart and two tours in Vietnam as an enlisted Army military policeman). You can bet that when Lieutenant Berryman called to speak with some high-ranking officer, civilian appointee, or congressional staffer, he didn't identify himself as Lieutenant but as Doctor Berryman in the office of the secretary of the navy. The ploy worked like a charm: He got to have the conversation and he got things done. I do believe that at one point my admin officer, Cdr. John Poindexter (who had a PhD of his own), got wind of the tactic and gave Lieutenant Berryman a proper dressing down. I do not believe that this had much if any effect on Lieutenant Berryman, and certainly not on my appreciation for heads-up, good old-style Navy initiative. Now a retired commander, Berryman continues to this day to work with me as a civilian personal staff associate. As I noted earlier, I have long had the habit, from my days as a Wall Street analyst, of creating and maintaining extensive files and memoranda; Berryman was instrumental in organizing the materials upon which I have drawn for this memoir.

Chapter 14

Secretary of the Navy:
Once and Forever—The Bicentennial

W e had not seen anything like it in one hundred years, and it was to be the only chance we would ever have to throw a two-hundredth birthday party for the nation. It began on the anniversary of Paul Revere's ride, April 18, 1975, ran through the high point of July 4, 1976, and continued to the end of that year. Under the general rubric of "if you're going to do something important, do it right," the Navy began serious planning for the bicentennial early in 1973, when Secretary John Warner established a bicentennial team in the office of one of the assistant secretaries. It was, and remained, a modest but significant effort, initially staffed by three people and coordinated by an officer in the office of the chief of information, Capt. (later, Rear Adm.) David M. Cooney. A thorough and methodical planner, Captain Cooney solicited ideas from throughout the Navy and put together a very comprehensive program, which was being implemented, I believe, before most other agencies of the government had even begun thinking about the bicentennial.

I learned of this effort when I reported on board as undersecretary, just about the time that plans were being converted into programs, and asked to have the project shifted to my office. It came with a team of two or three officers, headed by Lt. Cdr. William Eibert, who was the glue that held it all together right on through the end of celebration. When John Warner was tapped to head up the national bicentennial effort and I moved up to secretary of the navy, I picked up a program coordinator (Captain Harris, noted earlier).

The Navy Department had allotted some $4 million seed money for this effort, and the money was judiciously spread around the world. "Seed money" is the correct term, since many of the projects were expected to become self-supporting, and thereby return the investment to the U.S. Treasury.

Some of the projects were quite local: for example, a modest naval museum at the headquarters of the 12th Naval District in San Francisco, staffed by volunteers and with a grand mural painted by a well-known local artist. Some were global: We adopted the late 1775 "Don't Tread on Me" rattlesnake flag as the bicentennial "Navy Jack," to be flown when anchored or in port at the bow of every ship during the year of the celebration. We saw it as a colorful reminder to all, but especially to our own young Navy men and women, of our heritage as a fighting force. However, one timid politician thought that this aggressive motto might offend our overseas allies, and insisted that we clear this project with the State Department. There was no objection. (After 9/11, the flag was returned to active duty, at the suggestion of my former special assistant, to remind the world of the same.)

The bicentennial Navy Jack was one of the self-supporting programs: Each ship purchased the flags from central stores (as they would have done with the standard white stars on blue field version), which fully paid down the cost of development and production.

Another fully self-supporting program was the Navy bicentennial commemorative medal, struck in gold, silver, and bronze by the U.S. Mint and sold through government sales outlets. My office also served as executive agent for medals honoring the Army and the Marine Corps (the Air Force, not created until 1947, was out of the running). Each service decided for itself how it should be represented on its own medal. This seemed appropriate to me, but the chairman of the District of Columbia Commission of Fine Arts soon wrote an excited letter to the director of the Mint, Mary Brooks, in which he asserted that all the medals "were unanimously disapproved." Why? Some contained "items whose precise meaning was not clear and which did not seem to be particularly relevant." We—the three relevant services—liked our designs; *we* certainly understood the symbolism, and besides, the District of Columbia Fine Arts Commission did not have authority in this matter. In any event, by the time the chairman had raised his objection, the medals already had been struck.

Some projects didn't make it to the starting gate. There was a suggestion that the 1797-era USS *Constitution* be taken on tour all along the East Coast; visions of the proud old ship foundering in a gale put that idea to rest. A very politically well-connected man suggested that we paint the whole of the U.S. Fleet white, to emulate Teddy Roosevelt's 1907–1909 "Great White Fleet" world tour. He would have us also paint the words "Come Visit the USA" on the back end of each ship to help promote tourism. The man was well connected enough that we didn't just say, "No," but the idea crumpled under its own weight when we worked up the probable cost, just in paint.

The Navy took the lead in assembling a bicentennial military band, comprising members selected from the Army, Navy, Marine Corps, and Air Force bands and choral units, and organized a world concert tour. We also wanted to create a souvenir recording; millions of Americans heard these bands in concert every year, but because of long-standing opposition from the musicians' union, military band recordings could not be offered for commercial sale. They could be given away—say, to radio and television stations for celebrating patriotic events and late-night sign-off—but under the law governing military bands, the Defense Department could not recover even the cost of production.

We felt that an exception ought to be made for the once-and-forever bicentennial, with proceeds being applied against the costs of the record, and any surplus going to the Treasury. I certainly did not believe that this unique project would be in competition with any commercial endeavor; the musicians' union believed otherwise.

We asked Congress for permission, and the Armed Services Committee held a hearing. Rear Adm. Bill Thompson, the Navy's chief of information, made the case for the Defense Department: a one-time exception only, a purely commercial sale through a distributor to be selected on a competitive basis, all net proceeds to be turned back in to the bicentennial account. The members listened politely.

Sam Jack Kaufman, president of the American Federation of Musicians, offered his rebuttal: This would set a dangerous precedent; the livelihood of widows and orphans might be placed in jeopardy; military bands were not a good thing, anyway. If the military wanted music, it should hire union musicians. The members listened politely.

When Mr. Kaufman had finished—there were no questions—the chairman realized that he did not have a quorum, thus no vote could then be taken. "This hearing is in recess," he announced, "to meet at the call of the chairman." The witnesses and their respective advisers began to drift out of the hearing room. Mr. Kaufman's team was the first to leave; Admiral Thompson had been engaged in conversation by a committee staffer.

The moment the door had closed behind the union team, committee members slipped back into the room and the chairman rapped the gavel. "The chairman," he announced, "notes the presence of a quorum, and calls this hearing back into session. On the matter now under consideration, all in favor signify by saying 'aye.'" There was a chorus of "ayes." "Opposed, 'nay.'" There were no nays. The machinations of Congress can be, at times, indeed interesting.

Several projects had a much longer shelf life. One joint all-service effort, which we at first thought might be too difficult to bring off but which continues to this day, was to open up the Pentagon for public tours. It was not as if sensitive or classified information might be compromised—the Pentagon, after all, is an office building and offices have doors, and some offices have guards at the doors. On the other hand, there were some very good reasons for allowing public tours. The Pentagon had been demonized by the antiwar protestors, and we wanted to show that it was, in fact, just an office building, inhabited by normal, hardworking Americans. Ironically, until the early 1970s, the Pentagon had been an open public building. A few quarts of pig's blood dumped into files—including some in my office—and a few smoke bombs changed all of that. From that time to the present, access has been guarded by increasingly sophisticated scanning devices and entry controls.

There were two issues that had to be resolved. One: The Pentagon was a pretty boring place to visit. Through most of the building, there wasn't much to look at except formal portraits of mostly deceased officers and civilian leaders. Two: It would be impractical to let tourists wander around on their own, so we had to acquire and train tour guides. However, since "tour guide" is not a normal military specialty, how could we staff the tour? The question was answered, in a manner of speaking, by a directive from Secretary of Defense Donald Rumsfeld that said, in essence, "Just do it." So we gave each service a small quota, and created a team of outgoing, pleasant, interesting young men and women.

The "boring" issue was resolved by putting small exhibits (ship models and paintings) along the tour route—I contributed a nice collection of historic military recruiting posters—and the Navy's bicentennial office took the lead in drafting well-crafted scripts for the guides. The tours remain among the most popular tourist activities in the D.C. area, although the ground rules for joining a tour have shifted as the security threat has changed.

The goal of one project was to locate, and perhaps salvage some artifacts from, *Bon Homme Richard*, the most famous warship of the Revolution. This converted, aging, French merchantman, named for Benjamin Franklin's alter ego, "Poor Richard," and captained by John Paul Jones, was the first ship to carry the Stars and Stripes into battle, late on the evening of September 23, 1779, when engaged in a hard-fought duel with the brand-new British frigate, HMS *Serapis*.

Captain Jones is best remembered for the answer he gave the British captain, who called over in the gathering darkness to ask if the badly battered American had struck his colors. Jones' reply, as later reported by his first lieutenant and forever enshrined in the annals of naval lore: "I have not yet begun to fight!" He eventually won the battle, and transferred what remained of his crew to *Serapis*, as his own ship slowly sank into the North Sea, the tattered colors still flying.

The idea for the search came from Sydney Wignall, a professional British marine archaeologist, who offered to conduct the expedition—and to raise all necessary funds—if the Navy could give the effort status as a "Navy bicentennial project," which would allow the Navy to provide some support. Dr. Harold Edgerton—inventor of the strobe flash—heard of our plans, and came to my office to offer his help. Dr. Edgerton had recently perfected a "side-scan" sonar that, when towed along at depth, recorded an almost-photographic profile of objects resting on the bottom. Dr. Edgerton not only offered the loan of his unit, but pledged to send along a technician to make sure that it was working properly.

In the event, the sea bottom was littered with so many shipwrecks—and World War II aircraft—that the search was exactly like looking for a needle in a several-hundred-square-mile haystack. Wignall did identify a number of possible sites, but bad weather imposed too many delays; the search platform was needed on other assignments, and *this* search could not go on forever. However, about a year later, author Clive Cussler read about Wignall's effort and offered to provide funding for a loosely organized, purely civilian search from the proceeds of his 1976 best-selling novel, *Raise the Titanic.* Cussler did not find the ship, but he was encouraged enough to return for another try. However good the talent and solid the financing, they were not successful.

In spite of these failures, Cussler caught the maritime archeology bug. In the years since, he has financed more than sixty searches for historic shipwrecks. His interest ends with the discovery; he keeps no souvenirs, and turns the sites over to professional archaeologists and historians. Perhaps his most famous find is the Confederate submarine *Hunley,* which he located in 1995. *Hunley* was recovered from the bottom near Charleston, South Carolina, in August 2000.

As noted earlier, I did not, as a rule, inflict my own opinions in professional matters upon the uniformed professionals. There was, however, one notable exception: the naming of a ship. The director of naval history viewed the selection of ship names solely as the prerogative of his office, where lists of candidate names were always at the ready. In earlier times—not all that far back, really—the candidate names followed very traditional lines. Battleships recognized states of the union, cruisers were named after cities, aircraft carriers after historic ships or battles, destroyers after (deceased) heroes of the Navy and Marine Corps, submarines after creatures of the sea (real or mythical), and so forth. Today, things have changed a great deal, and "political" has long since pushed aside "traditional." Not only destroyers but also aircraft carriers, submarines, and cruisers are being named in honor of great men, living as well as dead. This was a change, I think, that can be attributed to Rickover, never one to let a political opportunity pass un-grasped.

However, the practice in 1975 was pretty much traditional, and my interest in naming a U.S. Navy ship after the French hero of the American Revolution—Comte de Grasse—did not sit well with someone (a senior flag officer) in the Office of Naval History. The U.S. Navy, that someone intimated, had never named a warship after a foreigner (let alone a titled royalist). That someone had a very inexact view of our own naval history. Four of the first five ships commissioned by the Continental Congress were named after "foreigners": *Alfred* (as in, "the Great," about as royalist as one might imagine), *Columbus*, *Cabot*, and *Andrew Doria* (an anglicized spelling of the first name of the sixteenth-century Italian admiral "Andrea" Doria).

I had two reasons for pursuing this matter. First and foremost, we were celebrating an independence that would not have been possible but for the assistance of the French navy. Second, relations with the French always seemed a bit strained, and nothing, certainly, would be lost by thus honoring Comte de Grasse with a Spruance-class destroyer, DD 974.

The wife of French president Valery Giscard d'Estang graciously accepted my invitation to be the sponsor of the ship, exclaiming, "I am very pleased to be the mother of this ship!" Her primary duty, at an event that would take place at the Ingalls Shipyard in Pascagoula, Mississippi in March 1976, would be to carry out the time-honored routine: Smash a bottle of champagne across the bow and proclaim, "I christen thee *Comte de Gras!*" My office assisted in arranging her travel and assigned one of our public affairs officers, Lt. Cdr. Jim Lois, to act as protocol liaison.

All was well until the party landed at the New Orleans airport, where they were to transfer to a motorcade for the two-and-a-half-hour drive to Pascagoula; the party landed, but the luggage couldn't be found; it seemed to have missed a too-tight connection in Houston. The fashion-conscious first lady of France was disconsolate, exclaiming, "My special dress! My makeup! My shoes!" Lois told her to go ahead in the waiting motorcade, while he solved the problem. He traced her luggage—it was coming in on the next flight from Houston—and then convinced a Coast Guard helicopter unit in New Orleans to postpone the transport of the body of a drowned fisherman—already in progress—and lend a diversionary hand, so to speak. The helicopter with the luggage landed at the shipyard just as the motorcade was passing through the front gate. The journey of the drowned fisherman from lakeshore to mortuary was delayed but a few minutes.

The best-known Navy bicentennial event—indeed, the best known event of the bicentennial, period—was the grand parade of ships in New York Harbor on July 4th. The official name was "Operation Sail and the International Naval Review," but most people, then and now, called it "OPSAIL" or the "tall ships thing." It included most of the larger sailing ships in the world, and representation from some forty of the world's navies, including the Soviets. Most of the navies sent at least one ship; those that did not have seagoing vessels—for example, landlocked Bolivia, which operated a patrol force on Lake Titicaca—sent delegations of senior officers.

The Review was a magnificent affair, hosted by both President Ford and Vice President Rockefeller (the former New York governor, who was not about to stay "home" in Washington), attracting a live audience of some three million and the world's largest television audience, two hundred million, to that date. We were told by many—not always as a compliment—that the Navy "stole" the Fourth of July from the other armed services.

And it almost didn't happen.

Originally, there were to be two separate events in different cities, on the same day. The organizers of the civilian-sponsored OPSAIL hoped to be in New York, the International Naval Review was planned for Norfolk, Virginia. Our Navy bicentennial office was working with Frank Braynard, the originator of OPSAIL, to arrange appropriate logistic support; many of the sailing ships were official navy training vessels and entitled to military courtesies and assistance. (One of them demanded more than mere "assistance," or it wouldn't participate—the Romanian *Mircea* wanted fuel, food, and money for miscellaneous expenses. I mulled this over with Holloway, and we agreed to more or less adopt *Mircea* for the duration.)

The suggestion for an International Naval Review, patterned after similar events in 1893, 1907, and 1957, had been submitted perhaps three years earlier, in the preliminary round of bicentennial planning. The suggestion had survived the initial winnowing process and was "on the books" as an official Navy project, along with a planning budget of $40,000. The actual costs—for fuel, docking fees, and so forth—would come out of normally budgeted operations and training funds. Well, "on the books" certainly is not the same thing as "under way." The responsible office at the Pentagon had taken no action, none, and had not even worked up a list of available ships. No naval command in the field seemed to be interested. As a result, with just about a year to go, our bicentennial office cancelled the nonexistent International Naval Review and released the allocated funds to the above-mentioned museum in San Francisco.

As these things sometimes happen, a new vice chief of naval operations, Adm. Worth Bagley, had just reported for duty. He called my special assistant for the bicentennial—Captain Harris was an old acquaintance of the admiral's—and said, "I understand you're coordinating the bicentennial projects for the secretary; how about dropping by and giving me a rundown?"

When the briefing was finished, the admiral seemed properly impressed but felt something was missing. "Gee," he said, "wouldn't you think that it would be a great idea to invite other navies to come and help us celebrate our big birthday?"

"Well," said Harris, "there was just such a proposal, for an International Naval Review, but no one seemed to care. The paperwork had been on the desk of a commander on the CNO staff, without action, for two years. So I cancelled it, for lack of sufficient high-level interest, and gave the planning budget to another project."

"Aw," said the admiral. "Gee, I'd like to know more about that naval review." That conversation took place around 3 PM on a Friday. At 9 AM on Monday, Captain Harris called the admiral and reported, with pleasure, "I think we have been able to locate sufficient high-level interest to ensure support, and we have put the review back in the plan." Harris did not need to tell Admiral Bagley that he had found that interest in the office files, in the form of a memo sent in with the original search for ideas, proposing the Norfolk International Naval Review—signed by then–rear adm. Worth Bagley.

Putting the Review back in the mix was one thing, but one reason the project had so long been ignored was the proposed location. Norfolk and environs are wonderful—packed with history, host to a great naval base and shipyard area—but are not a center of international media activity, are not easily adapted to grand public spectacle, and, for reasons of security, were not a port where any Soviet or client-state warship would have been welcome. Therefore, Harris redeemed his temporary lapse of judgment not only by resurrecting the Review, but by suggesting to me that the Review officially be combined with OPSAIL and the venue shifted to New York. This was not a decision that I could make on my own; however, it was not difficult to get approvals from OPSAIL, New York City, the states of New York and New Jersey, the State Department, and the White House.

We proposed to invite every navy that was listed in the authoritative *Jane's Fighting Ships*—it was not up to my office to decide what was, or was not, a "navy" (as in the case, noted above, of Bolivia), and we did not want political distinctions to mar the time-honored tradition of the brotherhood of the sea. We offered to provide an aircraft carrier as the official reviewing platform. Our plans were approved, but (ah, politics!) with one caveat: We were instructed by the (Republican) White House, "You can use any carrier except the USS *John F. Kennedy*."

In truth, we hoped to use *America* or *Independence* or even *Saratoga*—ships with some logical Revolutionary connection—but each was irretrievably scheduled for overseas deployment or shipyard overhaul. In the event, USS *Forrestal* was selected.

I wish I could report that everything was perfect, but we could have used two—or three—carriers and many more small boats to ferry people back and forth between shore and ship. If memory serves, there were some three thousand invited guests on board *Forrestal*. It took some of them longer to get back ashore than it would later take them to go from New York back to Washington. As for me—since Ford and Rockefeller had departed the area—I enjoyed a stint as surrogate guest of honor for a ticker-tape parade up Broadway, complete with falling confetti and cheering crowds.

I should report three other potentially fatal issues that arose during the final stages of our planning. One stands as a good illustration of how rigid and inflexible some military folk can be: The senior naval officer in New York, responsible for coordinating all local arrangements, became apoplectic whenever the *New York Times* neglected to include "International Naval Review" whenever they mentioned OPSAIL. The admiral's public affairs officer (PAO) was caught in the middle, trying to curry favor with the *Times*, for whatever good publicity might be generated, and subject to the admiral's wrath when the coverage didn't measure up to the admiral's standards. I did not want to become directly involved in this issue—again, I tried to avoid inserting myself personally into the operational chain of command. But I did ask a member of my staff to try to resolve the problem. He went to New York, met with the admiral, and explained that "Secretary Middendorf doesn't care what they call it, as long as they write about it." The problem was not resolved: The admiral was a good man, but could not let go of his fixation. So, the bicentennial team thenceforth dealt directly with the *New York Times*. The PAO, Cdr. Jay Coupe, who clearly demonstrated an ability to work under pressure, went on to promotion and a prestigious and well-deserved assignment as PAO for the chairman of the Joint Chiefs of Staff (JCS).

Another issue, which had the potential to close down our event before it got started, centered on some recently enacted maritime environmental protection laws. Vessels operating on the inland waterways of the United States—which certainly included New York Harbor—were required to contain sewage in onboard holding tanks, which could later be emptied at specified pump-out stations, or dumped overboard when far out at sea. The rules seem primarily to have been directed at small boat owners; the status of large ships—especially warships, none of which had been designed with sewage control systems in mind—was ambiguous. The status of many OPSAIL participants fell somewhere in between pleasure craft and warships.

At one of the New York planning sessions, someone raised the question: "What happens if a public-minded citizen tries to get an injunction stopping the whole thing on environmental grounds?" There was a long silence; our event was by this point a runaway train, with ships en route from as far away as Japan. Finally, a senior New York law enforcement official offered his version of "bold corrective action": "We'll have him arrested and held until after 4 July, then let him go and pay whatever damages he demands." That certainly would have been bold, although not necessarily corrective and certainly not legal. The true solution was more easily found. Someone who lived on Staten Island pointed out that at that very moment the Staten Island ferries were dumping raw sewage into the harbor with every crossing. An injunction aimed at the visiting ships would have to apply to the ferries—end of discussion.

Finally, we barely escaped one huge embarrassment. The Boy Scouts of America, Girl Scouts of America, and the Navy League Sea Cadet organization had an agreement with OPSAIL that selected groups of youngsters, representing every state in the union, could be on some of the big sailing ships for the last leg of the inbound journey, getting on board in Newport, Rhode Island, and riding to the parade in New York Harbor. We thought the arrangements for actual embarkation had been made by OPSAIL, but a few days before the big event we got a call from a reporter in, I think, Nebraska: "We hear that our kids can't get aboard the sail ships, as promised. Why is the U.S. Navy disappointing our kids?"

As it turned out, the managers of OPSAIL had told the youth organizations that the youngsters would be welcome, but had not shared this concept with the operators of the ships—the Germans, Romanians, whoever. By the time I learned of the problem, groups of boys and girls were assembling and happily chattering at Newport, the first of the ships had just arrived, and the rest were soon to follow. It was a bit late to engage the diplomatic machinery of Washington. Time for some more bold corrective action.

I said something obvious, like, "The U.S. Navy doesn't disappoint Boy Scouts," and sent the aforementioned action officer, Lieutenant Berryman, rushing off to Newport, there to board each incoming tall ship with a pleading.

Germany's *Gorch Foch*, Poland's *Dar Pomorza*, Norway's *Christian Radich*, the Italian *Amerigo Vespucci*, Romania's *Meicea*, the Soviets' *Tovarich* and *Kruzenstern*—all the captains were willing; of course the children could ride (although at first there was some hesitation about taking girls). In fact, the only real problem at this point was with the Soviets: they wanted to take *all* of the youngsters and didn't understand why they had to share the glory.

I might note that, a short time later, the Soviets were so irritated by the Israeli raid to free hostages at the Entebbe airport (July 3–4) that they pulled out and went home. Of course, by the time the news reached New

York, the Review had ended and the only damage, if you will, was to the Soviet sailors who missed some great liberty in New York. Perhaps a few also missed an opportunity to defect, an action that I understand was enjoyed in some numbers by sailors from the obviously impoverished Romanian ship. I understand also that some crewmen from *Amerigo Vespucci* (actual number unknown) embarked on matrimonial seas with Italian-American girls from Brooklyn. The "brotherhood of the seas" takes many forms.

For the most recent version of this event—OPSAIL 2000/International Naval Review 2000, celebrating the turn of the century—President Bill Clinton was the host and *John F. Kennedy* finally had its day as the reviewing platform. I also note that the celebration only attracted naval ships from fourteen nations.

Here's one more or less non-bicentennial event, but nonetheless linked by timing. The Smithsonian National Air and Space Museum, on the Mall in D.C., is the most-visited museum in the world; it is strange to note, though, that the original plans did not include a Navy exhibit hall. This was remedied when a committee, headed by Vice Adm. William Martin (Ret.) and largely comprising other retired senior naval aviators, persuaded the Smithsonian management to add one. This took the form of an aircraft carrier hangar deck displaying World War II–era aircraft, and a replica navigation bridge where the visitors would be able to listen to an audio replay of carrier operations.

The Smithsonian had a bit of luck with the equipment for that bridge: A Hollywood movie producer was just then preparing to film the movie *Midway*. He asked my office if he could borrow the bridge equipment from an out-of-service vintage carrier that was being kept in mothballs—as with my LCS squadron, closed up, sealed, against possible but increasingly unlikely future service—to use on a movie set. I agreed to let him do so, provided that, when finished, he would arrange to have it all shipped, at his own expense, for installation at the Smithsonian. The Sea-Air Operations Gallery opened to the public in July 1976, and along the way I enjoyed an invitation to socialize on the movie set, during a previously scheduled visit to the West Coast with naval reserve officers Capt. Jackie Cooper and Capt. Glenn Ford.

Another interesting but more significant non-bicentennial project grew out of the great Review. Felix de Weldon, famed for his magnificent sculpture at the Marine Corps' Iwo Jima Memorial, fell into conversation with Admiral Holloway and offered that he would be pleased to create a similar monument and ceremonial venue for the Navy.

Holloway was intrigued and passed the offer along to my office. I thought it was an interesting idea—the Navy could well benefit from a centrally located plaza large enough for band concerts, promotion and retirement ceremonies, and so forth—but I saw an immediate problem. We could not accept de Weldon's offer, which could be valued in the high six figures; I knew that selection of an artist would have to come through an open competition, and that could best be handled by a congressionally chartered, nongovernment, nonprofit organization. After some discussion, Holloway and former CNOs Arleigh Burke and Tom Moorer decided to call it the Navy Memorial Foundation. As Admiral Burke put it, "We have talked long enough about a Navy Memorial and it's time we did something about it."

I was pleased to serve as the founding chairman of the Navy Memorial Foundation. Rear Adm. Bill Thompson, by then retired, became the first president and is the man who brought it all to a successful conclusion through fifteen years of congressional hearings, the often-conflicting interests of local arts and monuments commissions, against the carping from interested citizens ("Why does Washington need another monument, anyway?"), and always up to his neck in the vital and endless fundraising effort.

There were many candidate sites for the Memorial, but most were out on the fringes of the central area and off the tourist's path. Thompson held off on site selection until he found the perfect spot, on land about to be reclaimed from the demolition of some worn-out buildings at Pennsylvania Avenue and 8th Street NW, just across from the National Archives. There was a problem, however, with one of the early schemes for the site; a committee formed by several interested agencies proposed a structure that was more or less a clone of the French Arc d'Triomphe. The U.S. Commission on Fine Arts sent us back to the drawing board, and it was the best thing that could have happened to the Navy Memorial.

As finally developed, the Memorial is on two levels. Below ground there is a visitor center with a movie theater and lecture hall, meeting and function rooms, gift shop, offices, and the computerized "Navy Log," a modest fundraising feature whereby anyone can purchase some space to note the service history or memories of anyone who has ever served in the U.S. Navy.

Above ground is a wide plaza, one hundred feet in diameter, with ceremonial fountains, twin flagpoles festooned with signal flags, and a series of bronze plaques celebrating various aspects of naval history.

Since we planned to use the Memorial for occasions of ceremony and to host concerts by military bands, I had hoped to include a covered bandshell. This was not a matter of acoustics, but protection: an open plaza of marble, concrete, and granite could, on a sunny summer day, cause the instruments to so overheat that they could not be played or might be damaged.

When I presented my idea before the Pennsylvania Avenue Development Corporation and my good friend, their chairman, J. Carter Brown, it was denied. I think they thought it would become a magnet for homeless vagrants. Perhaps, but I know for a fact that some concerts have been cut short because of the heat

The centerpiece of the Memorial, however, is indeed a statue. The contract went to Connecticut sculptor Stanley Bleifield in formal competition with thirty-six others. It is not a massive, heroic icon, but a quiet, only slightly above life-size bronze of the "Lone Sailor," hands tucked in his peacoat to ward off the chill and sea bag at his feet, as he looks out across an inlaid granite map of the world.

On October 26, 1976, just before the presidential elections, William Loeb, the idiosyncratic publisher of the Manchester *Union-Leader*, offered a compliment: "Middendorf," he wrote, has been the "most outstanding Secnav since Teddy Roosevelt." Setting aside the questionable merit of the statement, he was slightly off on the facts: TR had been assistant secretary. However, if Loeb had hoped that this praise for a hardworking member of the Ford administration would have some influence on the election, he was, well, greatly wrong. We lost.

I was flattered when president-elect Jimmy Carter asked me to stay on as secretary of the navy, but I had to tell him, in all candor, that it was the best job in government and therefore an insecure post for a Republican in a Democratic administration. I might be in the job for six months, I predicted, maybe a year at most, before the job was targeted by some political supporter whose interest the president could not easily ignore. After almost eight years in government service, I prepared to go back into the world of high finance.

However, I was proud of our record. When I took office, the three armed services had roughly equivalent budgets; by the time I left, the Army budget had remained relatively flat, the Air Force budget had risen slightly, and the Navy budget had soared by 60 percent. Most of that growth was in hardware—notably, the Trident, Aegis, and F/A-18 programs, which are still among our frontline programs.

As I noted above, we had obtained approval for a building program that would take us back to a six-hundred-ship Navy, sized to meet the threat. There was a plan, so many ships over so many years, most replacing older ships as they were scheduled for retirement. Sadly, Carter's new secretary of defense—Harold Brown—cut our shipbuilding program sharply. Brown was more of a strategic than a tactical type, focused on deterrence, not attack, capabilities; bargaining chips in arms limitation talks. He didn't seem much interested in ships—except for the *Ohio*-class Trident missile submarines. The Navy never recovered and I'm sure there are reasons (and villains) galore. Regardless, the surface warship level in 2005 was 111, the lowest since 1921, and the overall force level in 2007 was 279 ships, the lowest since the nineteenth century. For 2009, that number was 283; some folks may call that "progress."

On January, 7, 1977, winding down, clearing out my office to make way for Jimmy Carter's man, the excellent Graham Claytor, a call came in on the hot line: Rear Admiral Rickover.

"Hi, Rick. What's up?"

"I'm calling to wish you a happy New Year. Do you want the one I give my friends or to the bastards? Are you my friend?"

"I always thought I was."

"OK. Well, Mr. Secretary, I hope to hell you get what you deserve in 1977."

I don't know if it was meant as a blessing, or a curse. Little did I know, it would be the latter. The next four years were among the most difficult in my life.

Chapter 15

The Business of Banking

I was out of a job, and George Olmsted had a business proposition; would I meet him for lunch at the Metropolitan Club?

I had known Olmsted for many years, since my days monitoring the insurance and financial industries. A 1922 graduate of West Point, he left the Army after two years obligated service and, with his father, started Olmsted & Olmsted Fire and Casualty in Omaha. He returned to active service in World War II, retired as a major general and bought International Bank in 1954—a diversified financial enterprise with interests in insurance, manufacturing, leasing, financial services, and investments. However, despite the name, International Bank was not registered with the Federal Reserve Board as a bank, largely because the company did not think of itself as a bank. However, International bank did have a 22.2 percent controlling interest in a company that operated as a Bank, Financial General Bankshares (FG). The Fed had now determined that International Bank was in violation of the law; the cure was to sell the controlling interest in FG, and George Olmsted was looking for a buyer.

What he had to sell was a rare bird, indeed; a company that operated fifteen banks (with some 141 branches) spread among Virginia, Maryland, the District of Columbia, and New York, with total assets of $2 billion. The value of this prize had little to do with size. Under the antimonopoly interstate banking prohibitions enacted in 1927 (and in place until 1994), even the largest banks, such as Chase, Bank of America, and Riggs were limited to domestic operations in their home states of New York, California, and the District of Columbia, respectively (international operations were not so constrained). At that time, I believe that only three or four banking companies had multistate operations, FG among them, and they had been grandfathered, allowed to continue. Given the states in which it was licensed and the rising prominence of the national capital area as a center for business as well as government, FG—a thoroughly respectable company, dating back to 1925 and now headed by retired Army general (and former chief of staff) Harold K. Johnson—was more than a collection of banks; it was an untapped gold mine.

It was not hard to assemble a small group of investors, some of whom I knew, some not, willing to put up about $15 million. Armand Hammer heard about the deal; with typical Hammer insensitivity, he called me at 3 AM one morning and said, "Put me in for a share." I asked, did he know anything about this undertaking? He said, "If you like it, I want to be in with you."

Our offer to purchase the 1,204,231 shares of FG then owned by International Bank, at $12.50 a share, was accepted at the end of March, and within a month we began the transition from the old management to the new. I arranged to hold voting proxies from a number of major shareholders, giving our group effective control and demonstrating to the Fed that International Bank was no longer in charge.

The annual meeting was set for June, at which an expanded board of directors was elected to include representation from the new investor group, and without Olmsted and Johnson. At the following board meeting I was elected president, CEO, and chairman—and, to my surprise, one of the new shareholders handed me a fifty-three-page memorandum outlining *his* plans for the business. Some of his suggestions merited consideration, but the most surprising element was that he presented me with a bill for having drafted the memo. The next surprise: I hadn't been in the job more than a week when another investor let me know he expected to do business with the bank, selling us the services of his company. It began to look as if some of the investors thought they had bought into a private piggy bank. I said "no" to that foolishness, which did not sit well with that investor and a few of his cronies. Ten days after they had elected me chairman, they were secretly meeting to plot my downfall! It would be some time before I fully was aware of the behind-the-scenes maneuvering—which, before the year had ended, became absolutely Byzantine. Of this, more in a moment.

For a business run by military professionals, men whose careers revolved around such concepts as concentration of forces and force multipliers, the company had a strange hands-off philosophy. Olmsted believed that the most valuable asset was the image of each bank as a local, community-oriented institution, a position that might be damaged by too much centralization. Accordingly, they granted complete autonomy to each of the fifteen banks. In fact, when Olmsted announced the sale to the employees, he added, "We have insisted all along upon purchasers who would respect the long-standing Financial General policy under which its fifteen banks operate as autonomous units of a mutually profitable partnership."

In a staff memo, Johnson reaffirmed that philosophy: "Financial General, as it exists today, represents the philosophy of General George Olmsted. . . . Financial General has yet to determine the complete range of functions that are appropriate for a bank holding company that will continue to operate under a policy of autonomous operation for its individual banks. . . . Making things easier for the holding company is not our objective."

We respected their policies, to a point, but if Olmsted "insisted" that they be continued, it was not part of the purchase agreement. Johnson's somewhat confusing memo reflected a bit—a lot, actually—of management uncertainty. We had a pretty clear idea of what "management" ought to be: focused and successful.

In the meantime, and in happy ignorance of the cabal just then getting under way, my staff and I were busy getting organized. We centralized the purchase of supplies, made plans for the merger of three large Northern Virginia banks, the adoption of a common name—First American—and a common advertising budget for all our banks. In deference to legacy managers who had long enjoyed the freedom to run their banks as they saw fit, most changes were phased in carefully, and slowly.

We began promoting the national capital area as a business center—and what an easy thing that proved to be. The average household income in Washington was $21,000, 33 percent above national average; 75 percent of area residents had a high school or higher education. In addition to government-related professions such as law and accounting, there were more scientists, engineers, managers, and technical workers per thousand than in any other area of the country. Washington and surrounding communities hosted the headquarters of about 27 percent of all the trade and professional associations in the country. In 1978 alone, the area was to add 27,000 new jobs, only 5 percent of which were in the federal government.

In addition, not far to the north, is my often-overlooked hometown, Baltimore. It was then the nation's eighth largest city; as a percentage of the population, there were more home owners in Baltimore than in any other major U.S. city. The port of Baltimore ranked as the fourth largest in the United States in total value of shipments.

I carried the message far and wide. I sent a letter to 131 New York City–based CEOs, suggesting the merits of headquarters relocation to the D.C. area. Most responses were, "We have no plans at this time," or "We just signed a ten-year lease," but there were several positive inquiries. I made five trips to New York, for example, to successfully persuade Mobil to relocate corporate headquarters to the Washington suburb of Fairfax County, Virginia.

In an August 13, 1977 profile, the *Washington Post* noted, "An interview with Middendorf is like attending a one-man pep rally for Washington.

He believes, with an earnestness that's infectious, that the metropolitan area is in for a commercial boom and that his bank is bound to rise with the tide."

It did, indeed: We would enjoy a rise in earnings over seventeen successive quarters, possibly the best bank history on record (to that point). However, about the time the *Post* was extolling my virtues, the Securities and Exchange Commission heard rumors of a division between pro- and anti-Middendorf factions. The SEC sent a memo of inquiry, and wondered whether a proxy fight was anticipated. By then, the dissident group was not only trying to ease me out of control, they were trying to sell the bank without my knowledge and without permission of the rest of the stockholders. I was to learn some of the details along the way; others I did not learn until some years later, when they were revealed in a series of congressional hearings, in a 1991 report of the Federal Reserve Board, and in transcripts and press accounts of a series of criminal and civil proceedings—details of what was to become the greatest banking fraud in world history, the collapse of the Bank of Credit and Commerce International (BCCI).

In October 1977, Bert Lance—close personal friend of President Jimmy Carter—was looking for an opportunity, and he hooked up with Pakistani banker Aga Hassan Abedi, who also was looking for "an opportunity." Five years earlier, backed by a loan from the ruler of Abu Dhabi, Abedi had created BCCI with headquarters in London but with global ambition. He was off to a fast start, attracting deposits from rich Arabs who distrusted Western banks (which they believed were using Arab money to finance Israeli development), and Abedi wanted to establish a presence in the financial center of America, New York City. Abedi made a clumsy attempt to buy two banks in New York—one of which, coincidentally, was owned by FG—by sending in sham purchasers, but they had been rebuffed by the state regulators. (One of the applicants put forward for a multimillion-dollar bank was a young man with an annual income of only $34,000.)

Nonetheless, by the time Bert Lance entered the picture, BCCI had become the fastest growing bank in the world, with $2 billion in assets and 140 branches. It was, in fact, just about the same size as FG. "I am building a bank headquartered in London," Abedi told Lance, "that has a deep and abiding interest in the problems of health, hunger, economic development." Would Mr. Lance be interested in helping BCCI expand into the United States? Lance asked his attorney, Clark Clifford (the former secretary of defense under LBJ), to run a check on Abedi. When Clifford reported that Abedi and his associates were men "of integrity and character," Lance signed on as BCCI's agent. For his trouble, BCCI "advanced" Lance some

$3.6 million to pay off a loan and hired him, with a reported annual salary of $100,000.

And FG became the target, for the same reasons that I had become interested in the company: a multistate franchise with headquarters at the seat of government and operations at the center of world finance.

Lance sat down with the dissident group to develop a strategy, and they began contacting major shareholders with offers to buy stock on behalf of a "Washington law firm who was representing an undisclosed principal." Most of these shareholders would not sell to an anonymous buyer. Therefore, BCCI began buying shares on the open market.

To stay under the radar and not impact stock price, purchases were limited to ten thousand shares a day, and to avoid tripping the "5 percent" rule (which required an SEC filing if any individual holding in a company reached 5 percent of the outstanding stock), the shares were assigned to four theoretical purchasers. I say "theoretical," because as I later was to learn, the funds came from BCCI (as "loans" with no repayment obligation), BCCI held voting rights to the stock, and BCCI indemnified the "purchasers" against any possible losses. Unknown to us, they soon controlled 1,076,590 shares, about 20 percent of FG.

The increased activity in a normally sleepy stock prompted the American Stock Exchange to make inquiry, and we issued a press release (January 7, 1978): "Financial General Bankshares, Inc., today stated that it knew of no reason for the recent market activity in its Common Stock."[1]

We knew of no reason, but it was clear that something was up. We did learn that purchases were being engineered on behalf of an "undisclosed principal," but we assumed that to be one of the other stockholders. We knew, for example, that George Olmsted had sold his shares and that real estate magnate Frank Saul had not. We knew who had made the offers to those two men—one of the investors. I sent Jack Beddow, FG secretary and one of the finest men I have ever worked with, to see if he could find out what was going on. The investor—who I thought was one of my team—refused to answer Beddow's questions and summarily ordered him to leave the office.

Frank Saul was one of FG's largest stockholders and a very solid citizen, and at my suggestion he assumed my duties as chairman (leaving me as president and CEO), adding strength to our executive team. Then, the *Washington Post* (December 18, 1977) reported that we may have been targeted by some sort of "Arab raid," apparently being led by Lance, who was in negotiations with some "Middle Eastern financial interests" to establish "a holding company to direct their capital into banks and other U.S. investments."

Now that the game was afoot, Saul and I arranged to have lunch with Lance, to see where things stood. Lance was in fine form. He said something like, "Glad you came over, boys. I've got some good news and some bad news for you. Shall I give you the bad news first? The bad news is that you're outta there! We've bought 20 percent of the stock and we're in control; but the good news is, we're going to give you a big farewell dinner!" He made it abundantly clear that BCCI planned to buy more shares, and he told Saul that we had three choices: We could sell them our stock, join them, or be taken over by them. It didn't seem to make much difference to Lance; he told us he fully expected to become either chairman or president of FG.

I don't think I've ever heard of a theoretically responsible adult who was so blatantly unguarded in his comments. Lance had, in essence, admitted to material participation in a major securities fraud. Obviously, we lost no time in reporting the substance of this conversation to the SEC and the Federal Reserve. Then, Bert Lance called Saul and tried to change his story—the purchaser is not BCCI, he now claimed, but a group of "individual investors," a fiction that all parties would maintain to the bitter end.

On February 17, 1978, we filed suit against "Bert Lance, Bank of Credit & Commerce International, Agha Hasan Abedi," and members of the dissident group (who now were known to us as *Lance, et al.*) for "unlawful conspiracy secretly to acquire control. . . ."[2]

In March, two top BCCI officials admitted to the *Washington Post* (March 22, 1978) that the company indeed had a relationship with Lance, but they averred that he was merely "an informal adviser who pointed out investment opportunities in the U.S.," and they falsely affirmed that he was "not employed by the bank . . . was paid nothing by the bank . . . and had received absolutely no loans from BCCI or loans arranged by BCCI."

The federal court granted a preliminary injunction in *Lance, et al.*, agreeing that BCCI had been deeply involved in the takeover attempt. We thought that we had won the day, but, no. The federal court said, in essence, that BCCI's illegal activities did not prevent it from continuing the takeover attempt, only from doing so in secret.

In the meantime, we merged Alexandria National Bank, Arlington Trust Co., and the Clarendon Bank and Trust into First American Bank of Virginia, and the American Bank of Maryland and Chesapeake National Bank became First American Bank of Maryland, and we hired advertising agencies to promote the changes. We were among the first banks in the nation to install automatic teller machines (ATMs); we put them everywhere, dubbed them "the Money Exchange." We were very tough with our lending—no special favors to cronies. We did not try to compete for any and every loan opportunity that came along. We did not finance unproductive operations such as speculators, unproven real estate developments, or soaring consumer expenditures. In other words, we did not "buy" growth but continued to grow steadily based on prudent application of our own resources. And we were making money: Net income for the fourth quarter of 1977—fully under the new management—rose 37.8 percent over the fourth quarter of 1976. The first quarter of 1978 was the best in FG's fifty-two-year history, and a 26 percent increase over 1977. I thought the investors would be happy with such good performance; the other shareholders certainly were.

I thought that this was what it was all about.

BCCI charged ahead, always maintaining that the takeover effort was by a group of individual, unconnected investors who shared an adviser—BCCI. One of those investors stepped forward as the front man for the group: Sheikh Kamal Adham, former head of the Saudi equivalent of the CIA. Next—with the assistance of Clifford, who was now representing BCCI—they filed a suit against me and certain other directors (*Middendorf, et al.*), alleging that we had breached our fiduciary duties and wasted corporate assets by pursuing *Lance, et al.* There was a reasonably swift resolution to this nuisance, but Bert Lance, who had been kind enough to alert us to the secret plan, and who had expected to be appointed chairman or president of FG, seems to have reached, in his employer's eyes, the level of his incompetence and was eased out of the picture.

BCCI went full-frontal and announced a tender offer of $22.50 per share, which did not generate much excitement. Two months later, the offer was raised to $25—nothing happened. So BCCI took a new approach: to acquire enough proxies from existing shareholders to win a vote. They asked for the names and addresses of all FG stockholders. We declined to provide it. BCCI petitioned a court for relief, and the court granted the request. We gave them the list.

Sheikh Adham—the investor frontman—told the SEC he was willing to spend as much as $1 million to bring the matter to a vote for the 1980 annual meeting. Well, the tender offer was defeated, albeit narrowly, but, in truth, there was no end in sight. Hammer made an offer to Clifford: "Why don't we declare an armistice? This war goes on interminably, and I'll come along and we'll sit down and talk this matter out." After a one-and-a-half-day meeting in Clifford's office, the ante was raised: a cash tender offer for all of the outstanding common stock of the company at a price, net to the sellers, of $31.

It was clear that BCCI would never give up, walk away, and this was, after all, a good price for the stockholders (most of whom had paid $12.50 per share, or less), so the board voted to accept the offer. I added a clause that, in the event of any delay, the offering price would be adjusted to account for any increase in the book value at the time of actual sale. In the event, this added about $5 to the final per-share price. All in all, not a bad deal: My original investors got a 300 percent return in a little more than three years, and this in a time when the stock market was in disarray.

With the deal set and government approvals almost in hand, BCCI thought it was home free. Not quite. Virginia's chief bank regulator, Sidney A. Bailey, raised the most cogent question of the day: Why would anyone launch such a protracted, expensive campaign to buy the company at a price well above its probable value? He answered his own question: because of the company's unique position in the market, with operations in both the government and financial hubs of the nation. And, he wondered, what apparatus did our government have in place to ensure that foreign owners would abide by U.S. law, or to prevent them from stripping the bank of all assets?

This prompted a hearing of the Fed, on April 23, 1981, during which Clifford suggested it was the Fed's patriotic duty to assist the bank in attracting petrodollars, which were then leaving the country at a rate of ninety billion a year, back in the form of interest-earning deposits from the Middle East. BCCI, Clifford maintained, was not directly involved as purchaser but was merely an "investment adviser" to Adham and the others—similar to the role of, say, Merrill Lynch, independently looking at investment opportunities for its clients.

On the last day of June 1981, I resigned as president and CEO of First American "to accept a position as the United States Permanent Representative to the Organization of American States."[3] During the 1980 election campaign, I had provided Republican candidate Ronald Reagan with briefing papers and other assistance; after his successful election, I helped with some transition matters (more fully described in the next chapter) and had now been offered an interesting and challenging assignment.

I was satisfied that I had met any commitments to my investor group—indeed, to all the shareholders—by helping move First American from relative obscurity to the first rank of banking. At the same time, I was worn out from four years of fighting against what I knew in my heart but could not prove was the rape of my company. Frank Saul took on the responsibilities of CEO; Beddow became chief administrative officer.

In August the Fed approved the takeover, as did the office of the comptroller of the currency, noting, "It has now been represented to us that BCCI will have no involvement with the management and other affairs, nor will BCCI be involved in the financing arrangements." Sure—BCCI installed its own management team. Frank Saul was replaced as chairman by Clark Clifford, and Clifford's law partner, Robert Altman, became president.

Within a few years, First American was in big trouble. Clifford made desperate efforts to sell the bank; all fell through. There was a bailout of sorts: Federal regulators arranged for $200 million in new financing to forestall the risk of a bank failure.

In truth, the whole cloth of BCCI deception unraveled. On June 22, 1991, the UK branch of Price Waterhouse presented the Bank of England, the regulating authority in that country, with evidence of fictitious profits and concealed losses, fictitious transactions and charges, fictitious loans, misappropriation of deposits, shoddy lending, bad investments, off-book transactions, and falsified audits (juggled between two auditing firms that were not allowed to compare notes). Two weeks later, authorities moved in to close BCCI headquarters in London and branches in seventy-two countries around the world. At one end of the scale, at least a million small depositors lost everything; at the other end, BCCI officials were suspected of embezzling $2 billion from one depositor alone. Early estimates pointed, overall, to at least a twenty-billion-dollar fraud, and I don't believe that has been refuted.

Clifford and Altman resigned from First American. BCCI dropped the "adviser" pretense, pled guilty to illegally purchasing First American and three other U.S. banks, and forfeited $550 million in U.S. assets. Abedi, living in Pakistan, was under criminal indictment in several countries, but Pakistan denied extradition. Frontman Sheikh Adham pled guilty to criminal charges in New York and paid a fine of $105 million. I doubt that he was much bothered.

BCCI's day had ended, but litigation crept along. In 1998, Clifford and Altman agreed to pay $5 million to settle civil charges without admitting or denying wrongdoing. As the *Washington Post* explained (February 4, 1998), "The charges settled today involved the Fed's contention that Clifford and Altman lied when they told the regulators that BCCI would have no role in running First American."

A few years ago, when I was on the Hill giving testimony on another matter, one of the lawyers from the Treasury Department turned to me and said, "Weren't you the hero of that whole First American thing? Our records show that you tried to blow the whistle, and the regulators didn't pay attention . . . you even brought suit against them. Now, there's egg on our face, big time."

Indeed.

Chapter 16

CIA and OAS: Politics, Economics, Minutiae

As the next presidential campaign approached, I was no longer an official of the RNC or an official delegate to the nominating convention (held in 1980 in Detroit), but I was providing policy assistance to Governor Reagan as chairman of both the International Economic Advisory Committee and the Naval Advisory Committee. Thus, I was indeed on hand to participate at the convention. Just after Reagan won the nomination but before a running mate had been picked, we learned that a group of Republican insiders viewed the candidate as a political upstart, good at reading his lines but without a brain in his head. (Somehow, they seemed to have missed Reagan's two-term service as an elected governor of California who wrote all of his own speeches.) Clearly, to these folks, if he were to be president, he needed on-the-job assistance from an established professional. That would be the previous president, Gerry Ford, stepping in as nominal vice president but with authority to act as an extra-Constitutional "co-president" and behind-the-scenes powerbroker. Reagan did not reject the idea out of hand; there might be some merit, some extra credit to be gained to help win the election. Perhaps, he said, give the vice president some responsibilities in the international arena, as sort of an overseer of the State Department.

Well, I recall a meeting aboard the yacht of Republican fundraiser (and soon-to-be media mogul) John McGoff—with Henry Kissinger and Allen Greenspan representing Ford and with Dick Allen, Bill Casey, me, and a few others representing Reagan—to discuss possibilities or practicalities.

However, Gerry's ego got in the way. He told CBS newsman Walter Cronkite that he would have responsibilities across the spectrum, implying that he would, indeed, be an equal partner. Reagan saw the Cronkite broadcast and almost exploded: "I didn't say that!" And the deal, if there had been one, was off. Within hours, the vice presidency was offered to Poppy Bush.

I was on the convention floor, talking with Sen. Paul Laxalt, when Reagan made the announcement. Laxalt, who in his previous job as governor of Nevada had worked closely with fellow-governor Reagan on a number of neighboring-state issues and had placed Reagan's name in nomination at both the 1976 and 1980 conventions, thought he would be getting the VP slot on the ticket. If ever I saw someone who was visibly, viscerally shocked, this was it. As a consolation prize, I suppose, he was appointed general chairman of the Republican Party, a position, I believe, that was created for the purpose.

After the election, I served as finance chairman for the Inaugural, where I was asked to raise $15 million in ten days as a loan to cover the up-front costs; it was all paid back in about three weeks with the proceeds from ball tickets and trinkets. I even wrote a new march for the occasion, "Thumbs Up America." This one came with lyrics, provided by Sammy Kahn, head of the Songwriters Hall of Fame.

At the same time, Reagan offered me a new (but temporary) challenge: to head the CIA Transition Team. This is one of those generally invisible tools of our government, where an incoming administration sends representatives to meet with the leadership and examine the current policies of federal programs and agencies. The teams suggest replacements for jobs that are under political, not civil, service control; in some cases, they conduct a more formal inspection and suggest changes in policy or operation.

Such was the case with our review of the CIA. This was, to my knowledge, the first time that a transition team had been assigned to that agency—and it was sent, in part, because there had been worrisome signs that the nation's espionage machinery was at the least becoming rusty, if not being taken apart. The agency was shifting from an emphasis on "HUMINT" (human intelligence, or, basically, "spies") to the use of technological methods such as satellite imagery, and it had been pulling in spies from all over the world. Some of those had been in deep cover for years. We saw no evidence that the Soviets had been pulling in *their* spies.

Adm. Stansfield Turner was Carter's man at the CIA. Of course, I knew Turner—he had most recently been serving as president of the Naval War College, where he had done an outstanding job. As for the changes at the CIA, I don't know which may have been at his initiative or which could be attributed to President Carter and his team at the National Security Council, but I had the feeling that Carter was of the old Cordell Hull School, that "gentlemen don't read other people's mail."

The work of a transition team is "generally invisible" except, of course, when some insider—on one side or another—leaks information to the media. In our case, I believe the leaker to have been someone within the CIA who did not like the recommendations we were about to issue. The story played in the *New York Times* on December 8, 1980: "Reagan Urged to Reorganize U.S. Intelligence."

The "Middendorf-headed Team," the *Times* noted, was about to recommend "several sweeping changes in the organization and operations of the nation's intelligence programs." We were, indeed, about to issue a call for a return to emphasis on HUMINT and covert action abroad and greater attention to counterintelligence at home.

The *Times* alluded to some "tension" between the Reagan advisers and the CIA. "A spokesman for the agency," the *Times* reported, "described meetings between transition team members and Adm. Stansfield Turner, Director of Central Intelligence, as 'amicable sessions.' But Reagan advisers called the encounters 'hostile and acrimonious.'"

The truth? It depends on which session (or "encounter") is being considered. My meetings with Turner certainly were amicable. The meetings between some working members of the team and some agency personnel were not friendly. For one thing, the CIA regarded itself as a professional, not political, agency, and some in the agency resented the imposition of a transition team. For another, and perhaps more to the point, some of our recommendations may have put in question the agency's traditional dominance in intelligence affairs.

We suggested, for example, a competitive system of intelligence analysis: The CIA might have to defend its conclusions on any given issue against those offered by such other agencies as the Defense Intelligence Agency or the FBI. We saw a path toward wider debate; some in the CIA saw this as a threat.

We recommended the creation of a central records system that could be used by both the CIA and domestic law enforcement agencies. We saw this as one counter to a growing threat of international terrorism. Our critics saw this as a threat to civil liberties.

We called for tighter security checks on CIA employees. I was not trying to impugn anyone's loyalty and patriotism, but my heavens, you can't get a top job in the Navy Department—maybe almost any job—without the FBI crawling all over your past and present. The CIA assured us that we needn't worry; everyone was polygraphed and the polygraphs guaranteed legitimacy (as we later learned, all they actually did was validate the prejudices of the operators). I was blasted in the *Washington Post* for suggesting that Big Brother spy on the spies! Had the CIA actually undertaken proper surveillance we would surely have caught some of the more notorious of recent Soviet spies in our midst, especially Aldrich Ames, the head of the Soviet branch of the CIA's own counterintelligence group, whose treachery was said to have cost the lives of dozens of our own deep-cover agents in the Soviet Union alone. Ames passed a series of polygraphs with flying colors. In his 2009 book, *Advice to War Presidents*, Angelo Codevilla—a longtime staffer on the Senate Intelligence Committee and my deputy on the transition team—provided an update. Between 1984 (four years *after* our warning) and 1994, apparently all of the CIA agents in or from the Soviet Union or Russia were controlled by the KGB, thanks to Ames. What we ended up with was all of these spies in our own house, spying on us. So, were we so wrong for suggesting some oversight? Tighter controls should also have uncovered turncoat FBI agent Robert Hanssen and Navy communications officer John Walker (who warned the Soviets that their subs were too noisy and told them about SOSUS; the Soviets, as you can imagine, began a crash program to quiet the boats, which was well in hand when the Cold War ended). Walker, in fact, was unmasked by a disgruntled spouse.

Many of our recommendations grew out of work undertaken earlier by the Heritage Foundation, and most of our proposals had been debated for some time within the intelligence community. CIA-director-designate Bill Casey (a friend of mine from Wall Street days) was on our side, which should have given the report some status. However, even the hard-nosed Casey had a hard time penetrating the circled wagons of the CIA bureaucracy. Some of our recommendations for consolidation and cooperation were finally enacted (although we got no credit) some twenty-three years later with the creation of the National Intelligence Agency.

I soon enough was given the opportunity to take on a more permanent challenge, as ambassador to the Organization of American States (OAS). On the surface, this seemed like a rather sleepy posting to a venerable but little-known group. The OAS grew out of the 1890 International Conference of American States, which eventually became the Pan American Union. It was set up in a magnificent building (donated by Andrew Carnegie) at 17th Street and Constitution Avenue on the Mall, had a flurry of notice around the time of World War II, was reconstituted as the OAS, and then largely faded from public view just as a looming threat began to form against some of our southern neighbors.

As with my posting to the Netherlands—where I had some business connections—so, too, with Latin America. In 1955 I helped to found the International Fund, which, among other projects, built and operated a Cuban factory that turned sugar cane waste, known as "bagasse," into hardboard. We bought the rights to use the process from W. R. Grace, created jobs for four hundred Cubans, and began a successful effort to supply hardboard to much of the Caribbean—until Fidel Castro confiscated the business in 1958, staffed it with some Czech engineers who couldn't figure out how to operate the machinery, and it went bust. Of course, we lost our money, a couple of million dollars. An irony: We could have put the factory in, say, Puerto Rico, but I chose Cuba because at the time it had the most stable currency in the hemisphere. Oh, well. All our eggs were not in that one basket, and we did have mixed success in other nations. When we got hurt, it was usually from the runaway inflation that was so endemic in Latin America.

For a time, much of the world had been taken in by the "freedom fighter" propaganda of the American Left, which made Fidel Castro a national hero—in the United States. The then-senator John F. Kennedy said that Castro was following in the footsteps of Bolivar, the great liberator of South America; Ed Sullivan, in a televised interview, said Castro was "in the real American spirit of George Washington." Had anyone asked, I could have dispelled those notions. One night, before we lost our factory, Castro's freedom fighters blew up a building next to the one in which I was sleeping; at dawn, I was flown to safety in a private plane. There were bullet holes in the plane when we landed in Havana.

In December 1961—three years after he confiscated our factory—Castro confessed that he was a Marxist and always had been. It wasn't long before he began exporting arms, munitions, and revolution to Central America, a topic that will occupy much of the next few chapters.

Reagan understood that all of it, good, bad, and chaotic, was great preparation for my OAS assignment; he hoped that our major focus would be encouraging free trade and investment. And so it was—but not without some serious distractions.

The attention of most Americans had always been directed east to the ancestral homelands for most citizens (and the vast oil reserves of the Middle East), and west to the industrial and financial giants on the far side of the Pacific. Whatever was happening below our southern border was barely noticed, even though the capital cities of most members of the OAS are geographically closer to Washington, D.C., than is, say, Sacramento.

However, my watch was to be marked by revolutions in Nicaragua and El Salvador, the fight between Great Britain and Argentina over the Falklands, the U.S. invasion of Grenada, and any number of smoldering issues, one of which burst into flame as the Iran-Contra affair just a few months after I had left OAS for a new assignment. So much for a sleepy posting.

Let me set the stage.

Front and center was Cuba, not a member of the OAS but wielding inordinate influence throughout much of the region. Little wonder, because the Soviets were underwriting much of the Cuban economy. It had been twenty years since the "understanding" that followed the Cuban Missile Crisis, in which the Soviets agreed that they would put "no offensive weapons in Cuba." Now, however, with a series of U.S. administrations having been focused elsewhere, the Soviet military presence was strong and growing. There was a three-thousand-man brigade stationed near Havana (purely "defensive," I am sure) and twenty-five hundred advisers providing training and assistance to the Cuban Army; the Soviet air force flew long-range (defensive, of course) reconnaissance, and the Soviet navy conducted joint exercises with the Cubans. The Soviets operated the largest intelligence monitoring and telecommunications facility outside of the USSR. (One effort: Calls originating in the United States were monitored, and, based on key words and phrases, were recorded for further study.) In 1981 and 1982, Moscow gave 134,000 metric tons of military equipment to Cuba, valued at more than $1 billion; the Cuban air force, for example, had more than two hundred MiG fighter aircraft. One could quibble that none of these forces were Soviet-controlled "offensive weapons," but they came close.

The governments of Nicaragua and Grenada were solidly in the Cuban/ Soviet camp, El Salvador was just climbing out, and other countries were hedging their bets. When Belize celebrated independence from Great Britain in September 1981, the members of the Cuban delegation were in premium seats up front, the American delegation of Assistant Secretary of State Tom Enders and I were relegated to the back row, while in the sunset the British flag was being lowered and the band was playing the brand new "Belize Independence March" that I had been asked to write for the occasion.

Another nation hanging off to one side, always testing the wind, was Mexico, barely an ally and not really a friend. Mexico was suffering from serious growing pains: In twenty years, the population had doubled, per capita income had fallen in proportion, and the country's hidden asset—oil—was ripe for plunder. Cuba and the Soviets were circling, vultures waiting for the right moment, and Mexico had been hedging its bets by supplying Cuba with largely discounted oil. Part of my job was to be like Horatio at the bridge, to do what I could to keep things in balance and to court Mexican leaders. We had one important friend, at least: the Mexican ambassador to the OAS, Don Rafael de Colina. An ancient and very wise man, he had been in his posting since the 1920s. From the start, and with his tacit but not overt support, I worked diligently to bring Mexico to our point of view. One small but immediate contribution: a bit of music, my "Mexican Rhapsody," dedicated to Don Rafael and premiered in the great hall of the OAS building, to an audience including Mexico's first lady, Carmen Lopez Portillo, in 1981.

Don Rafael told me—many times—that he was under tremendous pressure from other Latin countries to vote against the United States; resentment ran deep throughout the region. We had long forgotten "gunboat diplomacy." We fought a war with Mexico; they lost. U.S. Marines occupied Vera Cruz in 1914, and in 1916 the U.S. Army wandered back and forth across the border without regard for diplomatic formalities, pursuing Pancho Villa. Nicaragua was occupied off and on by Marines from 1912 to 1933; Haiti, from 1915–1934; Guatemala, 1954; Cuba, the Bay of Pigs fiasco in 1961; the Dominican Republic, 1965. By 1981, we had forgotten. The "beneficiaries" of our care had not.

Most of my working days were filled with economics, politics, and the strange internal workings of the organization. "Internal workings" first, then politics and economics. One example should suffice. As an organization, OAS reflected the anti-American bias of many members in general and the personal bias of Secretary General Alejandro Orfila, an Argentinean, in particular. He was determined to reduce our share of contracts controlled by OAS. In 1982 the national distribution of purchase orders was striking: Argentina got 25 percent, the United States, 0.43 percent. In one report to the Permanent Council, Orfila juggled the numbers to make it look as if the rich U.S. was barely a player: "Of the total costs of OAS projects, the member states from Latin America and the Caribbean contributed 71.8 percent compared to 24.4 percent for the major [i.e., U.S.] contributor." By this focus on "projects," the reader was left unaware that the U.S. supported 66 percent of the overall costs of OAS. In the opening sections of a document issued in May 1983, Orfila criticized the U.S. for paying "less than projected" during the first quarter of 1983. If a reader were to bother to read on to page five, he would learn that the U.S. contributed 99.5 percent of *all* collections during the same period. You get the idea.

At the same moment, we were particularly irritated by Orfila's refusal even to consider the appointments of two highly qualified Americans to key jobs in OAS: director of the Tourism Department and director of the OAS Mission of Modern Art. However, thanks to a bit of fortuitous timing, I was able to apply a bit of leverage. I had just been handed a Treasury check for $11.6 million—the quarterly payment to the OAS. As I dangled the check in front of Orfila, I suggested that, if he wished, we would be pleased to reduce our contributions from 66 percent to the 24.4 percent with which he had credited us, while of course alerting the news media to the change. I left him with copies of the resumes of our two candidates.

Through it all, Orfila—a dedicated and hardworking public servant—and I remained good friends. Diplomacy and gamesmanship are often much the same thing.

Politics? As it had been with the Navy, a key part of my job was working with (or on) members of Congress to assure support for our programs. Successful votes on controversial issues do not come from a burst of spontaneous goodwill shared by all—they come from good organization, cogent argument, and some imaginative quid pro quo. This was often triggered by good intelligence, fed to me from friends who worked on the Hill, who might alert us to issues that I might address in a phone call or visit; Congressman So-and-So "feels that he has been neglected," and another "may be willing to soften liberal stance on El Salvador if approached personally by a prominent representative of the administration."[1] On one hectic day, April 26, 1983, I attempted to reach thirty-four members of the House, saw and spoke with sixteen in person and one on the phone, chatted with the legislative assistants of three others, visited two offices without meaningful contact, and ran out of time.

As for economics, I felt like a fox in a chicken coop, getting into a branch of government where I could push my own ideas forward—and get paid for it. I enlisted the brilliant Alberto Piedra as my deputy, with the rank of ambassador. Alberto had a law degree and two PhDs; he had been an official in Castro's ministry of commerce, saw the light in 1960, abandoned home and possessions, and fled Cuba. When he and I met, he was chairman of the Department of Economics and Business at Catholic University.

During my tour, I visited thirty-one of the OAS member countries at least four times each, to push for privatization of industry, free markets, encouragement of private property rights, sanctity of contracts, and a stable independent judiciary to ensure all—keys to working democracies, and our goal. In those days, more than 60 percent of economic activity in virtually all Latin countries (as much as 70 percent in Mexico) was controlled by the government. Growth was nil; poverty and unemployment rates were astronomical, tax avoidance and corruption were endemic, and black markets flourished. The countries were deep in debt, more than $300 billion; most were in default. Private foreign direct investment, one of the most powerful tools of growth, was barely noticed. Foreign direct investment is not the same as government-to-government grants and loans, which are often soaked up too quickly by the bureaucracy; direct investment brings new plants, technology, equipment, and jobs, while opening export markets back into the investing country. Foreign direct investment is a prime mover in growth, and every rational developing (and developed) nation is in competition for the funds—including, I would note, the United States, a prime beneficiary because potential investors recognize our relatively (compared with almost every other nation in the world) stable business and government environment.

In those countries that did encourage private investment, the encouragement often was premised on government greed. Local businessmen learned to keep two sets of books—one to show the tax collectors, and one for running the business. They exported as much of their production as they could, taking payment in dollars that were deposited in U.S. banks; Miami may have been the unofficial financial capital of Latin America. If the money was brought home it was savaged by confiscatory taxes, which largely disappeared into the pockets of some government official. It was generally held that if you were in politics and weren't rich, you weren't very bright.

I once suggested to a State Department official—in jest, I suppose, but out of frustration—that it would be more efficient if we just sent our foreign aid payments to corrupt governments directly to the Swiss bank accounts of the leaders, and avoided the middle-man charges.

I believe that one of the more important early contributions to OAS was when Bill Brock—he was then the U.S. trade representative—and I worked with his deputy, David McDonald (who also had been my undersecretary of the navy), to develop the Caribbean Basin Initiative (CBI), a comprehensive package of political and economic measures with the goal of stabilizing the Caribbean Basin. This multiagency (and highly successful) effort provided a much-needed, structured approach to encouraging economic growth throughout the region. It provided a radically altered two-way tariff structure between the U.S. and participating countries, and a framework within which American (and other) companies, banks, and individuals could safely invest in businesses in the region. To this point, foreign investors had lost billions and few had any interest in losing more. We wanted to provide increased and safe opportunities.

CBI was not meant to be a blanket, one-size-fits-all program. We included a country-by-country assessment, pointing out the business and industrial areas with the highest potential. What local government policies will help or hinder? What sort of technical assistance, management, or marketing training might be needed? Will the transportation infrastructure—roads, rail, port facilities—accommodate increased freight traffic? Is there a reliable supply of energy? What about telecommunications?

To participate, we stipulated that a country must have a non-Communist government, an extradition treaty with the United States, must agree to abide by copyright rules, and to cooperate in regional antinarcotics efforts. The initial beneficiaries were twenty-one nations in the Caribbean, Central America, and the northern coast of South America. The European Economic Community provided modest parallel efforts, and Japan and Canada increased aid to the region.

One of my tasks was to brief—and get approval from—the Cabinet, which was easily done. Next, Congress passed CBI, but under pressure from some labor unions exempted oil, shoes, and textiles. The Commerce Department set up a CBI business information center to assist interested companies and offer solid knowledge of policies and regulations in any target country. A little-known but important U.S. agency, the Overseas Private Investment Corporation (OPIC), stepped in with direct loans and insurance to cover the political risks of operating in developing countries—such as expropriation, war, and currency crises. The Export-Import Bank and the Agency for International Development (AID) provided loans and grants. The Agriculture Department developed a program of technical assistance, covering worker's health, guidelines for fumigation of crops, preparation for transit or storage, quality and labeling, how to adjust production to meet the needs of the marketplace, and the value of crop insurance to protect against loss. A wide range of non- and quasi-government agencies became involved, such as the U.S. Business Committee on Jamaica, Caribbean/ Central American Action, CBI Coalition, Council of the Americas, U.S. Chamber of Commerce, and the Association of Chambers of Commerce in Latin America.

Chapter 17

Organization of American States: Nicaragua and El Salvador

W hen I reported on board in April 1981, I was confronted by two regional crises playing out at the same time (and they would continue throughout my tenure). Each of these provided aid and comfort to those Americans who opposed—for whatever reasons, some of which I'll discuss in a moment—many of our efforts to provide economic and military support to Latin nations in need. The first crisis began two years before I came on board—with the overthrow of Nicaraguan strongman Anastasio Somoza—and the other was an attempted revolution in El Salvador that was triggered about the time I arrived. They were not separate and independent, because the former was helping foment the latter. And the former was hardly a free agent—it was fully supported, and goaded on, by the Soviet Union and Cuba.

The Nicaraguan insurgents, operating under the name "Sandinistas" to salute an earlier and failed effort by revolutionary Antonio Sandino, overthrew the authoritarian rule begun by Somoza in 1936 and carried on by his two sons. The United States—and much of the Western Hemisphere—looked on with relief, anticipating a new democracy under a new government. The Sandinistas pledged to establish full observance of human rights, a peaceful and orderly transition, civil justice, and to hold free and fair elections.

By January 1981 the United States had granted emergency relief and recovery aid to Nicaragua of $118 million; in fact, in the first two years of Sandinista rule, the United States directly or indirectly sent five times more aid to Nicaragua than it had in the two years prior to the revolution. If we were trying to buy friendship, it didn't work. The governme nt of Nicaragua treated the United States as an enemy.

Why? After the new government shoved aside more moderate allies, the incoming minister of defense declared their creed to be Marxism-Leninism and moved quickly to consolidate power. Business leaders were jailed. The government seized control of most media and subjected all media to heavy censorship. It denied the clergy of the Roman Catholic Church the right to give a radio Mass during Holy Week. It insulted and mocked the Pope and, most important, it drove the indigenous Miskito Indians from their homelands, burned their villages, and destroyed their crops. To my mind, that came pretty close to genocide. Somehow, this escaped the notice of the Sandinista supporters in the United States. The "shoved aside" Nicaraguan moderates formed a movement in opposition, dubbed the "Contras." This was quickly denigrated by the Sandinistas and their champions as a group of former Somozistas angry at having been removed from power. Some were, but most were not.

Under the Sandinistas, Nicaragua went on a military building spree, developing three times the number of military bases that were in place during the Somoza years. The new army numbered 25,000 men, supported by a militia of 50,000, supplemented by 2,000 Cuban military and security advisers. It was the largest army in Central America, equipped with dozens of Soviet-made tanks, 800 Soviet-bloc trucks, Soviet howitzers, antiaircraft guns, planes, and helicopters. There were thousands of civilian advisers from Cuba, the Soviet Union, North Korea, East Germany, Libya, and the Palestine Liberation Organization (PLO). About seventy Nicaraguans had been trained in Bulgaria to be pilots and aviation mechanics. Nicaragua became a willing platform for Cuban and Soviet covert military action.

Elections? Those who command revolutions are loath to surrender power. In July 1980, the Sandinista defense minister announced that there would be no need for elections, since the people had already "voted" during the revolution. Elections, he ominously declared, could not be held until the people had been reeducated. At last, U.S. policy switched and now supported the opposition—the Contras, aided and assisted by the CIA—but opposition in our own Congress made that support problematic. In amendments to several military appropriations bills between 1982 and 1984—known collectively as "the Boland Amendment" for their author, Massachusetts Democratic congressman Edward P. Boland—Congress prohibited military support "for the purpose of overthrowing the Government of Nicaragua." As you will appreciate, this was all quite controversial—could Congress thus interfere with the president's ability to conduct foreign policy? Did the prohibitions apply to the National Security Council? This was never resolved, and much of the support continued but went underground, so to speak, to surface as the chief embarrassment of the Reagan administration, the Iran-Contra affair. Then, a series of clandestine arms transactions in the Middle East resulted in cash contributions to the Contras, which was a possible contravention of the Boland Amendment. (A few years later, the Boland

Amendment was repealed, overt support was resumed, and the Contras prevailed over the Sandinistas in the 1990 election.)

But here's an interesting anomaly. Almost every month, in sessions at the OAS, I would berate the Nicaraguan government for not following through on their promise to hold free elections—but I never made it personal with the Sandinista representative, with whom I worked to maintain a proper and cordial relationship. I must note that, in four years, he never voted against us, on anything, through hundreds of votes. Even at the time of the Falklands dispute (see later), when Secretary of State Al Haig and I had to take a lot of heat from the Argentineans and several of their allies, the Nicaraguan ambassador did not join in the free-for-all. I can only assume that this was not due to my charm, but that he was a Nicaraguan patriot in the best sense, not a prisoner of his government, albeit otherwise powerless.

In the other immediate crisis, parallel to and connected with the Nicaraguan business, El Salvador was up for grabs, with the government under assault by guerrillas supported and trained by the Cuban-Nicaraguan cabal. And here, our Congress was ambivalent—help the government fight the guerrillas, or help the guerrillas? This got pretty murky. The government was greatly flawed; in fact, a staffer for Tip O'Neill (who was now speaker of the House) had a sister, a Maryknoll nun, who was one of four church women who had been raped and murdered in 1980 by Salvadoran National Guardsmen. A Catholic bishop had been assassinated, possibly by a government agent. The far left in America saw religious oppression and rallied behind the guerrillas.

Our unseen opponent was the concept of "liberation theology," which, anchored by notions of the Christian obligation to bring justice to the poor and the oppressed through political activism, should have been on our side. But things got pretty confused, and much seemed to depend upon which side got the most notice first. To my mind, "theologists" should have been firmly opposed to dictatorial Communism, but in Latin America, liberation theology had been so co-opted that it was supporting revolutionary takeover. Where we saw frightened, ill-trained soldiers and law enforcement officials, our opponents saw thugs and murderers. Where we saw the guerrillas as corrupt thieves and Communist partisans, the far left and some in the media saw "freedom fighters." However, I must point out, the guerrillas were not embattled peasants striving to break free of an oppressive government, but Marxist professionals with good training and weapons often better than those protecting the government's interests.

The United States established a program for training the Salvadoran army, but by the middle of 1983 only about 10 percent had been through the course—far fewer than the number of guerrillas that had been trained by Nicaragua and Cuba. On their own clandestine radio station, the guerrillas acknowledged getting arms and ammunition from throughout Central America "and other countries," while affirming their ties to Nicaragua, Cuba, and the Soviet Union. One Salvadoran guerrilla leader boasted that soon enough El Salvador and Nicaragua would be "arm in arm and struggling for the total liberation of Central America."

Nevertheless, O'Neill and friends gave us a hard time. The nuns were murdered by the government. Period. Nothing else mattered. Not the Soviet/ Cuban maneuvering for control over our soft underbelly to the South. Not the acknowledged intervention of Nicaragua. Not the avowed Marxist ideology of the guerrillas. The story told first gets remembered best. An error in the file is a fact, forever.

El Salvador held an election at the end of March 1982; it was both a tragedy and a triumph. The guerrillas destroyed trucks and buses that could be used to carry voters to the polling places and threatened to kill anyone who voted. "Vote today," they warned, "die tonight." Despite all, perhaps 80 percent of eligible voters showed up at the polls. One million people, in a nation of five million. One U.S. congressman, who went down as an observer, reported that one woman, wounded on the way to the polls, refused to leave the line to be treated until after she had voted. Another woman, who was warned that she would be killed upon her return from the polls, said she told them, "You can kill me, you can kill my family, you can kill my neighbors. You can't kill us all."

Did we acknowledge that El Salvador was far from perfect? Yes. There were human rights violations, a corrupt criminal justice system, and officially sanctioned violence against noncombatants. But this did not excuse the violence from the guerrillas, who savaged farmlands and destroyed more than half of the railway rolling stock, along with bridges, water facilities, and telephone and electrical systems. The guerrilla motives were clear enough, and they had nothing to do with overthrowing a repressive regime. Secretary of State George Shultz pointed out the conundrum: "The guerrillas," he said, "are deliberately and systematically" depriving the people of El Salvador of "food, water, transportation, light, sanitation, and jobs." And yet—they "claim they want to help the common people."[1]

We were accused of trying to impose the "will" of the United States on recalcitrant Central American neighbors, when in fact Costa Rica, El Salvador, Honduras, and Guatemala—all under threat from the Soviet/Cuban/ Nicaraguan coalition—were asking for our help to support their economic and military self-defense against real subversion. Further, we applauded the efforts of Mexico, Venezuela, Colombia, and Panama, assembled under the rubric of the "Contadora" movement, to broker peace in the region without participation by the United States. President Reagan said that we would support any agreement among Central American countries for the withdrawal—under fully verifiable and reciprocal conditions—of foreign military and security advisers and troops; that we would support efforts to settle issues by ballots instead of bullets; and that we would support efforts to control insurgencies based in neighboring countries.[2]

I learned that our erstwhile allies, the Brits, were hooked on the propaganda and not the reality. "My government," I wrote in a letter to the editor of the London *Times*, "welcomes positive European engagement in the search for solutions to the region's problems."

I did get a bit testy: "We would welcome as well an effort by Europeans to understand what we are trying to do and why." It was obvious that they knew little if anything of our economic support, only that somehow we were pumping in large sums of money to train thugs. There was little if any appreciation that the turmoil in El Salvador was caused not by the United States but by the intervention from outside agencies—i.e., Cuba and Nicaragua—supporting client guerrillas. "Vote today, die tonight" was not just propaganda but a real threat. To set the record straight, I wrote: "Nicaragua is characterized today by swollen military forces, pressure on those who do not support enthusiastically the regime, controls on trade union activities, persecution of the minority Miskito Indian population, censorship of the one remaining independent newspaper, closure of radio stations, disregard for religious freedom, continuing support for guerrilla subversion in neighboring countries, and the presence of some 11,000 security and other personnel from Cuba and the Soviet bloc." The London *Times* printed my letter on December 8, 1983. I'm not sure if it had any impact on British public opinion.

Chapter 18

Organization of American States:
Falklands and Grenada

E xactly one year into my tour, I was on a "mission" and things were going well. I had completed a round of official visits primarily with the heads of state of Brazil, Ecuador, Peru, Chile, Argentina, Uruguay, Paraguay, Belize, Honduras, Panama, Venezuela, Colombia, Jamaica, Barbados, Dominica, Costa Rica, and Trinidad and Tobago. Frequently, I enhanced my visit with a piece of music I composed—a march, a nocturne, a rhapsody—played by a local orchestra as part of the official ceremonies. (Overall, during my tour, I wrote nineteen such pieces, which I found to be a helpful extension of diplomacy—a concept affirmed when I later was given the prestigious Unity Through Music Award of the Inter-American Music Council.)

My message was clear: to champion the benefits of free markets, free trade, the right to private property, the value of a strong independent judiciary—those things that would contribute to a strong economy, protect the rights of citizens, and attract foreign direct investment. In many areas, I was going against years—centuries—of custom and tradition, but conditions in so many countries were so obviously troubled that I often found a willing and receptive audience. President Reagan came over to the OAS to announce the Caribbean Basin Initiative, and two new countries were admitted to membership in the OAS—St. Vincent and the Grenadines, and Antigua and Barbuda. A strong showing in the elections in El Salvador, the month before my first anniversary, was encouraging.

And then, a setback. On April 2, 1982, Argentina's president, Leopoldo Galtieri, elected to make a military issue of a long-smoldering dispute: "ownership" of the unprepossessing Falkland Islands, economically destitute, best known as a graveyard of sailing ships caught in the almost constant storms of Tierra del Fuego. The islands—the "Malvinas" to the Argentines—had been occupied by the British since 1833. President Galtieri decided it was time to take them back.

President Reagan called Galtieri to urge restraint, without success. Galtieri sent in an occupying force, but his motives were suspect. Argentina's economy had been run into the ground by gross mismanagement and most outside observers assumed, absent any real economic or humanitarian need to reclaim the Malvinas, that the government was waving the flag and flexing some muscle to shift the public focus.

Within a matter of days, Al Haig had flown to London and Buenos Aires, trying to mediate a solution. Secretary of Defense Caspar Weinberger made two trips to meet with British prime minister Margaret Thatcher. The OAS Council was called into special session but deferred action, as not to impede Haig's effort. A British armada set sail; the islands *would* be retaken. Haig convinced the British to hold the fleet at Ascension Island, about halfway to the Falklands, while diplomatic efforts continued.

Argentina called another special session of the OAS, to demand that the British withdraw completely. Haig made a plea for moderation, urging the Latins not to let their natural sympathies for Argentina impair a rational approach. He received polite applause, an embarrassing contrast to the standing ovation that had been given his Argentine counterpart, Foreign Minister Nicanor Costa Mendez. However, in voting a resolution, the OAS took a more even-handed approach and urged both sides to avoid the use of force.

Haig and Weinberger worked their contacts; Jeanne Kirkpatrick worked the UN; and my focus was the Argentine ambassador to the United States (and through him, directly to Galtieri). The ambassador was very open, and in a series of private conversations with Alberto Piedra and me at his residence, worked on a face-saving compromise: The Pope would divert from an already-scheduled trip to Latin America, visit the Falklands/Malvinas, and put up Vatican, British, and Argentine flags. We hoped this might defuse the passions of the moment and allow for withdrawal of forces, pending a calmer discussion of the issues.

Our effort was soon enough overtaken by events. Galtieri thought that Thatcher was bluffing, and he moved the cruiser *General Belgrano* into position. He called his ambassador, told him to thank me for our efforts, but that he could not accept the proposed arrangement; the ambassador asked us to hang on a bit longer. I was still with the ambassador at his residence, just before midnight, April 30, when I got a call from Haig. "Get back here quick," he said. "It's all over. The British are going in tomorrow." He added an unnecessary caveat: "Don't tell the ambassador."

May 1, the British bombed the islands; May 2, in a strange inter-generational juxtaposition, the pre–World War II *General Belgrano* (ex–USS *Phoenix*) was sunk by a British nuclear submarine firing a World War II–vintage torpedo; 321 Argentinian sailors were killed. On May 4, an Argentine fighter

aircraft hit HMS *Sheffield* with a French-built Exocet missile; 22 British sailors were killed. A territorial dispute became a war. By the time it ended, some
seventy days later, the British were in full control of the islands, but they had
lost 255 men, 6 ships (10 others were badly damaged), and 34 aircraft. The war
cost the Argentines about 700 men—and Galtieri lost his job.

Some members of the OAS accused the United States of violating the
Rio Treaty, which required all members to come to the assistance of any
American republic subjected to unlawful force from outside the alliance.
Our position was clear: In this case, the unlawful aggression came from
within the alliance, not from outside the hemisphere, and thus neither we
nor any other member was required to support Argentina. There were many
who disagreed, offended that we would back the British in a dispute against
a country on our side of the world. They had little respect for Galtieri, but
he was, after all, a member of their club.

Along the way, the world was treated to an audacious but blundering
bit of propaganda, in the form of "Department of Defense News Release
Number 217–82, May 5, 1982. Comments of Secretary of Defense Caspar W.
Weinberger on Support to Great Britain."

Although neither the Defense Department or Weinberger had anything
to do with this patent forgery, it was widely accepted as true. The following
are accurate excerpts, bad grammar and poor spelling, as found.

> The time has come when Washington cannot regard current Britain-
> Argentina conflict as a second performance of a 19th century com-
> ical opera any longer. The U.S. Has found itself in an unenviable,
> but not incapable to solve this complicated situation. . . . From the
> very beginning of the shuttle diplomacy of the State Secretary Mr.
> A. Haig I was in a position that this mission cannot contribute to a
> settlement of the conflict by diplomatic means in keeping with our
> policy. . . . Should the Premier Mrs. Thatcher's Falkland policy break
> down, for Washington would be evident to face the possibility of a
> future Labour Government in Great Britain.

The United States—according to 217–82—was "strongly opposed to Labour
Party power in Great Britain," and was therefore taking steps to ensure British
victory in the Falklands—including passing "intelligence information" which
"is taken advantage of as demonstrated by many attacks of British forces to
Falklands" and, without doubt, "will affect in a decisive manner the outcome
. . . of the conflict." In addition, 217–82 said we were providing material support in the form of fuel, food, and technical assistance. The ersatz Weinberger
was, in effect, announcing that we had entered the war and, setting aside fear

of the Labour Party, the real reason was "U.S. support to Great Britain will bring us future military presence in the Falklands which will assert our control of the whole of the Latin America continent."

On July 25, 1982, Al Haig, frustrated at what he saw as interference from the NSC and policy differences with our UN ambassador Jeanne Kirkpatrick, offered to resign. I believe that he had done so before, without result, but this time President Reagan—also frustrated, I believe, with the bickering—took him up on his offer. George Shultz became secretary of state.

As for the Falklands, the fighting had ended, but not the arguing. The Argentines affirmed that the islands were theirs, forever, but agreed that renewed hostilities were out of the question. Margaret Thatcher authorized British banks to participate in Argentine debt rescheduling. Wounds, perhaps, were healing.

And, in December 1983, I was honored to be a guest at the inauguration of the first president of Argentina to have been freely elected in twenty-five years, Raul Alfonsin. At this point in history, democratization had reached about 90 percent of the population of Latin America. Two major holdouts—Uruguay and Chile—seemed to be coming around. They did indeed: Uruguay in 1985 and Chile in 1988.

About halfway between the end of our unsatisfactory involvement in Vietnam and the successful Gulf War in defense of Kuwait, the U.S. military won a small, controversial, often-denigrated but highly significant bit of warfare—the temporary capture, if you will, of the smallest independent country in the Western Hemisphere: the island nation of Grenada. Located on the eastern fringe of the Caribbean, a bit north of Venezuela, Grenada is about twice the size of the District of Columbia, with a population then just over 100,000.

Once a British possession, Grenada was granted independence in 1974, but in 1979—with arms supplied by Cuba—a small group of perhaps twenty-seven revolutionaries staged a coup and Socialist Maurice Bishop was installed as prime minister.

Bishop was spiritually and militarily allied with Cuba and the Soviet Union, but he vowed to lead his country to a new and better future. When, toward the end of 1980, a large force of Cuban workers began construction of a nine-thousand-foot runway on Grenada, Bishop said the runway was to encourage tourism. Well it may have been, to a point; Bishop, indeed, Socialist or not, was trying to promote business interests and private-sector development. However, this seventy-one-million-dollar airport, sized to handle wide-body jet aircraft, was simply too big for the intended purpose;

the passenger load of two 747s would fill every hotel room on the island. Grenada already had an airport with a five-thousand-foot runway, and it easily handled aircraft shuttling in from, say, Caracas, Venezuela, only four hundred miles away. That runway was unlit, which the government said was a serious shortcoming; the government didn't mention that they could add runway lights for a lot less than $71 million. In fact, the World Bank estimated that a large, modern airport sized to handle all possible tourist traffic should only cost about $19 million.

Why such an ambitious project? The operational range of a Cuban MiG fighter was 690 miles. Put military air bases in Nicaragua, Havana, and Grenada, and you covered an area about as large as the United States. More to the point: Grenada was not included in the Missile Crisis "understanding." The Soviets would be free to put whatever weapons they wanted in Grenada. Do you wonder that we were concerned? With a Grenada base, Soviet aircraft could interdict the vital sea lanes of the Caribbean in time of crisis. Vital? In World War II, Adolph Hitler's U-boats sank more American tonnage in the Caribbean area than in the entire Atlantic Ocean; in the 1980s, some 52 percent of oil imported into the United States was carried in ships passing within a few miles of Grenada.

Cuba was indeed the driving force behind the airfield, providing most of the equipment and materials, and a couple of hundred construction workers and technicians. The United States—alarmed—took action by blocking loans from the European Economic Commission (EEC). In fact, Grenadian ambassador and UN representative Dessima Williams harangued the OAS Permanent Council with charges of U.S. "economic hostility" against Grenada. "They have started a hysteria in the international community that our airport is a Cuban base," she said. "Once again the world . . . has been confronted by a big, rich country like the U.S. trying to destabilize a developing nation like Grenada . . . through . . . unprincipled, unjust, inhumane acts," she said. "The United States . . . is trying to squeeze and crush Grenada, one of its smallest and poorest sister states." In any event, construction continued, with increased aid from the Cuban/Soviet axis. The number of Cubans on site—workers, or military forces, or both—was increased to one thousand.

June 1983. Prime Minister Bishop was scheduled to come to Washington and address the OAS Permanent Council—and, I was certain, to blast the United States. However, a few days before that event and to my great surprise, Dessima Williams took me aside and asked if I would be willing to meet, unofficially, with Bishop. I asked Bill Clark, the president's national security adviser, to join me at the meeting with Bishop and Ambassador Williams, which we held in secret in a back room at a local hotel.

Bishop was trim, athletic, bearded—and wary. He clearly wanted to talk, but I had the distinct impression that he didn't know what he wanted to say. He came across not as a hard, tough, uncompromising revolutionary, but as a worried, even haunted, man. In most of my dealings with the Soviets, for example, you could see the machinery behind the conversation, like a verbal chess match; you say something, they search their mental index and find the proper rejoinder, peppering the talk with the buzzwords of the day, "peace" or "harmonious relations." I did not have that impression with Bishop. Sure, he had the Marxist slogans down pat, but he didn't seem to believe them.

Bishop admitted that he didn't have a free hand; his government was dominated by the Soviets. His partner in the coup, Deputy Prime Minister Bernard Coard, was a willing slave of the Soviets. I believe that Bishop wanted to find a way to dump them but stay in power.

I was obligated to point out the issues that were impeding better relations: political prisoners being held without trial; suspension of press freedoms and the right of assembly; indefinite postponement of free elections; a foreign policy parroting the Cuban-Soviet line; the growing presence of Cuban and Soviet personnel and their involvement in projects that had serious implications for security throughout the area.

I appealed to his sense of national pride, to help his people. He grew up in a free country—it may have been a British Colony, but it certainly wasn't under British domination. Sure, it was fashionable for the residents to "hate" the British, but the British legacy was a boon—strong judicial system, organized government—and those nations that did not reject the legacy and stayed on as members of the Commonwealth prospered.

I said, "If you move toward freedom in your country, you will gain a tremendous ally in the United States. Trade, tourism, positive net cash flow to help your people. Direct investment. Right now, Grenada is a pariah in the Caribbean." Judge Clark and I both said, "Let's find some accommodation; perhaps [Bishop] could outline a path to democracy and allay our fears about the airport." I warned him that promoting the Communist cause while criticizing the United States would not be helpful.

Our conversation lasted for something more than an hour, without resolution.

Why did he want this meeting? I have no solid answer, but, from the look in his eyes, I believe that he was trapped between the hardcore ideology of his fellow revolutionaries and the geometric logic of benefits certain to arise from cooperative development and growth within the Western community of nations. And he didn't know how to reconcile the two.

We told the State Department that there may be an opening here. The State Department didn't seem too excited. They got the information, assessed the information, reported the information within their own chain of command, and filed the information.

Well, the day after our conversation, Bishop played to his militant supporters, blasted the United States, and accused us of planning an invasion. A reporter asked for my response: I said, "Bull." It was, indeed, accurate at that moment. (In January 1984, some seven months after we had, in fact, invaded Grenada, *Washingtonian* set the meeting with Bishop in April instead of June, and quoted me as saying, "Horse—." So much for accuracy in media.)

Unfortunately, here was a "Bishop" who ignored scripture: "For all they that take the sword shall perish with the sword" (Matt. 26:52). Bishop went back home, soon enough, to his death. There was a coup of the coup, and on Columbus Day Deputy Prime Minister Coard, backed by the army, threw Bishop in jail.

In the turmoil following Bishop's arrest, I had an urgent call from NSC staffer Constantine Menges—only a month into his job—to come to the White House and mull over the matter of Grenada. Constantine sketched out a plan: We could get the Communists out before the airfield was finished. There were almost seven hundred American citizens, along with several hundred other foreign nationals, enrolled at an American-run medical school, just about a mile from the airport. They might be in danger, a plausible reason for intervention. He said, "Let's be alert for an opportunity, then go in," and he asked for my opinion. I agreed, but added a Machiavellian joke, "Why don't we wait until they finish the runway? If they've spent fifty-seven million dollars on it now, why not let them spend the whole seventy-one million, driving themselves closer to bankruptcy, and then go in?"

I think he laughed, but he wasn't diverted. He asked, "Can you keep the Latins on our side?" I said, "Sure, if we win." They were all playing a game, playing the odds—Free World and the Rest of the World. Many Latin governments were hanging by a thread, hoping for support from one side or the other. Ideology was not an issue with some of them; they didn't care which, as long as they were on the winning side. The Soviets were giving out a lot of free lunches, the United States couldn't make up its mind, and everyone was hedging their bets.

Well, Bishop escaped from jail, rallied some supporters, tried to regain control, was captured, and seven days after his arrest was brutally murdered. The island lurched into anarchy and violence, and the head of the army, Hudson Austin, pushed Coard aside, took over, and established a revolutionary military council. He imposed martial law with a shoot-on-sight curfew. The safety of the American students was no longer theoretical; memories of the Iran hostage crisis were fresh, and we didn't want to see another.

Robert "Bud" McFarlane had just assumed leadership of the NSC and asked his new deputy—my former admin officer—Rear Adm. John Poindexter, to convene a meeting of the planning group for the next morning, a Thursday. I was there, along with Menges, Lt. Col. Oliver North, and some folk from State and the CIA. Menges offered his proposal; one of the State Department reps suggested negotiation, but several of us strongly urged a direct rescue that would lead to the restoration of democracy. Poindexter agreed.

Vice President George H. W. Bush chaired a cabinet-level NSC meeting later in the day: He sat at one end of the table, McFarlane was at the other. I offered my assessment. How would most OAS members react? They would support us. If we won. When he was briefed on the meeting, CIA director Bill Casey said, "Hey, f—k, let's dump those bastards." Bill had a way with words.

Someone noted that a Navy task force had just left Norfolk, headed for a routine and scheduled deployment in the Mediterranean; it could easily be diverted. JCS chairman Gen. John Vessey was concerned about interrupting this long-planned deployment. I spoke up, to the effect: "The Navy can adjust."

Reagan ordered the ships to turn around, with no public notice, to be available just in case. To provide cover, that all was business-as-usual at the White House, he stuck to his published schedule and left for a weekend round of golf in Augusta, Georgia. In the meantime, we had obtained an emergency resolution from the Organization of Eastern Caribbean States (OECS, a subset of OAS) with, I must note, my behind-the-scenes arm twisting. This called upon the United States to intervene. Eugenie Charles, prime minister of Dominica, and Edward Seaga, the new prime minister of Jamaica, held very real fear for the safety of their own countries and were not shy to say so.

Early Saturday morning, when he learned of the OECS resolution, Reagan consulted with Bush, Weinberger, and Vessey—who were back in Washington—and then asked McFarlane "How soon could we launch an invasion?" McFarlane said forty-eight hours; Reagan said, "Do it."

Almost twenty-four hours later, the president learned that 241 U.S. Marines had been killed in a suicide bombing at the Marine barracks in Beirut, Lebanon. Some pundits were later to opine that the invasion of Grenada was a retaliation of sorts. It was not; the order had already been given.

To maintain secrecy, Reagan continued on his published schedule: He stayed in Georgia through most of Sunday, playing golf. The president didn't even brief congressional leaders until the invasion was actually under way.

As wars go, Operation Urgent Fury was not very large: Perhaps seven thousand Marines and Army troopers landed on the island, most of which was secure by the second day. The whole operation was completed a week later. Total casualties: 19 Americans killed, 119 wounded; perhaps 49 Grenadians and 29 Cubans killed, several hundred wounded. Reagan said Grenada was "a Soviet-Cuban colony being readied as a major military bastion to export terror and undermine democracy. . . . We got there just in time."[1]

In truth, the military fell into a bigger war with the media, which had been excluded from participation in the first few days. The representatives of the media were livid. They offered allusions to "another Vietnam," based on nothing except misplaced emotion. Many—not prepared in advance—called this an unwarranted invasion of a peaceful independent nation, and the inevitable errors, especially from such a quickly planned operation, became the focus of the story: The troops were using out-of-date tourist maps; there were difficulties with interservice communications because of incompatible radio frequencies.

Why was media participation delayed? Two possible reasons. One is practical: The invasion was planned so quickly, and with such secrecy, that, as noted, even the leaders of Congress were not brought in on it. The other was philosophical, most certainly a carry-over from Vietnam: The military didn't like having the media second-guessing everything they did.

The media were angry; editorialists fumed; the First Amendment had been trampled by an arrogant president (who was not involved in the "exclusion" order, which may have been created by a committee at the Pentagon). The public, bless them, didn't care. *Time*, December 12, 1983, reported that *ABC News* anchorman Peter Jennings was astonished that 99 percent of mail from his viewers supported the way the media had been handled. In 500 letters and phones calls to NBC, the government was supported five to one; in *Time* itself, of 225 letters to the editor, eight out of nine supported the government. Max Frankel, then editorial writer of the *New York Times*, wrote that the most astounding thing about the Grenada invasion "was the quick, facile assumption by some of the public that the press wanted to get in, not to witness the invasion on behalf of the people, but to sabotage it."[2]

My assigned task was to "hold the Latins in line." Well, that sounds pretty arrogant; my job was, at the least, to keep OAS members, many of whom continued to harbor long-standing resentments against the United States, from making an all-out public assault. I called on dean of the corps, Don Rafael de Colina, at his home, to alert him that, at a session of the Permanent Council session called for the next day, he would be under a lot of pressure from the Bolivian ambassador (who was taking his turn in the chair) to second a proposed condemnation of the United States. "It would mean a great deal to us," I said, "if that condemnation doesn't take place."

The meeting began. The Bolivian made an impassioned attack on the gringo imperialists. His next order of business was to introduce a tape recording made by Dessima Williams at her UN office in New York (where she did double duty as the Grenadian representative). She wanted a resolution condemning the United States. I objected; entering a motion via tape recording was without precedent. The Bolivian overruled my objection: "I am permitting it!" So we sat and listened to a twenty-five-minute diatribe.

The Bolivian said, "There is a motion before the chair. Do I hear a second?"

All eyes turned to Don Rafael. It seemed to be a foregone conclusion that this senior representative of a nation that had fought one big and two little wars against the big bully of the North would wholeheartedly join in condemnation.

He did not rise. He did not speak. Ten seconds passed; twenty; a minute. He did not speak. The Bolivian called out, "Is there a second?" Don Rafael said nothing. Finally, after perhaps three minutes, the Bolivian backed down: "There being no second, the motion is withdrawn."

I embraced Don Rafael; other delegates came over and did the same. I believe the delegates truly realized that our action in Grenada signaled a sea change, the turning of the tide of Soviet incursions into the Western Hemisphere. This is not my assessment, but that of a former Soviet general I met at a Heritage Foundation board meeting in Moscow in the early 1990s. The Soviets thought, he told me, that by expanding their military presence in Latin America, they had a shot at a soft underbelly of the United States, and they were surprised to find that Reagan had a stiff backbone. In the general's opinion, the action at Grenada was one pivotal point of the Cold War.

Two weeks after the invasion, the medical school had been reconstituted in temporary quarters in New Jersey and was back in Grenada three months later. Last time I checked, it was going strong, now enlarged into a university with enrollment above two thousand.

And—a bit of a surprise—Dessima Williams, archrival and constant OAS antagonist, asked me to support her request for emigration to the United States, which, as a diplomatic courtesy, I readily did. She is presently a distinguished assistant professor at Brandeis University, and we have spoken since.

Chapter 19

The European Community

After the 1984 election, Ronald Reagan asked George Shultz if he would stay on at State for the second term, and George said he would be pleased to do so. I heard a rumor that he wanted to swap out the left-over Haig team and put in his own; word on the street soon had it that one by one, Shultz had been thanking various appointees for their loyal and valiant services, which were no longer required. My turn came: George called, "Can you come over and see me?" Our meeting was a Sunday morning, at his home. After the pleasantries—I'm sure that mine must have seemed a bit strained—he said, "Well, Bill, you know I've been asked to stay on and I'm going to make some changes." Indeed. I put on my best good-soldier smile and made ready to deliver the little speech I'd already rehearsed in my mind: "Grateful for the opportunity to have served the president, ready to assist in any way in the future, thanks, etcetera."

George continued, "I'd like to ask you if you'd be our new ambassador to the European Community, in Brussels."

I was startled and mumbled something about how much I was enjoying my position at the OAS, working issues close to my heart, such as promoting privatization and working toward free market economies. I would have preferred to continue meeting those challenges in our own hemisphere, but George pushed: There were greater challenges, he implied, in an emerging coordinated Europe; new barriers to trade to overcome; changes in customs duties to be dealt with; quotas on imports to be considered; attitudes to overcome. "Let me give you an example," he said. "One of the things that I find difficult in relations with Europe, is the French approach to trade. A very restrictive, narrow view, focused only on what's in it for France. With your quiet, non-judgmental approach, you're the right man for the job, and you are needed."

I had learned a lesson when I took the Netherlands posting without consulting my family, and I wasn't about the make that mistake again: I told

George I would have to get back to him. Well, Isabelle was not thrilled but finally gave her OK, although she and the kids, all very much involved in their own lives, were not going to join me on this tour.

My orientation was nowhere near as thorough as that for the Netherlands—I guess I was considered "qualified"—but I was treated to a bit of history, which I share. The dream of a unified Europe began to take shape as a Pan-European Union in 1924, which was derailed in 1933 when Germany refused to play, but was revived after the war. Winston Churchill called for a "United States of Europe," to begin, he suggested, with a partnership between France and Germany, one of a number of proposals that led to the European Coal and Steel Community (ECSC, comprising six nations: Germany, France, Italy, Belgium, Luxembourg, and the Netherlands), joined in 1958 by a newly created European Economic Community (EEC) and Euratom (for atomic energy cooperation). These three bodies merged under the umbrella of the European Community, EC, in 1965, informally known as the "common market" and after 1993, reconstituted as the European Union.

As for the job, George was right. There were real challenges, not the least of which was trying to learn about, understand, and deal with what may have been the most complex political organization in the history of the world. By the time I arrived in Brussels, August 1985, the EC employed some 12,000 staffers; conducted business in nine languages; had major offices in Strasbourg, Brussels, and Luxembourg; was organized into twenty departments; and was run by a policy-recommending Commission reporting to a policy-approving Council of Ministers, which listened to, but did not necessarily accept, advice from a fully separate organization, the European Parliament at Strasbourg, made up of an improbable collection of Reds, Greens, Socialists, Christian Democrats, and members of the far-right National Front.

The EC had ten member states: Those of the ECSC had been joined by Ireland, Denmark, Greece, and the UK (membership of which had been blocked for ten years in a French power play). Spain and Portugal were being added in 1986. (George Shultz and I formally encouraged the EC to add Turkey. The EC declined.) The original ten had a combined population about fifty million greater than that of the United States but with a smaller gross national product. There indeed was some incentive—economics, pride, take your pick—to move the numbers.

Most of my first few months on the job were taken up with the basic tasks of an ambassador: exchanging pleasantries with other members of the diplomatic corps; hosting visiting dignitaries, members of Congress, diplomats, and trade groups; making courtesy visits to member countries (in my eighteen-month tour, I was able to visit eleven of the twelve, missing only Greece). I was able to squeeze in a few personal trips, including a visit to the ancestral Middendorf family farm in Germany, where I met with thirty distant relatives and slept in the four-hundred-year-old farmhouse in the same bed as did many of my ancestors. And I occupied some of my weekend time with music, for example composing "European Overture," and was most pleased when it was recorded by the Symphonic Band of the Belgian Guides.

However, my real job was to participate in hard-nosed negotiations largely over trade issues involving, on each side, hundreds of thousands of jobs. The EC was represented by Willie de Klerc; our team included the new U.S. trade representative, Clayton Yeutter, who had taken over from Bill Brock. I was on scene as a facilitator and coordinator; Yeutter was the hammer who would willingly fly over on a moment's notice to help wrestle our opponents to the ground in long and exhausting sessions.

During my tour, the more important issues included: agricultural subsidies and tariffs; suspicions that the Europeans were trying to overwhelm the U.S. market with cheap steel; EC distress because the United States was reluctant to share advanced technology; disputes over alleged covert subsidies provided by the U.S. government to the Boeing Aircraft Company and open government subsidies given to Airbus (the prime European manufacturer of passenger airliners); and the EC refusal to accept American beef that had been fed growth hormones.

Let me start with the one that almost drove my whole team crazy: agriculture. The EC's Common Agricultural Policy (CAP) was created to ensure a stable farm economy by providing subsidies and supports (especially but not exclusively, I was told, to some very wealthy farmers in France). The goal was to encourage production, in part a reaction to the hard times that followed World War II. The reality? As reported in *Time*, September 8, 1986, "Too Much of a Good Thing," production was encouraged so far beyond the capacity of the marketplace, at home or abroad, that 1.4 million tons of butter and 750,000 tons of beef were sitting unsold in refrigerated warehouses (at a cost of $63,000 an hour). The stockpiled beef seems not to have been properly stored; what would *you* do with three-quarters of a million tons of spoiled meat? Turn it into fertilizer, I suppose. I don't remember what they did do with it. And, what about the 300 million gallons of what the *New York Times* of December 27, 1986, in "Food Surplus May Bankrupt European Bloc," called "undrinkable rotgut" wine? The whole program was costing $25 billion a year.

However misguided (and/or mismanaged), the CAP had a large impact on our trade. One of the first issues I tackled involved canned fruit, where European subsidies resulted in an unrealistically low price for their goods in the international marketplace. This was not a huge problem in the grand scheme of things—except, of course, to the American canned fruit suppliers who suffered from the unfair competition. Yeutter and I reached an agreement with the EC, but the agreement fell through. We revisited, and they finally agreed to reduce the subsidies.

Of course, full disclosure, the United States had (and still has) a massive farm-subsidy program of its own, and the goal in any of these international negotiations is to level, or at least moderate with some degree of fairness, the playing field. Subsidies and tariff protections are exercised to protect indigenous producers in whatever industry, often subsidizing overproduction while hurting consumers.

There were other agricultural issues and a lot of tit-for-tat. For the sake of brevity (and your sanity) let me offer an oversimplified but nonetheless accurate summary. One issue had been festering for sixteen years, EC tariff preferences that favored citrus fruit from Mediterranean growers—a clear violation of rules established by the General Agreement on Tariffs and Trade (GATT), sort of a supreme court on international trade matters. GATT had ruled in our favor; the EC ignored the ruling. Therefore, three months after I assumed the post, the United States increased duties on heavily subsidized pasta from the EC (largely, Italy); the EC retaliated by raising duties on lemons, almonds, and walnuts coming in from the United States. These issues were resolved after about ten months; at the same time we worked out an agreement on steel imports. We agreed to quotas that would not seriously harm European manufacturers who had long counted on the U.S. market, while protecting our own steel companies. Then we learned that Italy was going to veto the fruit and nut pact, as inimical to Italian farmers. So steel was put on hold for a few months, until we received assurances that fruit and nuts would be given a fair standing in the marketplace.

In the meantime, we calculated that the entry of Spain and Portugal was going to cost U.S. farmers some $400 million in lost sales of such products as corn gluten feed, a huge market, among our largest. That market would be compromised by favorable tariffs given to these new members of the club, not to mention new competition from Spanish and Portuguese fruit and vegetable farmers whose products would eventually enter the EC duty-free.

We threatened to impose 200 percent duties on wine, cheese, and brandy (directed like an arrow at France, the most adamant defender of CAP). The EC soon enough came up with a package to compensate us for the $400 million—by lowering tariffs on perhaps ten non-farm industrial products. (How much would that help the U.S. growers of corn gluten feed? Not very much, but such is the illogic of international trade.)

A small irony: It was just about this time that France was required to pay more money into CAP than the benefits being received by French farmers *from* CAP. France began to rethink the overall concept. In fact, as I write this chapter—almost twenty-five years after my posting—I read that France now wants to get beneficiaries of the program to return the money.

On to the sharing of technology: The Europeans were upset because the United States had a close hold on emerging military technology; we would sell them fighter aircraft but not release the source codes for, say, the fire control system. There was some logic to that—we had to keep the latest developments out of the hands of the Soviets. But what about navigation systems or computer programs or telecommunications technology that had relevance in civilian, as well as military, applications? Such dual-use technology fell into a murky gray zone, and the Europeans feared that they would fall behind. Of course, our policies gave them a marvelous incentive to go forth and develop their own technologies. They set up a ten-year, one-billion-dollar-plus research program to help them stay competitive with the United States and Japan. It worked. We lost business.

The Airbus-Boeing dispute: Airbus—at the time, a consortium of aircraft manufacturers in England, France, and Germany—was supported by government subsidies, which brought charges of unfair competition from U.S. aerospace companies, notably, Boeing. Airbus charged that Boeing received subsidies in the form of Defense Department development funds, the results of which often had direct application in civilian airliners. We were unable to come to either an understanding or an agreement.

Hormones in beef: On recommendation of their veterinary committee, the EC blocked the sale of American beef from cattle that had been fed growth hormones. It didn't seem to matter that there were no residual growth hormones in the beef (the hormone feeding stopped well before the slaughter), and that no one could show any harm to anyone who ate the beef. Our beef sales to the EC, more than $70 million, dropped to zero—another issue that has never been settled.

A new British commissioner arrived just before I reported on board—Lord Caulfield—and I believe he was not too excited about his posting. I heard that he had somehow gotten himself cross-threaded with Prime Minister Thatcher, a lady who seems to have made a practice of rotating less-favored ministers out of her hair. To an Englishman, anything outside of

Whitehall was exile. Mrs. Thatcher might as well have sent Lord Caulfield to Abyssinia.

He and I spent many hours in cordial socializing, and it was clear to me that he was a good man, careful and thorough, but at loose ends. I sensed that he was looking for a project, something that would prove that he was not the odd-man-out in Mrs. Thatcher's circle; something to let her know that she had made a mistake. During one of our conversations, we fell into discussion of the general dysfunction of the EC. The goals of the organization, laid down in the 1957 Treaty of Rome, included the elimination of customs duties among members, creation of a common tariff and commercial policy toward outside nations, development of common agricultural and transport policies, and removing barriers to free movement of persons, services, and capital—but little progress had been made. Most attention was focused on wrangling over tariff and quotas.

Lord Caulfield asked my opinion of a plan that could bring the European Community together, meet those goals, develop a common currency, and become a common economic force, a bulwark against Communism. I could only say that plan would have to be a winner! He came up with a magnificent white paper, listing some 315 action items to be studied and approved as the foundation for a true single market. Over the next few years, as most were ratified by each member government, full credit went to Lord Caulfield. I don't think he was thereafter concerned about his standing with Mrs. Thatcher.

A grand irony: Here at the height of the Cold War we encouraged Caulfield to pursue a unified Europe, as a stalwart partner against the Soviets. Somewhere along the way Henry Kissinger had warned me not to count on a true "partnership" with an emerging Europe; their goals would not always be our goals. Well, Henry was right. The Cold War is long since ended, and while the "improved" Europe has remained a strong trading partner, it also has been a powerhouse economic competitor. The recent Greek collapse and the emerging economic problems of the Southern Tier are, however, providing a real challenge for the Alliance.

As with my posting to the Netherlands, I had to deal with threats from terrorists or anarchists or just plain criminals; it's sometimes hard to tell the difference. The most significant: Late one weekend night, when I was alone in my residence, a security guard notified me that "two men" had been seen lurking in the bushes on the nine-acre property. A team of policemen and dogs searched around, without result, and I was told to "keep the doors locked." I didn't need much prodding, but I would have liked to have a very aggressive dog of my own, standing guard. In any event, a few days later,

I learned that two men indeed had been sent from some Middle Eastern country with instructions to "kill an ambassador." They had traveled separately, each carrying half of a torn sheet of paper with the name of their intended victim—me. They would not know the identity until they put the two pieces together. I do believe I was targeted as a protest to U.S. support of Israel, but the amateurish plan—like something out of the adventures of the Hardy Boys teenage detective novels of my youth—would have been laughable if the intended result had not been so deadly.

But I moved on and came home in 1987. The EC/EU continued to grow, today at five hundred million people in twenty-seven nations (fifteen of which have adopted a common currency, the euro). Something less than one-twelfth of the world population generates an impressive 30 percent of the world gross domestic product. During my tour, I am proud to note, our team resolved almost all of the pressing trade disputes of the day. However, squabbling continues.

Chapter 20

The New Russia

I had been fighting threats against America's freedoms—especially from the Bolsheviks—through much of my adult life, and, whatever my modest contribution, I am delighted that toward the end of 1989 and thanks to the unflinching leadership of Ronald Reagan, we could claim victory! The Soviet Union began to unravel, and along with chairman Ed Feulner and some members of the Heritage Foundation board, I wanted to see with my own eyes the dismantling of that ultimate symbol of the issues that divided us from the Soviets, the Berlin Wall. Happily, upon arrival at the scene, we learned how we could help speed the process: An entrepreneurial Berliner was renting the use of a sledge hammer, $5 for a few whacks. With great personal satisfaction, we vigorously contributed to the cause.

At almost the same moment, Poland formed the first non-Communist government that was more or less still within the sphere of influence of the Soviet Bloc, and the hero/leader of the "solidarity" movement, Lech Walesa, began exploring relations with other nations. (He was honored to address a joint session of our Congress, one of the very few non–heads of state ever to do so.) During a lunch we threw for him at the Heritage Foundation, Jack Kemp and I made so bold as to suggest that he take Poland "cold turkey" into real-world free market economics.

His interpreter asked, "What is this 'cold turkey'?"

We explained: Free your markets from state control, abolish state-owned monopolies, privatize all government manufacturing and financial businesses, create an independent judiciary to protect private property rights and validate the sanctity of contracts, make all commercial transactions transparent, slash tax rates, and provide for the full repatriation of dividends—all at once. If you do it piecemeal, I suggested, those folks who enjoyed special privileges under the Communists would find plenty of opportunities to preserve their advantages and defeat the purpose.

It must have seemed a bit overwhelming, but, I added, "By doing all this, Poland would attract massive amounts of foreign direct investment and could become one of the fastest-growing countries in the world." By the time he became president of Poland about a year later, something close to "cold turkey" was the name of the game. To what result? As foreign direct investment increased in Poland from $89 million in 1990 to $4.5 billion in 1996, Poland's gross domestic product grew from $59 billion to $134 billion.

Not too long after the fall of the Wall, our Heritage group made our first trip to Moscow. We stayed at the hotel Octobraskaya, dubbed thus in honor of the October Revolution of 1917. It was upscale and cheap; all of the extras were included in a government-subsidized fee, including a copious buffet with unlimited caviar—and unlimited vodka. The top Communists lived well.

How can I ever forget one dinner meeting, with a group of former Soviet (now Russian and aging) generals? Awash in the free vodka—I lost count at nine—they dropped all diplomatic pretenses and turned boastful. Most notable was one, first for his appearance, not to be believed had he been portrayed in a movie or a comic strip. Medals and ribbons in gay profusion, pinned to his left shoulder, chest, and upper stomach in sufficient numbers to provoke a permanent list to port. He was notable, too, for his role as one of the officers in charge of crushing the Czech uprising, the "Prague Spring."

"Crushing" was not my term, but his. Early in 1968, the Czechs began maneuvering for freedom from Moscow, led by a Communist functionary-turned-patriot, Alexander Dubcek. Dubcek sought, in his own words, "Socialism with a human face" to reassure Moscow that he and his government were good Communists, just working to clean up some internal problems. Moscow was not convinced, nor amused, and had dispatched my dinner companion to take care of the problem.

"First," he said, "We had to get Dubcek out of town." The tanks were standing by, ready to move in. But—how to move him out in some non-confrontational (as in, don't kill him) effort? Offer him an honorary degree from a distant university, or an invitation to an important meeting, even a bribe? The Soviets managed to get him out of the way on some pretext of which I am not cognizant.

And then . . . "And then we *rolled*! We crushed them. We *crushed* them." This was a line punctuated by an upward thrust of his right fist, leaving no doubt as to his meaning. His friends burst into applause. This had been his shining moment, the high point of a career perhaps floundering in stagnation.

A few vodkas later—a few, or many, memory fails—another general launched into the subject of Grenada. "We really had plans for that island," he said. Cuba was off-limits; they couldn't bring in any more Soviet assets. Too many people were watching, but Grenada, they thought, was off the radar. "We could hardly wait for the new airport," he said. "We had high hopes, except for that s—, Reagan."

I said, "I guess you'd have to call him a 'victorious s—.'"

"Big s—!"

"Yeah," said I, "but he's *our* big s—!"

Cheerful repartee except, at one point, these guys really wanted to kill us.

This dinner was during one of half a dozen trips I made into the former Soviet Union. I had pretty free rein, sponsored by a reformist, Deputy Premier Vladimir Shumeyko (whose confidence I gained when I offered him space and staff support for his U.S. coordination efforts in my personal offices in D.C.). I journeyed through much of the country, looking for signs of economic life; I didn't find any. The Soviet Union, it seems, had been a hollow giant, with the economic sins of Communism aggravated by a budget that devoted the bulk of GNP to building and maintaining military forces. When the country went bankrupt, industries collapsed, and millions of people were thrown out of work.

In the industrial heartland, I visited shipyards filled with rusting hulks and huge monster factories now cold, dark, and dismal. Those workers who still had jobs were sitting around with nothing to do, and I was reminded of an old anti-Soviet joke: "We pretend to work and they pretend to pay us." Once, I did spot a lathe operator working at some task way down at the end of one cavernous building. A few coworkers seemed to be watching but not participating—a handful of men being paid to watch another at work.

I visited a truck factory and got a firsthand look at the worst sort of Soviet production planning. The chassis were made at one place; the wheels, cabin, and engines came from factories each one thousand miles away—and maybe one thousand miles away from each other. In the United Sates, with an efficient transportation infrastructure to move the parts from one plant to the next, this is called spreading the wealth, ensuring jobs in more than one state (and therefore greater support in Congress). In the Soviet Union, it was called paranoia. Stalin, always on guard against revolution, scattered the elements of production. Thus, in theory, it would be difficult for a revolutionary group to seize control of one or another vital industry. In practice, all industries functioned as wards of the state, too inefficient to ever turn a profit.

Our Heritage group—which included Shelby Davis, Bob Krieble, Kim Holmes, Ed Feulner, and several others—saw fertile ground upon which to plant free market seeds, which we discussed with government officials. We explained the formula for success, what had worked elsewhere. Ah yes, they said, and I do believe that our listeners understood.

On one visit our friends asked, could we help them as they developed a proposed constitution for the new Russian Republic? This was a challenge eagerly grasped, and Heritage coordinated a draft, which among other radical Anglo-Saxon ideas called for the sanctity of contracts and the protection of private property. When we presented the draft on our next visit to Moscow, one official questioned the inclusion of that right to "private property," a foreign concept throughout the seventy-plus-year life of the Soviet Union. He wondered, if this was so important, why was it not included in the U.S. Constitution?

A fair question. It could be argued—and argue, we did—that the concept of private property was so well developed in English common law, which we inherited, that it did not need to be codified. As backup, we trotted out the Bill of Rights, which put "property" in a defensible framework; in the Fourth Amendment, "persons, houses, papers, and effects" were secure against unreasonable searches and seizures; by the Fifth Amendment, no person may "be deprived of life, liberty, or property, without due process of law; nor shall private property be taken for public use, without just compensation."

We won the argument with those officials, but not the vote in the Russian parliament, the Duma.

Some months later, I was in the balcony along with my Heritage comrades when the Duma considered the "private property" clause in the proposed constitution. Considered, yes, but barely, and it was defeated. The Russian parliament was like much of the rest of Russia: The labels had changed, but not the players. At that point, there was still a large block of Communists in the Duma and the private property clause might keep some from stealing everything in sight as they moved to privatize the oil companies and other major industries. Many of the Communists moved from being powerful but poor, to being powerful and rich. Some of those oligarchs are billionaires today.

After the defeat, the more sympathetic members of the Duma presented me with a marked-up copy of the draft. There was a lot of pencil scratching to indicate editorial emendation, but the essence remained as we had proposed. I was as honored as if I had been given a draft of the Magna Carta.

Our basic efforts continued. I was guest of honor at a dinner Shumeyko gave at the same Moscow hotel—Octobraskaya, of our first visit—now renamed The President to reflect the more or less democratic shift in political attitudes, and brought under the umbrella of a "free market" (to the extent, at least, that the vodka now was sold by the drink). The dinner was packed with power including the minister of agriculture (whose name—apologies!—I have forgotten) and the head of the Central Bank, Viktor Gerashenko.

Geraschenko was skeptical of my proposition, that a high priority should be attracting foreign direct investment to bring new technology, management skills, capital, and to develop export markets. He admitted to the need for a great infusion of capital, but was un-persuaded about the tactic. I argued that to attract foreign capital, Russia must establish a basis for reasonable taxation (low, and flat) and make a clear declaration affirming the rights of private property and the sanctity of contracts, all to be strengthened by an independent court system that enforced both.

Do these things, I emphasized, and after some seventy-three years of Communist misrule and with an enormous pent-up demand for everything, all else would quickly flow. Success. Employment. New markets.

Geraschenko, who was seated to my right, insisted that Russia had to move slowly, even on a reform as basic as privatization of farmland. This provoked a heated debate from the reform-minded minister of agriculture, seated on my left. As the man in the middle, I suggested that privatization should be "cold turkey," across the board, the same argument that we had used with Lech Walesa at our Heritage meeting. I argued that some 44,000 state-owned businesses—dubbed, by economists, "parastatals"—should be shifted from making useless things like tanks and submarines to meeting consumer needs—or shut down. Naturally, the central banker Gerashenko took a cautious view, but in the end I think he was beginning to soften.

Shumeyko was supportive throughout. He said that our earlier Heritage trips had been helpful by urging many of the free market reforms now taking place. However, he noted, if they eventually succeeded, he, of course, would take the credit. If they failed? He knew where to place the blame; he pointed a friendly finger at me, and smiled.

As I had in my work with Latin America, I continued to press for free market reforms, and as with my efforts in the Netherlands, to look for joint business opportunities. I helped set up and became chairman of a Russian-American business council. We easily signed up many leading American businesses to whom investment seemed like a good idea, and why not? Russia had by then declared itself open to foreign direct capital, and our members had checkbooks at the ready. Except . . .

Except for the corruption, the blackmail, the not-so-veiled threats of harm to local facilities and employees unless "protection" was purchased from some willing vendor—it was like the nineteenth-century Wild West (or like some mob-controlled industries in twentieth-century America). Promised contracts evaporated unless under-the-table payments were forthcoming; this was not a practical move for our member companies. They were subject to the U.S. Foreign Corrupt Practices Act, which provides draconian remedies against individuals who offer bribes, however defined. And, even when contracts were solid and legal, other problems arose. One of our drug company members sold $150 million worth of product to the Russian Ministry of Health for distribution to hospitals, nationwide. A thoroughly above-board transaction, except the bill was never paid. Upon frequent inquiry, the response was always, "You're on the list . . ."

The Russian-American business council staggered along for about five years, until our members grew tired of trying to deal with the corrupt Russian bureaucracy. Oh, Russia seemed to prosper for a while, aided by massive loans, when the economy had nowhere to go but up. However, without a firm free market foundation, any attempt at economic restructuring was doomed to fail. If only Russia had early on followed the lead of Poland—not to mention Chile and the Czech Republic, countries that exchanged state-controlled economies for the unseen hand of the marketplace—it would have attracted the one thing developing economies need most: substantial foreign direct investment. Instead, Russia got loans the oligarchs could (and did) convert into Swiss bank accounts.

There has been some improvement. The concept of private property has now been written into law, a flat tax instituted, and the economy has been growing. However, Russia is too heavily dependent on commodity exports, especially petroleum products. The country is seeking to diversify.

Maybe.

Chapter 21

Economic Freedom and Justice

B ack in 1985, as I was leaving OAS and headed for Brussels, President Reagan asked me to head a task force for an initiative called "Project Economic Justice." This major study was launched at the suggestion of Norman Kurland, president of the Center for Economic and Social Justice in Arlington, Virginia, and was funded by donations, not the taxpayers. "Task force" was an operative term: As chairman, I was nominally in charge but most of the work was done by a team of experts: businessmen, labor leaders, economists, lawyers, and at least one religious scholar.

We wanted to confront, head on, a key element that was keeping the Latin American nations from realizing their true potential (or, any potential at all): government regulation of the economy and state ownership of many major industries—typically, heavily subsidized non-competitive failures that were a constant drain on resources. We encouraged free and open markets, expansion of private property, and reduction of government ownership. As Adam Smith wrote in *The Wealth of Nations,* 1776, "Basic institutions that protect the liberty of individuals to pursue their own economic interests result in greater prosperity for the larger society." It wasn't even a new idea in 1776. Ibn Khalduun, a fourteenth-century Arab jurist and historian, wrote in *Muqaddimah: An Introduction to History*: "When incentive to acquire and obtain property is gone, people no longer make efforts to acquire any." Or, to take care of anyone else's. Larry Summers put it in contemporary terms: "In the entire history of mankind, no one ever washed a rental car." And, as Norm Kurland put it, "To paraphrase Karl Marx, you could sum up the entire philosophy of Communism in a single sentence: Abolish private property."

Some nations knew that state ownership was a recipe for disaster, but when the more enlightened governments moved toward privatization of industry, they too often were blocked by the workers' organizations that feared losing jobs. We strongly recommended Employee Stock Ownership Plans (ESOPs) as a vehicle to put ownership in the hands of the workers—whether in state-owned or private business. We found many examples of struggling companies around the world that became successful when turned over to employee ownership, including some that had been government owned (such as Britain's largest trucking firm, the National Freight Corporation). Here in the United States, you probably do business with an employee-owned company every day—especially if you buy groceries from Publix, Food Giant, or Hy-Vee, or do business with the 14 percent of companies on the 2009 Fortune Magazine "Top 100" list that are more than 50 percent employee owned. When you give the workers a stake in the future, they are motivated to ensure that there will be a future, and a profitable one to boot. Avis Rent-a-Car set up an ESOP in 1987. Profits for the first half of 1988 were 35 percent higher than those of the same period a year earlier; market share increased to 27 percent, and customer complaints were down 35 percent. (I should note, the employees were bought out when the company sold itself to a single investor in 1996.)

We presented our report, "High Road to Economic Justice," to Reagan in August 1987. In commending the task force effort, the president reminded us all that "I've long believed one of the mainsprings of our own liberty has been the widespread ownership of property among our people and the expectation that anyone's child, even from the humblest of families, could grow up to own a business or corporation." Reagan also offered a kind personal comment: "Scientists say a perpetual-motion machine is impossible. Well, considering that this task force completed its work without any appropriation from Congress, I think we ought to introduce Bill Middendorf to a few scientists."

At about this same time—an example of "government knows best"—Mexico had more than one thousand state-owned businesses, including some of the largest industries in the nation, most of which were unprofitable and struggling to survive. As a corollary to my work at the OAS and on Project Economic Justice, I helped establish and served as the first president of the Mexican-American Free Trade Association, which was one initiative leading to the North American Free Trade Act (NAFTA). Today, I am pleased to note, partly because of the influence of Project Economic Justice and the very positive impact of NAFTA, the number of Mexican state-owned businesses has been reduced by 75 percent and the economy is among the top fifteen or so in the world.

I also served on the Inter-American Foundation, where we pioneered small loans (dubbed "micro loans" by economists), often less than $100, used to set up small home businesses or village cooperatives in Latin America. The payback rate has always run around 99 percent. The concept had been developed some ten years earlier by Bangladeshi economist Muhammad Yunus (who was to receive the 2006 Nobel Peace Prize for this work).

A personal note: Isabelle and I decided to step in and directly help one small "employee-owned" industry get a leg up, and contributed $5,000 to a group of cheese-making families with a factory high in the Bolivian Andes, whom I had met on one of my OAS travels. Well, the women made the cheese, and the role of the men was to take it down to market in La Paz (where, it was rumored, too many of them drank up too much of the profits, until the women started riding shotgun). Because of rampant inflation, by the time our contribution had worked through the bureaucracy and into the hands of the women, it had become the equivalent of $50,000. This was truly a boon, because the cost of running the cheese factory had not much been affected by inflation, and the surplus was turned to road building and bridge repair—undertaken by a local labor force whose wages also had not ballooned. Better roads equaled more trips to market, which equaled greater sales.

I was invited to a ceremony, to thank us for the gift. Imagine the scene: a village square in brilliant sunshine and filled with several hundred people. A small table in the center of the crowd, upon which sat one bottle of Coca-Cola—a token reward for the honored guest. I think every child in the village was clustered around, longingly eyeing the Coke. I was almost too embarrassed to drink it, but I had been warned by an official that the women had gone to some effort to get that bottle (which was very expensive), and to not accept it would be a huge insult. I drank, slowly, to show my appreciation and to great applause, after which the women launched into almost an hour of dancing—at an elevation of ten thousand feet, wearing heavy clothing, under a hot sun. I was induced to join them and, unaccustomed to the altitude and overwhelmed by the heat, I was barely able to hang on until the dance was over.

Overall, it was one of the most rewarding experiences of my life.

Project Economic Justice worked with two giants of Latin American economic thought: Guatamalan educator Manuel Ayau, and Peruvian economist Hernando deSoto (author of the seminal books *Another Path* and *The Mystery of Capital*, must-reads for anyone interested in the field). DeSoto tried to set up a legal garment-making firm in Peru without bribing any officials. It took a team of four people (one of whom was a lawyer) ten months, working full time and dealing with eleven government agencies, just to complete the paperwork. When one member of the team tried the same new-business-creation experiment in Tampa, Florida, it took three and a half hours.

This—and a number of similar examples—got me to thinking: Since the difference between Peru and Tampa was easily measured (and so instructive), might not there be a method to compare all nations as well? Not just in the ease of starting a business, but in a range of activities? And would not this information be of great value to someone looking for a place to invest— or to avoid?

To my colleagues at the Heritage Foundation, I proposed what I called the "Index of Economic Freedom." We should measure every country on such vital factors as an absolute right to own property and a fully realized freedom of movement for labor, capital, and goods, protected by an independent judiciary; we should give each category a score and each country a ranking. Heritage took the idea and turned it into a masterful program. The first Index, covering 101 countries, was published in 1995. Today, administered by the Heritage Foundation and the Wall Street Journal, the index scores 183 countries in ten specific areas:

1. Business Freedom
2 Trade Freedom
3. Monetary Freedom
4. Government Size
5. Fiscal Freedom
6. Property Rights
7. Investment Freedom
8. Financial Freedom
9. Freedom from Corruption
10. Labor Freedom

The top ten rankings for 2009, in order: Hong Kong, Singapore, Australia, Ireland, New Zealand, United States, Canada, Denmark, Switzerland, and the United Kingdom. Eleven points separate the top. Hong Kong scored at 90.0, and the UK at 79.0. At the other end of the scale, Cuba is at 27.9, Zimbabwe at 22.7, and North Korea at rock bottom with 2.0.

Any award for "most improved" country in the fifteen-year history (1995 through 2009) of the Index would go to Azerbaijan, up 28 points, accompanied by measurable improvements in the standard of living. Over time, 200,000 citizens learned to read and write, three-quarters of a million gained access to clean water, more than two million escaped malnutrition and were getting enough to eat. The worst performance: Zimbabwe, which fell more than 25 points. In 2008 the government issued a note for one hundred trillion Zimbabwean dollars, worth, I suspect, a loaf of bread. The most telling proof that economic freedom works: The average gross domestic product per capita, a measure of standard of living in the seven countries at the top of the list, is $40,253, ten times as high as the seven at the bottom.

Why isn't the United States at the top of the rankings? Well, we do offer great freedom to conduct business, for example, under a strong regulatory environment, and in the "Business Freedom" category we score 91.9. However, the measures of fiscal freedom (burdensome tax rates) and government size (expenditures as a percent of GDP) are both below the world leaders and drag the United States down to number six.

The Index is widely used across the world; as a tool it helps the United States, the World Bank, and the International Monetary Fund (IMF) determine how best to apportion economic assistance to developing nations in Africa, Asia, the Caribbean and Latin America, and countries of the former Soviet Empire. Many countries have contacted Heritage, seeking guidance. "How can we improve our rating?" Implementation may be hard, but the answers are easy—and by now, having read through this memoir, you could probably provide them yourself: Reduce taxes, protect private property with an independent judiciary, do everything in the open for all the world to see, and thus encourage foreign direct investment.

I know I've hit on this topic so many times, but I can't emphasize enough that foreign direct investment should be the most sought-after commodity in the world. Why? It brings desperately needed capital resources and the technological and management skills needed to leapfrog years of bureaucratic backwardness. It creates export markets back into the countries in which the investments originated. After Chile, the Czech Republic, and Poland adopted free market practices, they attracted billions in foreign direct investment. From 1990 to 1996, Chile and the Czech Republic attracted more than $10 billion each, and Poland received more than $12.8 billion.

The United States, I might add, is proof of the concept: With our well-protected property rights and a strong currency, we've been the beneficiary of one of the highest rates of foreign direct investment of any country in the world. It's sort of a mixed blessing, because the flow of so much foreign money into our coffers for so many years allowed us to live beyond our means. We have at the same time been leveraging the future with massive amounts of additional debt, some held by foreign investors but most by our own citizens. Excess leverage leads to bubbles, and bubbles eventually burst. (Famously, the Dutch tulip bubble in the seventeenth century, the South Sea bubble of the eighteenth century, and our own Dot Com bubble of 2000, where technology stocks were selling at 150 times earnings and Silicon Valley became a—temporary—wasteland.) Our latest bubble, fueled by sub-prime mortgages, burst in 2008–2009. Recovery will be prolonged while banks desperately try to replenish lost assets.

In the spring of 2010, I gave a dinner in Washington to recognize this year's winners of the Index, along with those countries, some still on the poor side, who had shown the most improvement in the past year. We honored ten ambassadors and two foreign ministers. Bob Mundell (winner of the 1999 Nobel Prize in Economics and "father" of the euro) added his praise for these economic heroes.

Coda

My days as a formal diplomat came to a close, but not my participation in world or military affairs—I'm still on a mission. For twelve years I was co-treasurer (with Lord Jeffry Rippon) of the International Democrat Union (IDU) started by Thatcher and Reagan, with members in Europe, Asia, Canada, Latin America, and including foreign ministers and heads of state. We promoted the idea of democracy across the world. In 1984, along with Fred Biebel, Frank Farenkopf, and Dick Allen, I participated in the founding of the International Republican Institute (IRI) that, today chaired by John McCain and with Lorne Craner as president, is working with the similar National Democratic Institute (NDI) to develop democratic institutions in fifty countries. I helped establish the Center for Advanced Research at the Naval War College and put up an annual, personal award for the student contributing the most to the goals of the Center. I also endowed a Naval History Research Chair at the Naval Historical Foundation.

I kept my hand in the world of business and public activities, serving as chairman of two banks, and for more than thirty years I have chaired both the Defense Forum Foundation (as noted earlier) and the Committee for Monetary Research and Economics (CMRE). I've not had much to do with Wall Street, which is just as well, I think. It seems to have lost the human touch. In my day, our job was to serve our clients, research opportunities, make recommendations to buy or sell this or that security. It was careful, painstaking, labor intensive—until the Wall Street boys brought in computers to run the numbers, to quantify everything (they even developed what they call a "Quant" theory). They determine cost/benefit ratios and measure risk, all within a matter of seconds. Today, many Wall Streeters don't even bother with clients but are traders, moving stuff around for their own account, putting together, for example, blocks of sub-prime mortgage-backed securities (unaccountably given AAA ratings) to sell to Italian or

Chinese pension funds. For this, they are richly rewarded. Many of these transactions have turned out to be worthless.

As a trustee of the Heritage Foundation, I continue to be involved in worthwhile and interesting projects. One memorable day in 1993, Heritage president Ed Feulner organized a board meeting with Vaclav Havel in Prague on the day he was sworn in as president of the Czech Republic. Here was a truly amazing fellow: He shunned American-style celebration and braggadocio to meet with us and, later that evening, Howard Phillips and I were walking down a street of beautiful old Prague, past a row of austere cafes showing the wounds of the Communist past, bare light bulbs hanging down from the ceiling, and in one of them was the president—discussing literature and poetry with three or four friends. This great man never lost his common touch.

Over the years, I have learned a few political lessons of my own. Let me touch on a few, beginning with Barry Goldwater's guiding rule: If you want to run for office, arrange your financing well before you announce your candidacy. I certainly agree; too many times, I've seen wannabes announce against patronage-laden incumbents with not much more in their favor than an attractive family. They have an oversized ego and—too late—find that they must spend most of their campaign time in suburban living rooms pleading for funds. They go up against entrenched incumbents, where the incumbent reelection rate is above 90 percent. Incumbents are well supported by lobbyists representing industry or labor (something like 23,000 are currently registered in D.C.) who know how to stick with winners. Especially "winners" who have risen to positions of power and authority (particularly committee and subcommittee chairs) where they have significant influence on the fortunes of the lobbyists. There is a pattern here, and a strong argument for term limits. I thank God for the wannabes, but let us hope they can learn to play the game before the game is lost.

Should you make it into elective office—or score a significant government appointment—don't spend your time trying to make a grand impression on the world outside your office door, pontificating or holding gratuitous press conferences. Spend your time working to ensure the success of things that will be important in, say, ten years. Don't try to upstage your boss or anyone else in leadership, and, if you want to accomplish anything, never go around a key player in the legislative process, such as the chairman of a committee.

Do your job, and if you deserve some credit for your accomplishments, let other people point that out. Like most games, politics (and for that matter, almost any job) is a team effort, something too easily forgotten in the heat of the moment. If your team does well, you may win the election—or solve a problem or create a life-saving program, in which case you may be given some token of appreciation, perhaps a medal bestowed by a grateful government or an engrossed certificate suitable for framing. You may be justifiably proud, but don't get caught up in the fantasy that these tokens come to you because you're such a wonderful person. They are more often symbolic representations of the work of your team. I have thus been honored, as noted earlier, with almost a dozen honorary degrees and foreign decorations and another half dozen awards from state and defense, but I know what most of these really mean: that my team's efforts were considered important or successful or both. Choose *your* team members wisely and reward them handsomely, especially with well-deserved praise. It may well be more important to them than money (although a promotion would also be nice).

May I offer another bit of advice? Great ideas will always present themselves to those who are skillful enough to notice, understand, and take action . . . but they may come disguised (and be improperly derided) as "bumper-sticker wisdom." For example:

- The Sage of Baltimore (and America's prototypical cynic), H. L. Mencken, said, "Every election is a sort of advance auction of stolen goods."
- In Washington, a friendship might last at least through lunch; make an enemy and the relationship will last forever.
- The most intolerant politicians are those who congratulate themselves on being open-minded.
- Assume that the one-hundred-year-flood will come every ten years.
- To paraphrase the Cheshire Cat in Lewis Carroll's *Alice in Wonderland*: "If you don't know where you want to go, it doesn't matter which path you take."
- And—a line from a 1960s newspaper ad for a men's clothing store— "You never get a second chance to make a first impression."

This last item is brilliant. Now, whether or not it was fully original with the copywriter I have no idea, but it is at least an accidental restatement of something Samuel Johnson wrote in *The Rambler* No. 166, October 19, 1751, which is just as cogent although not as succinct: "Few have strength of reason to overrule the perceptions of sense, and yet fewer have curiosity or benevolence to struggle long against the first impression: he who therefore fails to please in his salutation and address is at once rejected, and never obtains an opportunity of showing his latest excellences or essential qualities."

America's chief foreign adversary, the Soviet Union, is gone, but Bolshevik ghosts still animate much discourse. I don't suppose the term should apply to the Chinese Communists, but as a practical matter, I don't see a dime's worth of difference. As noted earlier, China has embarked on a naval building spree—submarines able to launch nuclear-armed intercontinental ballistic missiles, a new shore-launched antiship missile with a range of one thousand miles, an aircraft carrier on the drawing board, increasingly sophisticated cyber warfare (each day we see thousands of "attacks" on Defense Department computer systems), and electromagnetic pulse (EMP) capabilities—and clearly seems focused on projecting military power and political influence well beyond its traditional areas of interest. Add the bellicose North Korea (a nuclear power) and Iran (which wants to join that club), along with the possibility of nuclear proliferation spreading among al Qaeda, the Taliban, and freelance terrorists. Add regional disasters visited upon their own people by ignorant tyrants, and we have a world where people are far from safe.

Some people argue that enlightened diplomacy will always trump military confrontation. This may—or may not—be true; I believe that history tells us otherwise and when the Great Nightfall comes, if it ever does, it will likely be a big surprise. Those men and women who have been given the responsibility to protect America must prepare to handle the "capabilities" of potential adversaries and not be led astray by arguments about "intentions." Intentions can change overnight.

But we don't have to focus on people who might want to kill us, just on people who with their vast oil and gas reserves might be happy to control us. Russia and the states of the Persian Gulf sit on two-thirds of the world's proven oil reserves and about 70 percent of the natural gas. Even the most casual strategist—on their side, or ours—could devise a plan whereby, in concert, Russia and Iran could gain control of all that oil and gas. If Iran succeeds in developing a nuclear weapon and forms a nuclear axis with Russia, how long could the oil-rich states of Saudi Arabia and the Emirates remain free? Would we go to war to save the Saudis and protect our access to the region's oil?

If not contested, where would a Russian–Iranian energy monopoly leave the United States (not to mention our allies and the rest of the world)? A United States, I must point out, that restricts drilling and exploration for oil in our own territory because of the assumed impact on the environment. We are so energy dependent that if we lose access to even the one-third portion of our imported oil that comes from Russia, the Middle East, and Venezuela (now being drawn into the Russian orbit), we will see a chaotic rise in energy prices, runaway inflation, and won't be much worried about the environment. Oh, some pundits might argue that we will just increase our reliance on wind and solar energy. When and at what cost? In my judgment, it will be twenty or thirty years before development of those alternatives will reach an economically rational level and have any impact on reducing our dependence on oil or natural gas—and I doubt that we will ever see battery-powered airplanes or ships.

A footnote, of sorts. In 1969 I was co-founder of the first mutual fund to invest in alternative sources of energy such as wind, solar, and wave action. The Oceanographic Fund prospered for a year or so, then faltered as the companies invested in those programs could not make them profitable. I lost a lot of money. Four decades later, has anything changed? As Cicero said to Atticus, "It is the right given to any man to err, but to no one unless he is a fool to persist in." However, lest you think I am an environmental Luddite, opposed to progress, I should note that, today, I frequently drive my 1896 Roberts Electric Car (to my knowledge, mine is the oldest electric car in the world). It can go forty miles on a charge. My car was featured at the December 2010 Boston Auto Show parked next to the brand-new Chevy Volt, "Car of the Year." The Volt also can go about forty miles before the battery has to be recharged. The issues I note are issues of the next few years, and unless we prepare to deal with them, what "might" happen in twenty or thirty years will be moot.

Even more important, perhaps, is the wedge that Russian-Iranian energy domination would drive between us and our allies, who are vastly more dependent on imported oil and natural gas than are we. All of them have greatly diminished military capabilities and would likely be forced into uncomfortable agreements and accommodations with Russia, Iran, and their allies.

Eternal vigilance, as wise men have noted, is the price of liberty. But vigilance just means watching, being aware. Unless you are ready to act on what you learn or when you must, you lose. Our nation's security must come before all else. I fear subtle disarmament—one ship, one division, one squadron at a time—pushed by politicians who believe that they can talk everything out and, oh, by the way, just now need the money for something else. Politicians who forget, or have never learned, just how long it takes to build a ship or to develop a state-of-the-art aircraft or missile, or to recruit, train, and equip a division of combat-ready soldiers in today's high-tech military world.

Over the last 150 years or so, the United States moved from an agricultural economy to a manufacturing economy, and today we are immersed in a communications revolution that, on the one hand, spreads knowledge across the developing world—a wonderful thing—while reducing the need for much unskilled labor in our own world. At the same time, much of our manufacturing has been lost to other nations so that, more and more, we are moving toward a service economy. Soon, there may not be enough jobs in America to keep everyone employed in just taking care of each other.

We long assumed that our technological leadership would always keep us out in front of the rest of the world . . . until much of the rest of the world, especially Japan, Korea, and China, learned the secrets of reverse engineering. They bought our goods, studied our goods, copied our goods, and improved on our goods. Now we buy "our goods" from them. And China is kind enough to lend us the money to do so.

And . . . just at this point in our nation's history, we can't seem to agree on much of anything economic. I need mention only the controversies over tax rates. I submit: High rates drive a lot of choices. Ronald Reagan the actor only made one movie a year, because his fee took him into the 91 percent bracket and it seemed pointless to put in the effort for another movie for, basically, no compensation.

If taxes are too high, a person might choose to invest in tax-free municipal bonds that create not much of anything, rather than taking a risk at setting up a new job-creating company. A person might move their business, or some part of it, to a no- or low-income-tax state. (It should not come as a surprise to learn that high-tax California is losing jobs to low-tax Texas, which, last year, by the way, created nearly half of all new jobs in America.) Or, a person might move their operations to another country altogether.

JFK, Reagan, Bill Clinton—each cut tax rates and saw revenues rise. More people had more money to spend, and they spent it on whatever they liked. The companies that made "whatever they liked" hired more people to keep up with demand, thus more people had jobs and money to spend. I am astounded that, today, a running argument continues that we should raise rates "because we need the money."

We already seem to have over mortgaged the future; let's not also just give it away.

An Epilogue of Sorts:
Thoughts on Reaching Eighty-Six

The path through life is a checklist of things you don't have to do again. Life is all about seeking equilibrium, the rarest of human conditions; we are always a little off balance. It's about moving forward without going over the cliff, finding success without losing our way, smelling the roses without getting stung by the bees. As Prescott Bush told me, when I was about to be confirmed to the post in the Netherlands: "It's not important how many friends you make when you're in the job, any important job—you'll have lots of them. What's important: How many of them you have after you leave."

I've learned that the dreams I've spent so much energy chasing are worth less than what I had at the beginning but tossed aside. I can stop running after shadows and be happy with what I've got—at long last, to discover happiness in things that so many others take for granted, like a loving (and loved) family, one or two good friends, and a simple sunset.

Sadly, these insights only arrive about the time the old joints give out.

Notes

Chapter 1. Down to the Sea, in a Ship

1. "Pacific Fleet Confidential Letter 14CL-45," declassified and reprinted in the United States Naval Institute *Proceedings* (January 1956).

Chapter 3. Presidential Politics: Goldwater, the Draft

1. F. Clifton White with William Gill, *Suite 3505: The Story of the Draft Goldwater Movement* (Ashland, OH: The Ashbrook Press, 1967), 121.
2. *New York Times*, April 15, 1963.
3. Personal conversation with the author.
4. Cited in White, *Suite 3505*, 146.
5. Robert D. Novak, *The Agony of the G.O.P. 1964* (New York: Macmillan, 1965), 197.
6. Ibid., 208–209.
7. White, *Suite 3505*, 160.
8. Ben Bradlee, *Conversations with Kennedy* (New York: Norton, 1975).
9. Fred J. Cook, *Barry Goldwater: Extremist of the Right* (New York: Grove Press, 1964), 161.
10. Barry M. Goldwater with Jack Casserly, *Goldwater* (Garden City, NY: Doubleday, 1988), 151.
11. Ibid., 154.
12. *New York Times*, January 4, 1964.

Chapter 4. Presidential Politics: Goldwater, the Nomination

1. Theodore White, *Making of the President 1964* (New York: Atheneum, 1965), 103.
2. White, *Suite 3505*, 268.
3. Lee Edwards, *Goldwater: The Man Who Made a Revolution* (Washington, D.C.: Regnery, 1995), 207.
4. *Time*, March 20, 1964.
5. Copy in file.
6. "Editor's Notebook," *Detroit Free Press*, June 21, 1964.
7. *Time*, July 17, 1964.

Chapter 5. Presidential Politics: Goldwater, the Convention

1. White, *Making of the President*, 200.
2. Ibid., 201.
3. Ibid., 201.
4. Ibid., 201.

Chapter 6. Presidential Politics: Goldwater, the Campaign

1. *Newsweek,* July 27, 1964.
2. Memo, Jack Valenti to Lyndon Johnson, cited in Jonathan M. Schoenwald, *A Time for Choosing: The Rise of Modern American Conservatism* (New York: Oxford University Press, 2001), 154.
3. Goldwater, *Goldwater,* 201, 204.
4. Edwards, *Goldwater,* 340.

Chapter 7. Presidential Politics: Nixon

1. Undated clip in file.
2. Undated clip in file.

Chapter 8. Ambassador: Netherlands, One

1. All State Department instructions and embassy guidance from author's personal files.

Chapter 9. Ambassador: Netherlands, Two

1. *The Letters of John and Abigail Adams,* ed. Frank Shuffelton (New York: Penguin, 2004), 393.

Chapter 15. The Business of Banking

1. Copy of press release in personal files.
2. Copy of filing in personal files.
3. Copy of resignation letter in personal files.

Chapter 16. CIA and OAS: Politics, Economics, Minutiae

1. Staff memos in personal files.

Chapter 17. Organization of American States: Nicaragua and El Salvador

1. Quoted by Ronald Reagan, Address to Joint Session of Congress, April 27, 1983.
2. "Contadora: a process for Central American Peace." U.S. Department of State Bulletin, January 1985.

Chapter 18. Organization of American States: Falklands and Grenada

1. Ronald Reagan, *An American Life* (New York: Simon and Schuster, 1990), 456.
2. All cited in *Time,* December 12, 1983.

Index

About the Author

Twenty years out of Harvard, investment banker Bill Middendorf was at the helm of his own firm, Middendorf, Colgate and Company, with a seat on the New York stock exchange and offices in New York, Boston, Baltimore, and San Francisco. But he was restive. "I had learned how to make money," he writes. "I wanted to learn how to make a difference."

Thus he became actively involved in politics, first at the local level and then as a leader of the presidential campaign of Senator Barry Goldwater (1964) and as treasurer of the Republican National Committee (1964–1968). There followed a series of challenging public service appointments: ambassador to the Netherlands, secretary of the Navy, ambassador to the Organization of American States, and ambassador to the European Community.

Middendorf has experiences to share, from his World War II Navy service to an effort to bring a U.S.-style constitution to post-Soviet Russia. Tales of villains and heroes at critical moments in the Cold War, tales of narrow legislative victories on vital programs, tales of behind-the-scenes efforts to forestall war in the Falklands and to counter growing Communist control throughout Latin America. Through all, he has been an outspoken champion of the free market and a strong national defense.